Phänomenologische Erziehungswissenschaft

Phänomenologie als internationale Denk- und Forschungstradition ist in der Pädagogik bzw. Erziehungswissenschaft eine eigenständige Forschungsrichtung, deren Potenziale in dieser Reihe ausgelotet werden. Anknüpfend an die phänomenologisch-philosophischen Neubestimmungen des Erfahrungsbegriffs ist es ihr Anliegen, pädagogische Erfahrungen in ihren sinnlich-leiblichen, sozialen, temporalen und machtförmigen Dimensionen sowohl theoretisch als auch empirisch zu beschreiben, zu reflektieren und handlungsorientierend auszurichten. Sie versucht, in pädagogischen Situationen die Gegebenheit von Welt im Vollzugscharakter der Erfahrung sichtbar zu machen. Wichtig dabei ist auch die selbstkritische Sichtung ihrer eigenen Traditionen und ihrer oftmals kontroversen Geltungs- und Erkenntnisansprüche. Phänomenologische Erziehungswissenschaft bringt ihre Erkenntnisse im Kontext internationaler und interdisziplinär wissenschaftlicher Theorie- und Erfahrungsbezüge ein und versucht, diese im erziehungswissenschaftlichen Fachdiskurs kritisch zu bewähren.

Malte Brinkmann, Herausgeber

More information about this series at
http://www.springer.com/series/13404

Luigina Mortari

The Philosophy of Care

 Springer

Luigina Mortari
University of Verona
Verona, Italy

ISSN 2512-126X   ISSN 2512-1278   (electronic)
Phänomenologische Erziehungswissenschaft
ISBN 978-3-658-35174-8   ISBN 978-3-658-35175-5   (eBook)
https://doi.org/10.1007/978-3-658-35175-5

This Springer VS imprint is published by the registered company Springer Fachmedien Wiesbaden GmbH part of Springer Nature.
The registered company address is: Abraham-Lincoln-Str. 46, 65189 Wiesbaden, Germany

Contents

The Primacy of Care: Some Points for Reflection

In the field of human experience some things are essential and indispensable. Sometimes, however, this very essentiality, though clear in daily life, may elude the work of the thinking. It is often the case that the essential—the fundamental and inevitable part of experience—is what is proximal to us, but just because it is ontically so close may paradoxically be hidden from us and its ontological meaning remains constantly overlooked (Heidegger 1962, p. 69).

This is particularly evident in the phenomenon of care. An indisputable and evident fact is that care is something essential and pivotal, because life cannot flourish without it. For this reason "all people want to be cared for" and "the world would be a better place if we all cared more for one another" (Noddings 2002, p. 11). There is need for goodness as well as for protecting oneself from suffering; care is the necessary response to these needs.

Knowledge about the ontological necessity of care has ancient roots. In the *Phaedrus*, care is considered an essential trait not only of mortals, but also of gods. Indeed, Zeus is said to exercise his divine power when he disposes and cares for all things for the best (Plato, *Phaedrus*, 246e). In Book VII of the *Republic*, Socrates explains to Glaucon that it is fair to ask and compel philosophers to "care for and guard" other citizens, because they have acquired a proper vision of beautiful, right and good things through the uplifting path of knowledge and therefore are able to govern the city (520a).

When we think about birth, about our coming into the world, we envision light that opens on to being. For this reason, we can affirm that coming into being is like coming into light as an enlightened entity. According to Heidegger (1962, p. 401), care enlightens the essence of the human being, since care is the essential onto-logical trait of being-there, or in other words "Dasein's being is care" (1962, p. 329). The essence of human being "lies in its 'to be" (Heidegger 1962, p. 68) and in order to realize existence it is necessary to care for life. To be in the life means being called to care (Heidegger 1962, p. 332). Indeed, from beginning to end of life, human being has to care for her/himself and for others, and to take care of some things. Since the human being is brought to life with care, we can say that "each one of us is what he pursue and cares for" (Heidegger 1988, p. 159).

Stating that we become what we care for and that the ways of caring shape our being means that if we care about certain relationships, our being will be formed upon the various components of these relationships, whether beneficial or harmful. If we care about certain ideas, the structure of our thought will be shaped by this care. In other words, our mental experience will rely on the ideas that we have cultivated and will suffer the lack of those we have neglected. If we take care of some things, experiencing them and relating to them will structure our existence. If we take care of certain people, whatever happens in the relational exchange with these others will become part of ourselves. Care, in fact, could be defined as a *fabric of being*.

Care is imposed by the ontological quality of our being-there, which once it enters our lifetime "is already encumbered with the excess of itself" (Lévinas 2001, p. 15). Solidity is a quality which is opposed to lightness and a human being cannot live like a puff of wind. From the beginning, when, at birth, her/his body is touched by light, s/he has to take up a heavy burden: the duty of caring for her/his life, to care "for its endurance and conservation" (Lévinas 2001, p. 10).

When Hannah Arendt (1958) distinguishes between different forms of human activities, she talks of "work" as being constituted by those continuous, never-ceasing actions geared to satisfy primary needs. Care can be defined as the work of living and existing, because the lack of being that makes care necessary never finds a solution. We shall never attain a position of sovereignty over being, nor do we ever fully possess our condition. The intimate fragility of being-there, caused by lacking of sovereignty on life, makes care necessary along all the life. This work takes one's breath away, allows for no pause. It is a work that occupies every single moment.

Even in the most perfect of worlds, with no horror of war or starvation and where everybody has enough to sustain their life, there will always be a need for care. In some phases of life, a state of fragility and vulnerability makes us espe-cially dependent on others—in childhood for instance or in illness. In other phases, like adulthood, even if we have some degree of autonomy and self-sufficiency, without the caring help of others we cannot cultivate and express our possibilities of being, nor can we find comfort for our pain. Care is ontologically essential: it protects life and helps make existence possible. Good care keeps one's being steeped in goodness, and it is this goodness that gives shape to the generative basis of our living and that structures that layer of being that keeps us firmly among things and among others. Practicing care is therefore putting ourselves in touch with the heart of life.

It is often the case that a theoretical bias makes us lose our way among irrelevant issues. As Hölderlin reminds us in his poem *Remembrance*, it is not beneficial for the mind to wander far from thoughts inherent to life, while thoughts from the heart should be expressed; if truth be told, we should cultivate thinking which is rooted in the things essential to life. If we accept the presupposition that when we examine issues related to our being-there the discourse that starts with what we can define as experiential evidence is meaningful, then it is obvious that we should consider care a pivotal issue because its value for life is unquestionable.

Although care is an essential life experience and despite the widespread usage of the term, we lack an adequately rigorous and precise knowledge on this subject. It is indeed true that fundamental ontological experiences, those that mix the texture of daily life, are the most obvious, and it is probably because of this that we are far from having developed an interpretative theory able to define its original meaning. That is why we need to elaborate a phenomenological *analysis of care*.

The demonstration of a subject's relevance is the necessary condition towards the legitimation of engaging the work of thinking in examining it; in this specific field, it means supplying arguments in favour of the thesis of the necessity of care in life. To provide this thesis with a solid foundation, we must *design a phenomenology of fundamental qualities of the human condition and then supply the evidence that care is an essential element in the maintenance of those qualities.*

At this point, we have an eidetic problem: to deal with the epistemic passage mentioned above we must understand what we are discussing. This requires knowing what is meant by care. However, the identification of the essence of care constitutes the objective of an analysis of care. We may extricate ourselves from this discursive loop by adopting the strategy Socrates applies in the maieutic dialogue: for instance, we may consider the *Charmides*, in which Socrates asks his interlocutor to define the concept of temperance, and then proceeds to dedicate the action of the dialogue to discovering its essence. Taking the Socratic method as our point of reference, we will start with a temporary and introductory definition of care, and then allow the unfolding of the theoretical argument to find a rigorous and precise conceptualization of this term.

A simple and essential definition of care, which emerges from a phenomenology that methodically researches the simple and the essential in daily experience, is the following: *to care is to take to heart, to worry, to have consideration for, to dedicate ourselves to something.*

Once we have formulated this simple and at the same time essential concept, we need to verify if the human condition presents qualities which render necessary a way of being that involves taking existence to heart. Therefore, the questions that we ask are these: *what is the essential structure of the human condition? And what is the relationship of care to this essence?*

Being-There While Lacking Being

When the human being is born he/she has not a complete and well defined shape. When the mind thinks of the divine as the opposite of the human, this is perceived as fully completed and perfect form, since nothing divine needs further development. Any finite entity, on the other hand, is an imperfect and limited presence. It is substance without form, it takes shape with time, and its development is stimulated by the tension toward the search for shape. It is not for us to exist in reality in a pure and simple way. We cannot be at one with the world, as migrating birds are at one with the skyways they have always followed and who seem to have always inhabited the horizon. We carry within us a rupture with the world's order and because we are lacking this order, we are called upon to search for a meaningful balance to maintain us in a good relationship with reality.

We are incomplete beings, in a continuous state of need. We are not rounded off, autonomous and self-sufficient beings in our existence. This ontological state is proved by the fact that we are always desiring a full life that is never achieved. Since we are made of material and spiritual substance, we constantly need to nurture and preserve our body and our soul.

We are lacking in the sense that each of us is an entity without the power to switch from nothingness to being and in our essence we are something that can be, and within this "can" there is all the risk of not coming into being. Our ontological essence is "having the possibility of being" (Stein 2002, p. 34), in the sense that we have a disposition towards being. Having the quality of being possible does not mean not being, but rather the ability to become, and that transition is the passage from "being possible" to "being real".

Our own being, insofar as we know it is an inconsistent entity; we do not exist by ourselves and by ourselves we are nothing. At every moment we are facing the void and we must receive being as a gift, moment after moment. Even though this inconsistency we exist and at every moment we are in touch with the fullness of being (Stein 2002, I vol, p. 55).

The entity we are does not possess its own being, but is given it from elsewhere. The lack of self is caught in our enigmatic origin and in our end, in the emptiness of our past, in the impossibility to call into being anything that strives to become. We are dependent beings, depending on where we come from, on the world we are living in and where we are measuring our being. The weakness of the human condition consists in not possessing its being, but in needing time to become a being. Our being is transient, meaning it becomes from moment to moment and thus it is irrevocably exposed to the possibility of nothingness (Stein 2002, I vol, p. 58).

Our incompleteness is manifest when we are born without a shape to our being and we have the duty to forge it as time goes by without clearly being told what we are supposed to do to give good shape to our development and its unpredictable possibilities. In this sense we are essentially a problem for ourselves.

Just because we are lacking being and exposed to the possibility of not fulfilling our potential being, an empty abyss can yawn any moment under our feet. From the moment we come to life, we start losing life, because while living we consume the substance of life which is time. If only what is current is real, then our being caught between not-being-anymore and not-being-yet suffers a radical inconsistency. If we stop thinking about our being-there, we cannot but feeling its powerlessness. An impotence that, although it can rely on the power of reason, makes us very similar to other living beings. Semonides reminds us that: "As leaves on the trees is the lot of men" (fragm. 29). It is this ontological weakness that makes us beings who are destined to constantly question our presence.

We feel this exposure to nothingness very deeply. We start to feel it at the moment we become aware of the finiteness of our being-there, of the fact that death annihilates life. Death looms over the being-there simply because the being-there is constantly developing within a limited time and without any power over the scheme of its existence. When we reflect on our experience, we discover ourselves to be inconsistent, and this inconsistency is manifested by the fact that, even if we don't plan it, even if it is undesired, at any moment life can disappear. The possibility of no longer existing, that sets an end to the being-there, is a constant aspect that follows the entire span of existence in the world. From this feeling of losing existence instant by instant derives anguish, the anguish of an unpredictable and inevitable disappearance into nothingness.

It is, however, not only the void that nullifies life, that death which takes life away forever, but also the void that eliminates valuable things, such as the ties of friendship and love, but still leaves us alive. And it is that very feeling of the possibility of losing what we value, without the power of keeping these things within being, that generates a sense of our ineffectuality together with a feeling of lacerating despair. Death looms on the horizon and when it comes, we will no longer exist. Instead, the disappearance of good things—which occurs when we are deprived of them—erases the value of our being but without liberating us from the work of living, forcing us to endure the void we are dragged into.

Precisely because we experience good things with our entire being, with our mind and with our heart, and in the case of love even with our body, the pain of a friendship that ends or of a love that finishes makes us feel as if our soul has been flayed, excoriated, devoured bit by bit, and we are unable to weaken our sensitivity to the suffering. We must, perforce, deal with our powerlessness before reality, perforce be subjected to it, since "all can be borne" (Sappho, frag. 3). And here is the problem: the heart can stand anything, it cannot break, it does not disappear, therefore we feel the full force of pain and are spared nothing.

If, on the one hand, we face the undeniable reality of a fragile ontological substance since it is prolonged from moment to moment and because of that it is acutely exposed to the possibility of disappearing, on the other, we experience that despite our fragility instant after instant we are preserved into being. This is the paradox of our existence: experiencing the fragility of our being, that is kept together moment after moment, without exercising any sovereignty on its development, and at the same time discovering ourselves bonded to the responsibility of answering the call of our being. As far as the fragility of our being is concerned, we cannot rely on our habits or on any other peaceful and reassuring routine. The poet Bacchylides (fifth Century BC): "Being a mortal, you must cultivate twin thoughts/that tomorrow will be the last day you see/the sun's light/and that you will complete another fifty years/of truly prosperous life" (*Epinicians*, p. 80). To be destined to act as architects of our own existence is a difficult assignment, because the scheme of our being-there requires us to think long term, and this intellectual action implies that we isolate the condition that makes us feel postponed from one second to the next while knowing and feeling our profound fragility.

Not only we are born with a lacking being, and remain like this forever, but we are also trapped by the onus of becoming our own potentiality-for-being. This is the root of all the difficulty of living: we cannot exist in the lightness of a pre-established scheme of life free from the responsibility of finding the right direction in our own path in time, but we find ourselves immediately burdened by the encumbrance of an existence which must be devised instant by instant, having to make decisions without any definite orientation, in obscurity.

The first fact apparent to the mind is its own being, we can talk about the certitude of our existence, but this certitude is not reassuring, because from its beginning it becomes a certitude of the burden of our own becoming and of the impossibility of eluding it. The exertion of our soul in sustaining the art of life derives from finding ourselves involved in actions that seem useless or in some cases completely futile; and even trusting that all the effort of "struggling out of children's shoes" (Rilke 2000) is not a fruitless effort, we cannot evade the responsibility of giving shape and meaning to our own development. Lacking being does not mean lightness, but weight, a weight which this responsibility makes more and more evident. We are born with the obligation to become our own being-there. The human condition does not permit us to evade the imperative of being there. If thoroughly reflected upon, the "impossibility of nothingness", of abstaining ourselves even for a moment from being there, makes it evident why freedom is so sought after.

The Directionality of Care

Preserving Vital Strength

Our ontological weakness makes us needy. Life constantly needs something and if it has to go without it, it ends. The problem consists in the fact that this something needs to be found. The continuous urgency to find things for ourselves represents an ineluctable necessity. Being thrown into the world means dealing with the permanent task of coping with life. This leads to the ontological burden of caring for life. In the first place, the care for life manifests itself as a search for things that nourish and preserve the life cycle. Care is essentially care about the being-there and the being-there which may be identified as care as care is "being toward something" in order to actualize the "uttermost possibilities of its own can-be" (Heidegger, 1992, pp. 312 and 313).

In Ancient Greek, the word *mérimna* [μέριμνα] defines care as the action of providing everything necessary to preserve life.[1] Care as *mérimna* is the way of being that represents the answer to *hormé* [όρμή] as referred to by Stoicism, or in other words the tendency to persist in being, an inevitable inclination since we are all called to live the life. The being-there is constantly expected to face the threats of a world that tests our capacity of staying in the here and now and deals with this through the way of being of provision which is in itself care.

The term *mérimna* recurs frequently in the Gospel and describes the concern of dealing with life, safeguarding the possibility of the continuation of being-there, having always continuously to find things in order to keep on existing. Even if our

---

[1] Please note that Greek translations are mainly made by the author herself directly from the originals.

culture considers the life of the mind, and then the spiritual activity, "the highest and perhaps purest activity" of which human beings are capable (Arendt 1958, p. 5), however the action of procuring material things to preserve life is not a kind of less valuable action. Taking care of things, so that we satisfy the needs that we have in the world, is not a degraded level of life in comparison to another spiritual level of existence, but it is the way of being that belongs to us, that coincides with us, because we are embodied entities that live in the world. The care for things is our care for life.

Although the care to save life from its weakness is inevitable, it can assume enormous proportions because of the anxiety that affects our soul when faced with our ontological fragility. Our lack of sovereignty over life engenders apprehension and anguish, which can lead us to a frantic seeking of things with the illusion that acquisition allows us to find a shelter for our fragility. It is this very craving, however, that ends up consuming our life itself.

In the parable of the birds, Jesus invites us not to worry [μή μεριμνᾶτε] too much about life and to consider the birds in the sky (Matt. 6,25), since the excessive concern for things and the attachment to material riches suffocate the search for the authentic sense of the life (Matt. 13,22). In inviting us not to care too much about material things, he uses the verb *merimnao* [μεριμνάω]. Concern for life, which is necessary in order to protect the continuation of being, can be transformed into excess, into a form of relentless perseverance in collecting what might be useful, and this excess that leads to anxiety can be interpreted as a consequence of the anguished realization of our condition of lacking, needy, beings.

A blessed life is perceived as "sine angore curae", or in other words without the anguish of care (Augustine *Epistulae*, 55, 17), a necessary condition that helps us to find the middle way in caring. The awareness of being needy and unable to find a permanent defence against our want is transformed into a feeling of impotence that, if it is allowed to burgeon in our souls, can cause us to act compulsively so as to quiet our sense of lack, filling our life with an excess of things that make us feel anchored. For this reason, even though the following poetic fragment is referring specifically to her love life, we perceive as universal Sappho's prayer: "vex not my soul with agonies and anguish" (1, frag. 1) and in this case anguish translates the term *mérimna*. And we can add: *nurture it in the hope of finding the right balance of care.*

Care that Makes Being Flourish

Taking things to heart however, does not only mean providing things to maintain life the way it is. For the very fact that every human being comes to life lacking some form of being-there, her/his duty is to find the shape of her/his own presence, and that the very best possible. We are called to shape our life. Even if the human being-there is fragile and vulnerable, he/she has an important ontological task: being called to transcend and seek further forms of being. Besides having to find things to preserve life, every human being has the obligation to care for existence so that s/he can become her/his own potentiality-for-being. Care, in point of fact, may be understood as making bloom the ontological possibilities of being-there.

Our ontological fragility makes us incapable of being-there in a pure and simple way; it calls us irrevocably to accomplish the duty of becoming our potentiality-for-being, by responding positively to the commitment of existing. If we share the same intimate *logos* that permeates the world with all other entities, our obligation to constantly become other alienates us from this world, rendering us unable to live with an immediate simplicity at the hub of things. The human being is not a fixed point in the becoming of being, it is neither accomplished nor complete. Rather, it is a nucleus of being in continual transformation, driven constantly towards and beyond the way it exists. It is a self in search of its own shape and because of that it is forced to depart from what it is, to overtake itself. The essence of being-there lies within this lack of shape of being that calls for constant transcendence. To take upon ourselves the duty of transcendence means *to care for the span of life*. The *proprium* of the human condition is to submit to its own transcendence (Zambrano 2004, p. 13), because its living nucleus is a potentiality that needs to overcome what already exists and look towards further horizons. To submit to our own transcendence means that our being is always what it has to be, and it is called upon to become everything that it is not yet, but that it could be.

We can therefore say that there is a task for care to provide things which nurture and preserve life, as well as care seen as a search for evidence-based conditions that allow for transcendence and surpass what is already given in order to create new kinds of being-there. This is how I interpret the "double sense" that Heidegger confers on care: as providing things and as dedication to improve the quality of life (1992, p. 303).

Among the studies discussing care, there is a prevalent, not to say almost exclusive, attention for care as an answer to the need to find what is necessary to live, what Bubeck (2002, p. 161) defines as the labor necessary to maintain and reproduce ourselves, disregarding the idea that devoting ourselves to the search for the best quality of life possible, while permitting the realization of various possibilities proper to being, is just as necessary. There is a need for care that knows how to «awake souls and make them greater» not in order to «make human beings more efficient in action» (Cicero, *De officiis*, I, 12) but to better fulfill that adventure which is the human life.

Good maternal care does not consist only in satisfying the needs that are expressed by the baby, but also in offering those experiences that stimulate its self to grow and to flourish in all its ontological dimensions. A good teacher not only organizes the learning activities as presented in the syllabus, but tries to comprehend the needs of each student in order to offer those experience which nurtures the cognitive, ethical, aesthetic, social and spiritual potential of every one of them. A caring nurse not only provides competent therapy, but takes the time to put the patient in the condition of regaining his or her autonomy as soon as possible.

Propitiating the potential to transcend what we are in order to open ourselves to greater things is proper to the essence of the soul, which Heraclitus said is a *logos* that makes it grow (frag. 14 [A11] in Colli 1993, p. 29), a fruitful and seminal *logos* that nurtures the being with seeds of possibilities and with the necessary energy to make it bloom. The soul that follows its *logos* is always in search of its best shape. This potential towards expansion can give rise to fear and a propensity to retreat, without the realization that useless struggle is a waste of time. On the other hand, when the soul listens to its desire for transcendence and persists in the search for that source of knowledge that helps in finding the right way of living, then "it is the wisest and the best" (Heraclitus, frag. 14 [A52] in Colli 1993, p. 61). For the very reason that the human being lacks shape, our self is in continuous potential becoming and during the process of transcending it takes on a shape of sorts, even if this shape is always provisional and ahead-of-itself. If care is essentially care of the being-there and the being-there implies the possibility of being, then care as in the care of the being-there has the potential to realize the possible within its best form, that in which we can feel the positive sense of existing.

To be bound to the care that responds to the necessity of transcendence means the inability linger in the mode of existence most proper to us, because we have not been granted the possibility of existing in calmness. Care is an action that is ontologically necessary because human life is uncertain and incomplete. This way of being of mine, that I find prolonged moment by moment, never comes in a complete shape nor is it ever possessed, but needs the effort of caring that is necessary to give it shape. The work of living is incessant since we must perform our lives from moment to moment. In this continuous flowing we never attain true sovereignty of our existence (Stein 1950, p. 91). It is alive, gifted with vital strength, with potentialities that are expected to be actualized, but at the same time, it is vulnerable and fragile: it has to continuously work on preserving its life and on nurturing its existence.

In order to care for oneself it is not sufficient to accept the burden of transcendence, of the search for forms that overcome the existing situation, but it is also necessary to care for what is happening within our own being quite apart from any intentional investigation. The condition of the human subject is characterized by the fact that any action towards its own being intended to give it a shape, even if it is unsuccessful in what it set out to do, ends up by being effective in giving it some shape all the same. This pliability of being makes constant vigilance necessary regarding the modes of our own development. In this sense, the work of existing does not know the quality of lightness, and always imposes a presence that is extremely attentive and intensely responsible.

Being born without shape and with the onus to find one, the human being is therefore called upon to care for itself. To care for ourselves in order to look for the better kind of potential self means to search for a horizon that radiates significance. Caring for ourselves is a tiring job. It interweaves the threads of being-there, but without ever completely accomplishing the realization of its pattern, because the human being finds it impossible to realize all that s/he considers essential to the planning of a good life. From the beginning of her/his life s/he is bound to the task of giving a shape to her/his own individual way of existing without having any control over the steps of her/his own development. We care for ourselves in order to cope with the fragility and vulnerability of the human condition, without being able to reduce our intimate fragility and vulnerability, either in our flesh or in our soul.

From the analysis of the lived experience care manifests itself as being out for something that still is not (Heidegger 1992, p. 308). In this action, our being-there tends towards something that does not yet exist and for this reason we can say that care is the answer to the condition of being underway towards something that is possible towards the actualization of some of our potentialities. Caring for the self does not only mean finding what is necessary to live, guarantee our own lifespan and preserve it, but also how to build a living space in which we can fully realize our own potential for existence.

The lacking of a full and entire being that characterizes human life is at the same time openness towards the becoming of being-there, towards further and not pre-established possibilities of existence. Our state of existence is actually that of finding ourselves always open to possible ways of being regarding the how and why of our current being. Existing means answering the appeal to realize concretely the possibilities of being. This takes some care. To care for life therefore means committing to the duty of actualizing the possible in such a way that we can fulfil the life that makes the best part of the human being flourish so that it may be worth living.

We are always running the risk of a fragmented life, in other words one that it is divided into periods without a centre, periods without connection between themselves. The soul feels the necessity of finding a centre, a living heart, from which it can draw the necessary energy to walk with joy in time. Caring for existence is about making life a living whole.

As a non-finite entity, the human being is called to transcendence, and this call to realize our own possible being by transforming possibility into reality never ceases. If transcendence towards what still is not is something that the human being has to be subjected to (Zambrano 2004, p. 8), undertaking the care for our own existence is accepting the call to transcendence, to work on the possibility of the possible and to transform it into reality. Seizing the possibility of existing and projecting our own way of being-there to facilitate the actualization of the existential possibilities means to stay in the world with a project. Being in the world with a project of our own is a way of existing. This way of existing, which consists in taking upon oneself the burden of giving a good shape to our own becoming, is not meant to be explained technically as a managerial approach to the possibilities of existing, because the project is typical of a being thrown into life, and therefore immediately aware of not controlling what happens for his development. This type of awareness manifests itself in emotional phenomena (anguish, fear, apprehension...) that constantly reveal to our conscience the weakness of every existential project.

Having care for existence as a project for the actualization of our own possible being, and therefore as an opening to transcendence, finds its most significant enunciation in the dialogues of Plato, where we find Socrates engaged in theorizing the priority of care for ourselves as care of the soul.

In *Laches*, Lysimachus begins the dialogue by affirming that adults have the duty to care for young people and this care means that the adults have to take upon themselves the responsibility of the education of the young so that they may excel in the art of living (179a-d). In the *First Alcibiades*, Socrates explains that in order to learn the art of existing, that constitutes the meaning of life itself, we have to learn how to care for ourselves. We find the same concept in the *Apology*, where Socrates, while setting forth the original meaning of educational practice, affirms that it is the duty of every educator to cultivate the other to care for himself in order "to be as good and as wise as possible ἐπιμελεῖσθαι τῆς ψυχῆς (*Apology*, 36c), and he explains that the essence of care for oneself consists in caring for our own soul [™pimeleîsqai tê$ yucê$] so it acquires the best shape possible (*Apology*, 30b). Education is therefore a practice of care and the person-who-cares promotes at the same time in the other who is cared for the ability of caring for himself; since the self corresponds to the soul *(First Alcibiades,* 130e) so caring for ourselves means caring for our soul *(First Alcibiades,* 132c). Starting from the assumption that the soul is the most valuable of things, in the dialogues where he discusses the sense of education, Socrates talks about care and precisely of caring for the soul [ψυχῆς ἐπιμελητέον] *(First Alcibiades,* 132c), and while talking about this type of care he uses the term *epimeleia* [™**piméleia**]. *Epimeleia* means care that nurtures the being in order to make it flourish. It is not an answer to the urgent demand for survival, to feeling bound to the necessity of persisting, but responds to the desire of transcendence, to the need of horizons of meaning in which to actualize our own being as a possibility of being.[2] Caring for oneself to plan our own time meaningfully signifies allowing our being to be born into existence. Since everyone's existence always takes place within a political sphere, Plato uses the word *epimeleia* for the art of successful government, and he actually talks about "caring for the city" *(The Republic,* VI, 499b).

In the Gospel of John (3,5) the possibility of a birth from water and from breath is announced. Only those who are capable of this birth may attain the knowledge of the truth. If we put aside the religious interpretation of this passage from the New Testament, we could interpret that birth from water and from air might indicate the possibility of being born to a different way of thinking, one capable of helping us find a way to be-there with fluidity and lightness and that does not let the burden of conscience or the difficulties of existence prevail. Water washes away, it flows, and air allows us to breathe. We are all born from flesh (John 3,6) and our being remains flesh throughout our lifetime, but precisely because we are able to think, and through our thoughts we experience something else, we can be born to the other, to another sort of breath of life, unburdened by the feeling of emptiness caused by the work of life. But as we are relational beings, this possibility can only be disclosed to us by others, by those who know how to have care for.

We all would love to live a good life; the Gospel is also called the text of joy, because our soul thirsts for joy. Life, however, rarely spares us from difficulties, moments of more or less intense pain and anxiety. The burden of anguish can be sustainable or it can break down all resistance, and destroy every positive energy for life. If in our life we have experienced a type of care that has given our soul vital energy, we are then able to face anxiety and anguish without being overcome.

---

[2] The term transcendence is generally used to indicate something beyond the self, that is actually both the outside and the inside world that reveal themselves to the conscience, which is the sphere of immanence since it is inseparable from the self; here, instead, I use the term in the sense indicated by Zambrano, as the ability of going further that what is given, a leaning out towards the ulterior.

The newborn who is held in arms that not only carry her/his body but also her/his mind has experienced a calm source of energy that nourishes the being; the child who finds a teacher who supports it with his or her presence, who accepts it as it is and with trust leads it to other possible forms of its own thinking and feeling, can move forward without being alienated by anxiety.

Suffering can tire our soul to the point that we can see no way out: care is like a light that expands itself over the soul, letting us discover a crack through which we can get a glimpse of something else. This is not the cold light of that knowledge which is understood as *logos matematicos* but the warm light of a seminal reason, the *logos spermatikos* of the Stoics, a spiritual breath that warms time and fertilizes life with the seeds of possibility. The absence of care, on the other hand, makes us weaker, more fragile, more vulnerable to pain. Having care is taking away the burden of suffering, as far as is possible, lifting up the sufferer from her/his lonely thoughts and emotions and together finding the right pace for their journey through time.

Care that Heals the Injuries of Being-There

Another type of care is necessary sometimes. It is the care that mends the being in moments of extreme vulnerability and fragility, when the body or the soul become ill: it is care as therapy [Θεραπεία]. Therapy is the care required to reduce pain.[3] Our body is an extremely vulnerable entity, because it may suddenly stop working properly and when this happens we experience physical suffering. For this very reason "the art of medicine cares for the interests of the body" (Plato, *Republic*, I, 241e). Therapy is a perpetual necessity: indeed it is true what the poet Menander says pain and life belong the one to the other (Plutarch, περίευθυμίας, 466b).

---

[3] To indicate therapeutic actions in Greek we have two words: *therapeia* [Θεραπεία] and *iatreia* [ιατρεία]. The first word indicates an action that takes into consideration the person and his/her complexity, also including the spiritual dimension of experience. The second word specifically refers to the activity that is exercised by physicians to treat the diseases of the body. We can say that this distinction corresponds to the English distinction between 'care' and 'cure'. In order to better distinguish the difference of meaning between care as *therapeia* and cure as *iatreia* we can consider two English words: "disease" and "illness". The first term indicates the condition of break of the balance in the body, the second word indicates the experience of the subject in his/her condition, and consequently the elaboration process of the meaning of the disease. A caring action that conceives a condition of sickness only as "disease" is qualitatively different from that one that considers it as an "illness": in the first case we apply "cure" as *iatreia*, in the second "care" as *therapeia* (Benner and Wrubel 1989, p. XII).

It is not only a question of bodily pain, but also of soul suffering: we find ourselves immersed in bodily pain, whereas as far as the pain of the soul is concerned, it is something that arises from the deepest part of our interior life. Episodes of temporary pain accompany our daily life, letting the rhythm of existence carry on; but there is also a kind of pain, continuous or intermittent, that absorbs vital energy, and grinds the soul down in a way that seems to strip the very flesh from it.

Disease brings starkly to light all our dramatic ontological weakness, that of an entity that finds itself thrown into the world of life and has to continue its being-there without any sovereignty over the becoming that drags the potentiality-of-being through time. In the experience of illness, the feeling of interruption, if not the shattering of the normal rhythm of life reveals the weakness of the human condition.

My being-there exists, even if inconsistently, because it lacks power over the becoming of experience, and due to that it feels the pain when it penetrates the flesh, or expands in the recesses of the soul, in all its reality. When we suffer, we feel the true weight of our bondage to being–there. When the body is healthy and when the soul is well, the task of taking care of our existence, difficult though it may be, makes it possible to perceive being as a gateway towards the possibility of positive development, opening to the world and growing towards our potentiality-for-being. When we feel well, we perceive our being as a vital centre, able to produce forms of existence, where the life-force that nurtures our development can be materialized in experiences that represent necessary stepping-stones for the way of adventure that is life.

But when our body sickens, or when pain invades the soul, then that ontological weakness, which our mind—though feeling it in all its reality—can ignore for few moments in order to contain the sense of anguish, is experienced in all its heaviness. Being-there is suffered in all the difficulty of finding oneself tangled up in forms of becoming which have not been chosen and have proved to be unavoidable. We experience the impossibility of an ontological alternative, of backing away from being-there, we are aware of a deep-rooted passivity, and it is the awareness of this which generates anguish. This anguish becomes bearable only if the extreme passivity we are subjected to is accepted and the soul knows how to cultivate the art of patience. What we have to find is not the supposed innocence of lack of thought, that clear and calm simplicity of being-there that could be compared to the flight of a bee following in the air itineraries that have already been traced: this natural condition is not given to us because in our essence we are thinking beings. We should rather learn, in this case, to implement thought as the ability to accept what we are. Acceptance of our ontological quality, without resort to fantasizing or ungrounded imagination, and the resulting gain of momentum necessary to reinterpret existence, requires work on the part of mind and heart that is an essential part of care for the self.

The condition of illness makes the person feel that s/he is not only at the mercy of biological life, which follows its own rules, but also at the mercy of other people, who have the power of decision on their behalf. Losing that small amount of control over our being-there, gained with difficulty over time through the noetic and praxic acts constituting the establishment of our individual mode of existence, means losing the condition of being a subject and feeling that we have been reduced to an object. Not, however, simply to something inanimate, but to an entity that is intensely sensitive, that feels the lightness of a smile and the sweetness of a caress, but also the pain of an insult, the inexorable passage of time and suffers the diminishment that suffering produces in the being.

A life full of sense is a life that is experienced in its fullness in every moment, in every action, even the most apparently meaningless. In a good period, every moment is perceived as precious, because every event, even that which may appear less meaningful, can open a path to unexpected existential paths, where our being can be nourished by something quite new. A period of illness, on the contrary, radically changes the way of perceiving our own being-there. If in good times we aspire to the fullness of being-there, in difficult ones we would like to be relieved from being: to feel a reduction of the life-force, to find ourselves on the borders of our being, to reduce our sensitivity to reality. This type of experience happens not only in the case of a diseased body, but also, if not especially, when the spirit is unwell. If we accept that the core part of every human being is her/his spiritual activity, then when pain penetrates the flesh of the soul, the subject feels threatened in her/his innermost being. When pain persists and seems as if it will never stop, as if it will never give any room to breathe or to accede to other modes of existence, our only desire, is paradoxically, to lower the level of that vital energy which keeps us in touch with the real part of our being.

The substance of life is time. Life-time flows into the present to make us feel as if we ourselves were actually happening, moment by moment. This feeling of happening as a succession of punctual events, even if it does not rescue us from experiencing the anguish of our relentless disappearance, can however shine out in its meaning, full of the pleasure of fragments of being, which, kept together by thought which is engaged in building worlds, give the happy sensation of consistency. When we are in pain, on the other hand, time changes its quality: it becomes mute, impenetrable, there are no longer moments to invent, to light up with meaning. Time becomes something solid and relentless that oppresses the soul by robbing it of its very essence, the breath of life. The trickling away of time that during good moments is perceived with anguish, because it reminds consciousness of the vanishing of life and therefore of the fading of any possibilities of becoming our potentiality-for-being, can instead become, when we experience pain, especially pain caused by diseases that leave their mark, something that we almost aspire to. We would actually be glad if existential possibilities disappeared, as a consequence of the passing of the time, if this disappearance might become, indeed, the structural quality of the present. We crave the possibility of becoming other, of passing into another substance, less vulnerable and lighter. We would like to become the cherry tree, when at the end of flowering it loses its petals in the wind, becoming a branch that can let pain go, so as to feel the suffering of our material being no longer.

When we are well, our mind distances itself from every negative image. Not only does it wish to continue being forever, without suffering the human finitude, but also it craves the possibility of feeling the self in its fullness. The human being would desire to embrace the whole of its contents in a changeless present instead of experiencing their continuous disappearance almost at the very moment they come into being, since every lived moment after ascending into the life it sinks in the past (Stein 2002, p. 56). On the contrary, when we experience pain, what imposes itself on the mind is far from our own wishes. We would still like, and probably even more than before, to exercise a control of sorts over our being-there, not to feel vital energy intensely, but in order to weaken, to numb our sensibility to the point of no longer feeling at all, of escaping pain, so as to slacken the suffering that consumes our vital force. In this situation, the inconsistency of being sensitive and somewhat mentally weak can almost be beneficial. In this case, ascetic disciplines of diminishing, of clearing space in order to experience the essential, is an ethical activity, since it prepares us for some of the more difficult moments of existence, making us ready for the traversing of thorny paths.

There are philosophers who, through the use of sophistically honed metaphors, put into words emotions and thoughts that are part of ordinary life. This the case of the Platonic image of the soul which would like to attain the ability of detaching itself from the ties of the body, an image representing the desire for an existence that is relieved from the burden of material life. In the *Phaedo*, Plato talks about the body as a prison, where the soul, the only noble part of the human being, finds itself confined. When the soul remains tied to the body and tries to satisfy its innate thirst for knowledge through exploiting the senses, it is destined to wander, "as if drunk", among irrelevant cognitive data, since the senses, as they keep the mind connected to the material world, allow reference only to secondary and conditional knowledge that reveals nothing essential. On the contrary when the soul is free from the chains of the body and seeks only what is "pure, ever existing, immortal and unchanging" (Plato, *Phaedo*, 79d), it remains faithful to the quality of its essence that consists in searching for what is indispensable for a true life. The idea of a soul that frees itself from the burden of the material and being so light can access another level of reality, where nothing can trouble it, is not an absurd invention, because it expresses the profoundly human desire of avoiding a merging of the spiritual breath with the flesh when the flesh is suffering, the desire to feel the soul as free from the body when it is ill and, more radically, to avoid material life when it is too exhausting.

When pain overpoweringly affects the body, suffering penetrates the tissues of the soul. At this point it is possible that the quality of inner life seems to eradicate the life-force necessary to sustain a positive response to the striving towards transcendence. It is as if the material body consumes every drop of spiritual energy. At these times we would like to feel the soul take flight (Plato, *Phaedrus*, 246c) and, in a wingbeat, free itself from the burden of material life to fly elsewhere, to soar into the blue sky, where only good things can find a dwelling and where it would experience "true reality that is colorless, formless and intangible" (Plato, *Phaedrus*, 247c) for the very reason that there is nothing connecting it to material life, nor to cause it distress, leading it only to wisdom. The Platonic idea of "a pure and tender soul" [ἀπαλὴν καὶ ἄβατον ψυχήν] (*Phaedrus*, 245a), that knows how to approach perfect and simple things, contemplating them "in a pure light" as the soul itself is pure (*Phaedrus*, 250c), expresses not only the desire for truth that everyone feels trembling in their minds, that tension that becomes stronger when live is more burdensome and more difficult, but also the desire for a different life, inaccessible to the upheaval of pain.

We tend to see in Platonic thought the root of the dualism between soul and body, which has since then encumbered Western culture, permitting reductive approaches to every aspect of life. It is true that reasoning across separate universes is a risky simplification, since the quality of the real, where everything is interconnected, is betrayed in its integrity. However, the idea that the soul is something that can escape the material world should also be analysed from another perspective. This vision, actually, represents a human aspiration to be able to live a life that is not threatened by possible injuries to being-there and that is not mingled with things which degenerate, lose their shape and order. The idea of a pure thought,[4]

---

[4] It is probably not by chance that Plato uses the term *abatos* [ἄβατος] to indicate the quality of purity of the soul, as it also means inviolable, inaccessible, prohibited, sacred. Perhaps it was to remind us that this condition of the soul, which would make it unreachable by things that happen, is that of being inaccessible and forbidden to those who live on earth. Curiously, the term *batos*, from which derives the privative *abatos*, does not only mean "practicable" and "accessible", but also "bramble", "thorn". Even if the platonic *abatos* does not have any relation to *batos* that indicates the bramble, it is easy to think that an *abatos* soul, far from earthly life, is that which knows no earthly thorns.

that is not merged with the matter of the sensible world, in which no form is permanent because of its constant development, far from being a deceptive epistemological fantasy, is the answer to a typically human desire to tap into a sure and certain source of ideas. A desire that for us, who are finite and fragile, may possibly evoke a different space from that in which we now find ourselves.

Reality, however, differs from our ideal. It is, in fact, the condition in which our body and soul are united, not seen as distinct substances only temporarily bound together, but inextricably mingled one with the other. If phenomenological philosophy invites us to transcend the dualism of body and soul, Edith Stein goes beyond this because, in order to do so, she does not suggest an associative logic, which considers body and soul as united entities. In this case the idea would be that of two separate substances that cohabit one next to the other. Instead, she invites us to consider being-there as one single entity, composed of a body that subsists by means of its spiritual breath and of a soul which needs to be embodied to exist at all. If we cease to consider body and soul as two separate entities, but rather conceive of the body as spiritual substance and the soul as corporeal substance, then our way of relating to the other necessarily changes. Caring for a newborn means dealing with a body that feels the touch of its carer in a spiritual way; in the health care field, to touch the body of a sick patient is identical to touching his or her soul, because just as physical pain penetrates the soul, the soul's strength overflows into the body. Since the soul lives within the body, permeating every single atom of substance, actions we are subjected to though the body are also felt by the soul. Treating a baby without gentleness is an action that takes no thought for his or her soul. Prescribing therapy mechanically, without taking time to listen with empathy to the patient is an action that reduces him or her to an object. Handling the body of an elderly person without the requisite gentleness means abusing his or her intimate feelings. Any invasion of the other is not "only" carried out on the flesh of the body, but goes deep into the flesh of the soul.

What the ancients used to know has been forgotten by modern medicine. Forgotten is the fact that body and soul are one and that chemical care has to be integrated with spiritual. In the *Charmides* (155e), Plato explains that the remedy for a disease does not consist only of organic medicine—herbs—but also of medicine made of *logoi*, in other words by good discourse. Both have to be used together. Socrates, addressing the young Charmides, explains that: "one must not to attempt to cure the eyes without the head, or the head without the body, so neither ought you to attempt to cure the body without the soul" (*Charmides*, 156b-c). For a certain type of rational and reductive medicine a patient is nothing but a body. He or she, on the contrary, is a person. He or she is not an unimportant, insensible substance but an incarnate soul or a spiritual body. This indivisibility of substance and spirit makes the human being a material structure that breathes in a spiritual way. A person feels the quality of corporeal life in the soul, because our body has a spiritual substance. This spiritual life, diffused in the material structure, is sustained by bodily energy and, precisely because it is incarnate in the body, it shares its quality of life.

One type of pain is engendered in the flesh and another comes from the soul, but rarely are they separate. When they occur, they are indivisible: the one overflows into the other contaminating the different levels of being. Spiritual pain, when it is not processed and therefore becomes unbearable, finds the body a perfect place in which to develop and manifest itself. Physical pain can overflow into the soul, sometimes a slowly spreading stream, at other times a flood that devastates the soul, to the point that the soul is no longer aware of itself but only of pain. Faced with pain, which ruthlessly exposes the mind to the vulnerability of being-there, the heart suffers all the impotence of the human condition.

The sick person, thinking of the experience he or she is undergoing, cannot help perceiving her/his being as if it had been engulfed by a profound darkness, whose *logos* remains indecipherable. With disease, the sense of life's precariousness becomes a terribly heavy weight, bringing sharply to light the fragility of human life. We would like a pure and simple existence, and instead feel it shattered and randomly redistributed on to multiple planes, tugged this way and that by burdensome thoughts and pierced by contrasting feelings. Planning, an essential quality of existence, has always to measure up to an unclearly defined development, because of our constant conditioning by other things. However, during disease the mere idea of forward thinking becomes painful, because while suffering the actual meaning of planning disappears.

When we experience good care in life, that care that fills the soul with trust, then we are able to deal with pain without letting it overwhelm us. The absence of care, on the other hand, makes us weaker, more fragile, ready to be nullified by pain. The Gospel of Matthew, quoting Isaiah, states: "He took our infirmities upon himself, and bore our diseases" (Matt. 8, 17). There exists suffering that we feel we cannot bear alone. Only a god can bear it and lighten our load; perhaps there is a disease of the soul that only the source of a transcendental energy can cure. We, however, live among others just as fragile as we are; but it is precisely these others that help us to bear our burden without feeling that we will collapse. Being able to care for the other is also to being there when the other feels all the fatigue of the effort of life, being willing to share what we have in order to bear together the interweaving of existence, so that cold loneliness may not extinguish vital energy. There is no existence without self-care; but self-care needs the sustaining care of others. For this reason, care for others is a great and inalienable value. When care as therapy takes on the responsibility of the person in its entirety of mind and body, then it is not merely mending what was broken in the body, but care of the entire being.

The term care, therefore, as it is charged with different meanings, is polysemic: there exists one type of care necessary to go on living, another necessary to existence, so that it may tend towards transcendence, and sustain the being-there of sense, and yet another that mends both the spiritual and the material being when body or soul are sick. The first one is care as work to preserve us as an entity, the second is the art of existing in order to make the being flourish, and the third is a sort of mending technique, a "sewing-up" of the wounds of being-there. The essence of care responds to an *ontological necessity*, which includes a *vital necessity*, that of continuing to be, an *ethical necessity*, that of being-there with sense, and a *therapeutic necessity*, that of repairing being-there.

The Thoughtfulness of Being-There

Relationality as Primary Ontological Data

Because we are lacking in being and therefore destined to try to become our possible self, we cannot be exempt from care for our existence. However, dedicated and intense though it may be, this commitment is not enough, because we are relational beings and because of that, we need others.

The fact that that life is not a solipsistic event constitutes a phenomenologically evident given, because one life is always intimately connected to the life of others. For every human being, to exist is always to co-exist, because nobody can fully accomplish the project of existing singlehanded. In the *Nichomachean Ethics* Aristotle speaks of the human being as an entity that is political by nature [πολιτικός] (I, 7, 1097b11), or in other words the human being is someone who exists with many others [πολλοί] who bring the city [πόλις] to life.

If we consider the person from the point of view of psychic development, we can see how the relation with the other is the primary condition of being-there. As is explained by Donald Winnicott (1987, p. 11), the origin of everything is the relationship with the mother, in which the baby does not initially exist as a separate being, but rather as a primary identification with whoever takes care of its being. For the newborn, the most urgent need s/he has is that for a mother, that is, somebody to care for him/her, and within this relationship s/he begins to constitute her/his being. The relationship with the other person who receives me is therefore the matrix structure of the being, since to be in a relationship with a caring for means receiving material, mental and affective nurturing.

We are lacking being and for that very reason we feel an intense need to be in relationship with whoever, like us, has an ontological need of the other. This tensional relationality could explain the phenomenon of the intense attachment of the baby towards whoever takes care of it (Bowlby 1969). Recent behavioral studies have revealed an elevated rational competence in the very first days of life, evident in the quantity and in the complexity of the interactions that the baby establishes with others. This relational competence is of primary value for life.

Since at the beginning of our life, ontological weakness is at its highest, the attachment of the baby towards its mother is a vital need. And if, with time, this need fades, and a sort of precarious autonomy is developed, the search for meaningful relationships, different and of varying intensity though they may be, is evident in the life of each of us. This happens because relating to others is an ontological structure of being-there, in the sense that living is being-there and "there" discloses on entity who lives as "being-with-others" (Heidegger 1992, 253). Relational substantiality is something radically inevitable, because even when the entity that we are withdraws into an intra-subjective space, the space where the mind debates with itself, relating to others continues, because even when we are alone our thoughts maintain the relationship with thoughts we formulated with others and the feelings that move our hearts are threads that keep us connected. This is the relational substance of being-there, or in other words, to say it with Rilke, within a network of relationships, we are not like flowers that live only for one season, because our feeling comes from far away: it is like sap that is fed not only by present relationships, but also from past ones, which, even if forgotten, structure the vital background of being.

This evident ontological givenness becomes the first problem to face for philosophies of relationality. It is by starting to think about this phenomenological reality that we underline the non-relational quality of some orientations of thought, those that conceive of reality as constituted by separated entities. Indeed, some philosophies that express themselves as ontologies conceive of being as an entity circumscribed within specific and discrete borders, and consequently when they discuss intersubjectivity they conceive of it as the result of the encounter of individualities that pre-existed as single entities before their meeting with the other. Instead, whatever exists, from the moment it does exist, coexists; that means that plurality is the generative matrix of the being-there (Nancy, 1996, p. 49). It could be posited that it is being-with which makes being-there, rather than something that is added to being. Relating to the other is so intimate and significant that when we lose someone it feels as if a part of us has gone with them.[5]

---

[5] The twentieth century witnessed the affirmation of the relational vision not only in philoso-

If "being-with" is the core of being, then for all discussions which contend with ontological issues it is necessary to change the traditional order of discourse, which requires that we first address being as an undifferentiated entity, only after that may we speak of "being-with" (Nancy 1996, p. 50). This redistribution of rationale is a sign of the distortion of our perspective, that compromises all future discourses on being. Also, since ontology has important repercussions on ethics, a distorted argumentative division translates to a distorted orchestration of being.

We are not simply "surrounded" by beings and things" (Lévinas 1987, p. 42) with whom/which we would be free to decide whether or not to relate, but we are indeed profoundly relational, since the morphogenetic matrix of the being of each of us is shaped by vital energy that derives from the network of relations within a

phy but also in other subjects, such as psychology and psychoanalysis. We may affirm that psychology took a paradigmatic swerve when it abandoned an atomistic vision in order to develop a relational, intersubjective theory of the human being; we no longer conceive of the mind as confined within a single individual who enters into contact with other equally autonomous minds, but we talk about the mind as "the meeting point of a wide range of structuring influences" (Harré and Gillet 1996, p. 25). Our mental pasts emerge from an extended social mind from which we derive sustenance, while we contribute to its structuring. In psychoanalysis, there was a paradigmatic change when from the Freudian era, based on the concept of impulse, we arrived at relational culture, which regards relating to others as the fundamental aspect of life (Mitchell 1988). A characteristic of the psychoanalytic theories inspired by the relational model is the idea that the way of being of a person does not depend only on internal impulses, but also on the matrix of relations that structure his/her vital space. The experience of the self is now theorized as taking shape within intersubjective fields, where personal identity, self-confidence, the vision of the self, depend on the quality and quantity of caring relationships that we undergo. If the experience of the self takes shape within intersubjective fields (Stolorow and Atwood 1992, p. 22), then taking care of someone means looking after his/her way of living his/her relationships; it means thinking about the mental life of the other not within a mental space that is conceived of as within a subject, separated from others, but within an interconnected space. The psychoanalytic care with a relational matrix conceives of the patient as a subject who cares for and is concerned about maintaining certain relationships and keeping at a distance from others. The object of the analysis is not the single individual considered as a discrete entity, but the network of interactions, desires and anxieties stirring therein. The kind of therapy that puts the individual in the centre, that conceives of her/his internal life as something that happens exclusively inside the person, can only encourage the harmful fantasies of self-sufficiency and autonomy, that disregard relational interdependence. For the very reason that the individual has an intimately relational nature, analytical theory must take into consideration his/her intimate weakness. In fact, only by re-thinking the whole web of relationships that structure vital space can we reach a different configuration of experience. Any modification of the self that is oriented towards finding another existential position and other ways of functioning of the mind has to deal with the relational reality that follows its movement, and it is not always possible to harmonize with this.

space where we develop and with our actions we contribute to structuring. The ontology of relationality becomes then the horizon in the light of which we interpret our being-there with others in the world.

Consequently, our attention to the other's aspect, feeling the other's existence as something that closely concerns us and therefore formulating existence as co-existence is not the result of one of the many possible decisions to move beyond ourselves in order to meet "another", it is not a compulsion to go outside ourselves to take a chance on a space foreign to our ontological quality, but rather the answer required by the intimately relational structure of being-there.

Being Alone with the Other/the Solitude of Being-With

The difficulty of considering ontogenesis in relational terms is evident in the fact that according to Nancy (1996, p. 50), even Heidegger, who is, in spite of everything, still the philosopher who introduced the concept of being-there as being-with-others, made an initial non-relational assumption, because he only speaks about being-with after indicating the origin of being-there. This difficulty in dealing with being-there in relational terms, which translates to the tendency to name it in its singularity, is evidence of the complex quality of the human condition, which we intimately feel when we perceive that our social being with others is strictly connected with the existential solitude which does not permit us to share our feeling. Possibly the difficulty of conceiving reality in relational terms is connected to the pressure we all feel to make our uniqueness and singularity concrete, because if it is true that plurality is the condition of existence, is also true that each human being is unique, never the same as any other.

Ontological concepts are fundamental and because of this are included among the structural elements of a paradigm of thought. We can verify how non-relational ontology contaminates many types of discourse, including the ethical and the political. The shortcoming of Western political thought is that of founding itself on a conception of the human being as an independent, autonomous and self-sufficient individual. Preconfigured thus, it overlooks the condition of dependence on others that characterizes significant phases of each of our lives and that is a lasting condition for many. Theories of equality are based on the idea of a citizen who, being an individual or in other words a single entity, possesses certain rights. Even Paul Ricœur, when dealing with care to reinterpret the object of ethical discourse, envisages the subject according to tradition, forgetting that each person inevitably contains his or her never accomplished autonomy, and will always be dependent on others. In fact Ricoeur affirms that the person "is a being able to act on reasoned initiative and from choice in order to establish and attain a hierarchy of goals". The other (autrui) is imagined as "the one who can say "I", just as I can, and, like me, may consider himself an agent, an author and responsible for his acts" (2007, p. 36).[6]

Eva Kittay, on the other hand, basing herself on relational ontology, disputes western political thought as being founded on a non-relational vision of human life and, with the affirmation "I am also a mother's child" because "everyone is some mother's child" (1999, p. 23), reminds us that we all come from a relationship and because of that we are undeniably relational beings; consequently equality is invoked not just as something that refers to us as individuals, but as a characteristic we share with the other. The first relationship that each of us experiences is with our mother, an essential relationship because it is our welcome into the world. In being born, we immediately become dependent on others and because of that we need care: it is being dependent that makes care necessary. Re-conceptualizing the ontological status of the human being in terms of dependency obliges us to radically rethink ethical and political theories. Assuming relationality as a primary ontological category leads us to a political conception which is "connection based" rather than "individual based" (Kittay 1999, p. 28).

The fact that we find ourselves dependent on the other constitutes an inevitable trait of human life, which means the effort of care is seen as "dependency work". If political theory could not only highlight the relational vision of the human being but also the centrality of care as a primary need, then the theory of equality, concentrated on the principle of satisfying rights could be transformed into the responsibility of caring for others. Until the principle of equality is developed in terms of having equal responsibility for what is essential for everybody's life, there will always be some who cultivate a vision of justice as the engagement to satisfy the necessities of others and others who do not consider it imperative to act in the same way (Kittay 1999, p. 24). However, if we make care the foundation of political philosophy it means also re-thinking the primacy of the concept of equality, because the relationship of care is a relationship between unequals, between the person-who-cares-for who has the power to do something and the person-cared-for, who is in a state of dependence.

Though relationality qualifies as being phenomenologically evident, it is not axiomatic—as is held, on the contrary, by Lévinas (1987, p. 42)—to state that "we never exist in the singular", because it is easy to disregard this essential quality of the human condition because of the existential loneliness in which we all find ourselves. I am with the other, but I am not the other: I am alone. If we examine the

---

[6] Translation from French by the author.

quality of human experience, the first phenomenological finding is that of feeling infinitely alone, since we feel alone with the burden of an ethical duty to give shape to our own life, to give significance to the fragments of time delineating our individual existence. Reality continually reiterates to me "I am alone", in the sense that my existence is an absolutely intransitive element (Lévinas 1987, p. 42). Each singularity is an original access to the world, that makes us feel unique though being among others. In this singularity, there is not only the value of the exception, of the unique, but also the whole drama of loneliness.

Only during a few exceptional moments of being, such as when we experience an intense, reciprocal love for another, when body and soul are one and even thinking is weightless, is the loneliness of the relationship with our own being-there unperceived. A caress from someone who feels intense love for you manages to reach the skin of your soul, words seem to come from within and connect the breath of one with that of the other. This feeling of oneness with the other, part of the absolute peak of ecstatic fusion in love, is a condition that is absolutely different from normality, so that the thoughts and the emotions of daily life seem to become unrelated to the life of the soul. While loving each other intimately, we breathe in the soul and taste in the flesh that lightness of being that is nowhere else to be found. These are privileged moments of being, because they are radically different from ordinary experience. The ecstatic fusion with the other allows the lovers to live a quality of being beyond the normal, one that makes it seem possible to share existence, to reciprocally participate in the most intimate movements of being-there.

On the contrary, in ordinary life people can share everything except existing (Lévinas 1987, p. 42), that has nothing to do with anybody other than the existing being her/himself; in this sense the existing being is an isolated monad (Lévinas 1987, p. 42). We are alone, faced with our responsibility for the existential project, faced with the demand to give a fully human meaning to our time, faced with pain when it penetrates the soul like fog in autumn. When we have to face the most important things in life, when we are required to make crucial decisions, we are often inexpressibly alone. Solitude is not a condition open to choice: everyone is inevitably alone. The art of existing has to deal with this irremediable loneliness, and even while co-existing with others in the world, it is possible for us to imprint traces of meaning in so far as we manage to give voice to our singularity, our originality.

The evidence of my solitude is the work of my conscience. But my conscience, which is mine and mine only, has its generative matrix in the plurality of being-there; it is, in fact, the emerging form of the silent dialogue of the soul with itself, which is possible because the soul may become two in one: I who converse with myself. In this ontological tangle lies the difficult part of the human condition: my conscience, where I experience all my solitude and which evinces my singular being, has its own matrix in the plurality of two in one that structures the relational quality of being-there. It is this knowledge of endless solitude even in the intimate plurality of being-there which is the cause of the tragic and indissoluble loneliness every being experiences in the singularity of the act of existing.[7]

The most intense figure of solitude is Jesus, when facing his destiny alone in the olive grove (Matt 26, 36–46). When first he begins to pray, he orders his disciples to stay where they are, as he will go a little way away and pray alone, but then at the moment of solitary contemplation, he feels pain and anguish so hard to bear that, turning to his disciples, he asks them to keep his vigil with him. There is all the ontological depth of the meaning of being human in this need for others, an indisputable need, especially during the most crucial moments of existence, both when joy cheers the soul and when pain becomes unbearable. The disciples, however, fall asleep and Jesus points out their failure to remain "just one hour with me" (Matt. 26, 40). In moments of hardship, when our soul is confronting the more dramatic events of life and is overwhelmed by pain and anguish, we feel the need for others in all its ontological intensity, even if the burden of living remains something absolutely personal. And when those others are absent or have gone away, we feel as if we are in a wilderness, rootless and abandoned in the world.

---

[7] For the construction of ontological prerequisites on which to found the philosophy of care, the natural philosophical reference comes from Heidegger, for it was he who refocused our attention on care. Together with his, we may refer to other philosophies of relationality, such as those of Arendt, Nancy and Lévinas, who, as we will see, enable us to theorize essential qualities of care, such as responsibility. Nonetheless, at the moment of formulating the ontological frame to support the discourse that we are here developing, it does not seem justifiable to draw on either Heidegger or Lévinas, since as the first puts being-with-others as a priority of existence, thus locating relationality at the core of being-there, while Lévinas—though openly declaring his intention to distance himself from the ontology of relationality as a primary structure of being (1987)—affirms that the existent is immediately and always alone, and it is by starting from this solitude that he/she meets the other. But these two ontological visions far from being incompatible, are actually complementary, because only if they are considered together do they express the true quality of existence. We are born alone, it is true, immediately compelled to shoulder the responsibility of being-there, we all come to life lacking being, but with a porous substance that nourishes itself through the relationship with the other. For this reason, the first relational experiences play a fundamental role in the construction of identity. Consequently, it is not possible to maintain that there is a contradiction between the experience of solitude and that of sociality, because solitude is perceived as such simply because the pressure towards sociality originates within us just as powerfully. In other words, relationality is perceived in its essentiality for the very reason that we possess the ontological experience of being alone with ourselves.

The Neediness of the Other

The very task of cultivating the art of existence, the only thing able to transform the feeling that one is intolerably confined within the solidity of being into the possibility of being-there according to a scheme open to further events, evinces the inseparability of our being from that of others as an undeniable fact. Intense as it may actually be, the care each of us can implement towards our being-there is not sufficient to make life possible, since we all need to relate to others. The neediness for the other is immediately evident in the attachment of newborn to the maternal figure, and then reappears again in different forms all through life. We look for a friend with whom to feel we are sharing the essential core of our soul, a lover with whom to feel at one and to be able forget all else, a comrade with whom to plan a political project. When Heidegger (1988) talks of the existentive comprehension which prepares the project of being-there, he specifies that understanding is something that does not have as its subject an isolated self, but rather one who is together with others and with the world.

Each of us seeks the truth of existence, but when this search is conducted in solitude, even if many things can be recognized, none of these really is the truth. Just because we experience relationships that forge the substance of our life, the truth is the result of meeting with the other, of dialogue, of a path trodden together. Our ontological structure is essentially relational, in the sense that our being-there is developed through relationships with others. The essence of being is singular and plural at the same time (Nancy 1996, p.19) and this really means that the uniqueness of our being is possible starting from our development together with others. We do not come into our being through a single action but through exchanges of being taking place in the community where we live. The "fabric of being" (Murdoch 1997, p. 323) does not belong to the singular individual but is co-constructed by thoughts we have and gestures that we make together with others.

The difficult part of living consists in understanding the entire singular responsibility of the project of existing and at the same time realizing the inevitable need of the other for her/his own freedom. The decision not to be a passive subject regarding the inevitable materialization of time but to give it a form of our own, requires a thoroughly personal effort, an endeavor to face up to the evidence that solitude is not a metaphysical invention at all, but an existential givenness. At the same time, however, we shall perceive that the vital force making possible the ontological and ethical work of forging our being-there derives originally from the community that we belong to, because when we are searching within ourselves for the strength of the ontological and ethical breath we need, we find people with whom we intimately become our being-with-there.

When Iris Murdoch affirms that human beings are naturally selfish (Murdoch, 1970, p. 30), she uses as an example what happens when, too involved in the effort of living, we tend to perceive only our own being, completely isolated and responsible for our specific self, without simultaneously managing to see the relational substance of being-there and the fact that a self-referential vision of life is completely disastrous. It is precisely at the moments we suffer the sense of cold ontological solitude most intensely that we discover the inevitable essentiality of the relationality with the other. The fact of being alone becomes particularly evident when we begin to analyze past experience and cannot help thinking about certain existential mistakes, making us realize the whole weight of having missed something important. It is at those very times, however, that relating to the other, the person who helps you to retrieve the breath of being, is vital. The ontological structure of the human being is not monadic. On the contrary, it is a network, closely connected with the being of others. Therefore, if the essence of being is co-existence, we must acknowledge that if we cannot refuse a caress that communicates the nearness to another, a welcoming glance, or a word that makes our past seem less bitter, this is not mere sentimentality, but something human and vital.

When a human being is born, he/she actually begins to coexist; when he/she comes into the world, before being greeted by time or space, he/she is welcomed by a look. When the baby opens its eyes to the light it is at one with being accepted by the look of whoever will care for it. It is the maternal embrace that calms its primitive terror of finding itself exposed to the world. Birth coincides with finding ourselves exposed and care is the act of acceptance of the responsibility to offer protection from the threats that this exposure implies. When Kant indicates the fundamental categories of space and time, his statement is certainly essential, since those are basic ontological categories. However, he distracts the mind's attention from what takes precedence over everything else. Before time and space where the being will come into existence, there are the gestures and words of care of whoever welcomes a new life into the world and each of us has a categorical need for gestures and words that prove we are part of a caring relationship for the rest of our lives.

If existing is co-existing, then it is essential to find a rhythm to sharing with others in life. The ontology of relationality, while underlining the undeniable neediness for others that characterizes the human condition, shows the unavoidable necessity for an ethics of sharing. The basic epistemological structure of our culture makes us think of reality as a set of discrete entities holding together thanks to dynamic forces that act on them adventitiously. This is because we believe that an analytical philosophy, one that fractures the substance of life into separate parts, thus respecting a logic of division in order to discover the basic units, is the fundamental heuristic procedure to follow. Within this atomistic and disjunctive vision, the image of our person takes form as a being whose boundaries are constituted by our skin; but this atomistic vision does not correspond to the essence of the human condition, that is fundamentally relational, since personal identity is the evolving form of relationships that structure our vital space.

Socrates in the *Theaetetus* states "that nothing exists as invariably one, itself by itself, but everything is always becoming in relation to something" (157a-b). The path of life is always trodden with others, since no one can exist alone. To utter words, which is the same as creating the space in which to manifest our own essence, we need the other. Neither can we perceive our own body if there is no one else with whom to relate. Being aware that living is coexisting means knowing and feeling that our life, even if we are on our personal path, is intertwined with that of others and it is precisely as plural beings, not when we are on our own, that we are always able to find spaces and times to exist. When the awareness that our being is inexorably linked with the being of others fades, then we face the risk of madness. It is the ontological quality of our being-there that requires us to learn and cultivate the practice of sharing, to entwine our rhythms of existence with those of other beings. Since the path of life is never travelled alone, the wish for considerate and responsible coexistence should guide our being.

To sum up the statement above, it could be said that *if care qualifies as a significant ontological phenomenon of being-there and if existence is closely relational*, since being-with-others is the innermost essence of the human being, *then the caring for the being-there is identical to caring for the being-with and therefore with the caring for the others*. Being-there is to care for and in this care I find myself-with-others. Care as concern for the other, as solicitude for the well-being of the other, is an indispensable condition for a good life.

If we therefore share the assumption that care is *something ontologically essential*, then acting with care is a primary value, not only for those who receive care but also for those who give it. It is a value for those who receive it because without care they cannot become their potentiality-for-being, and it is a value for those who give it because taking on responsibility for care means placing oneself where it is indispensable for life itself. For this reason, the relationship of care brings value both to those who receive and to those who give care (Kittay 1999, p. 25).

The Conditionsnees of Being-There

Vulnerability

For the very reason that we are intimately relational beings, we depend on others; in this dependence on other-than-ourselves lies the typical vulnerability of the human being. The fact that our being is in a body and that the body has precise boundaries leads us to think of ourselves as discrete and distinct entities from others. Instead, our ontological matter is not something compact and confined within the skin of the individual being, but it is *porous*: it absorbs reality around it and models itself in relation to the other. This porous vision of being is implied by the words that Socrates pronounces in the *Phaedrus*, where he speculates that his learning may be due to the fact that the knowledge he has acquired is a result of being "filled in the manner of a vase, I know not from what sources (Plato, *Phaedrus*, 235d). It is the porosity of being that puts us in communion with things, but this being exposed to the quality of the events that invest our being-there not only makes it possible for us to gain sustenance from the other, but also to absorb what may harm us. If the porosity of being opens us to others by making a relationship possible, at the same time it becomes vulnerability.

It is true that relatedness shatters the solitude of being-there and allows us to share existence, but at the same time it renders us vulnerable, since we are constantly being subjected to the actions that other entities and other living beings set in motion. Such actions may nourish our being but can also place us in jeopardy.

The relational bond with others is translated into dependence upon others, that finds its reciprocity in power over others and also power which we are subjected to. In childhood we depend completely upon those who care for us, for everything from food to affection. Throughout life, we find the nourishment of ideas that the mind has need of in the exchange with others. These others may ask for help to put their life back together after a difficult period or to be looked after when injured in body or soul. The power to decide for oneself, which is the first condition in the exercise of freedom, an indispensable asset of life, can become the authority that decides the daily possibilities of the other's being-there. Our state of close connection with the world makes us dependent and inasmuch as we are dependent on the other we become vulnerable.

We come into being in a reality that possesses us and from which we cannot escape. We are not possessed of self-sufficiency. So, to be able to be, we turn to others and to the world. This being so, however, we come to depend upon these others and upon this world. The relationship with the other feeds our being, but at the same time limits us. We have need of the other and for this reason we try to relate to each other. We cling to the other, but the threat from which we seek shelter by holding on to that other can come above all from those who are closest to us (Rilke 1992, p. 21). In the plurality of the human condition the limitation we exercise towards each other is unavoidable. In this depending-on lies all the vulnerability of our being: of our project to exist, of our desires, of our affections.

What are we? "a potter's vessel, to be broken by the slightest shake or toss" (Seneca, *De consolatione ad Marciam*, 11.3). We are vulnerable in our bodily and spiritual life: we can be subjected to adverse environmental events that put our life in danger, we can fall ill, we can be hurt by someone else's actions with the consequence of losing good relationships that were built up with care, we can lose the job that allows us to lead a tolerably good life, we can lose our freedom, or we can simply lose our peace of mind.

The body is vulnerable because organic life can be affected by almost imperceptible changes. Situations of illness, disability and suffering that are intermittent or of short duration are more likely to be dealt with successfully if we hold on to our sense of self-sufficiency and autonomy. But life can also be affected by acute and chronic pain, by invalidating diseases, by a persistent weakness or disability, by traumatic events that cause lasting pain to the body and corrosive suffering to the soul and radically change the quality of life.

The relational essence of our being also conditions us in our search for excellence, since like any other relational being, we look for excellence in our relationships. Plurality is not only "conditio sine qua non" for existing, but also the "conditio per quam" each of us looks for the meaning of his or her life (Arendt 1958, p. 7). As a matter of fact, what mostly gives sense to life are relationships, like friendship, love, political connections intended to build shared spaces, and with these also all the actions that are related to qualities that create good relationships: kindness, courtesy, solidarity, compassion, generosity.

When you experience true friendship, you feel a vital force that nothing else can give you. You know you matter to someone, and that someone matters to you. We find support and we return it to the other and in this reciprocity of acknowledgement we truly experience the value of being-there. When life gives you an authentic love relationship, then the ontological solitude which is a crucial condition of our being-there seems to be something that has nothing to do with us, it seems to evaporate from our soul like the dew from the grass on a summer morning. Normally, we exist far from the living, pulsating center of things, we are not granted the possibility of experiencing the secret rhythm of the real, or at any rate only a fleeting suggestion of it now and then. But when our desire for good corresponds exactly to that of the other, then it is as if the innermost pulsation of being beats in our heart. We no longer feel ourselves to be simply one entity among many others, but to exist in harmonious duality with the other, and, in this way, we savour life to the full. This, indeed, is to experience the intensity and lightness of the joy of being-there.

The best things are, however, also those less subject to our will and more fragile, more at risk. Friendship and love transcend our will, they refuse any exercise of control. According to Simone Weil, friendship is something that should not even be desired. When we happen to experience it, it cannot be considered the result of our will, but as something unpredictable and gratuitous that denies itself to logic: it belongs to the order of grace […]. it is part of those things surplus (1970, p. 43). Friendship is not to be sought, but achieved, implemented just as with any other virtue. This is also true for love: it is not something that we can plan, that we can control, that we expect, but it is something that we accomplish, that we experience. And to further this possibility of cultivating friendship and nurturing love, we depend overwhelmingly on the other. The most valuable things in life belong to a transcendent order, they come about according to a logic foreign to any desire of control. They must therefore be removed from the egocentric exercise of imagination, from the desire to impose our own project. When we feel that it may happen, friendship is not to be managed but simply welcomed, with gratitude and generosity. When we realize that love has the potential to blossom, we should simply let it flourish.

As Socrates explains, love, a feeling that when experienced even for a few moments allows us to enjoy the presence of good, comes from Penia, that means poverty, lack (*Symposium*, 203b-c). To be poor means to lack something; we are poor because we lack the good, not being, but the good. Paradoxically it is that very state of poverty that allows us to experience things that are worthy of love, because it is the feeling of lacking something that make us strain to seek the good. It is indeed in this sense that Ulysses' refusal of Calypso's offer to make him immortal should be read, because only the state of weakness, lack and poverty allow us to experience good and beautiful things, friendship and love. Poverty seen as essentiality is a blessing: to be poor in spirit and pure at heart. Because only by reducing our being-there to its essence and eliminating most of our desires, aspirations, passions and beliefs, can we come into contact with the things that constitute the heart of the real.

The statement that excellence should be sought in relationships with others conflicts with the idea, one that has ancient roots in our culture, which affirms that it should actually be sought in the work, which consists in producing a world of durable things that are capable of withstanding the passage of time (Arendt 1958, p. 8). Paying attention to relationships means investing in precarious things which, even when they show themselves reliable, do not last longer than a lifetime. To devote ourselves to producing valuable things and actions means to invest in something that might last longer than a lifetime. These are not radically alternative visions, they may coexist, but they certainly are different: the first seeks for excellence within the limits of the human condition, the second reveals the aspiration to last beyond a lifetime, almost as if to follow a dream of immortality.

The assets of a relationship, at least the most valuable ones, not only transcend our will, but are also extremely delicate; Martha Nussbaum defines them as "vulnerable in an especially deep and dangerous way" (Nussbaum 1986, p. 344). They are vulnerable because they are exposed to jolts from reality, to the events of the world that can weaken or destroy relational connections. When a meaningful relationship falls apart, the pain is very intense: when we disengage from a political project shared with others, when a friendship dissolves, when a loving relationship comes to an end, it is at these times that we experience a sense of loss, not of a thing, but of a part of ourselves, because, while we are living a relationship, our development is closely entwined with that of others and when the other leaves, s/he takes a piece of us with her/him. If, generally speaking, no possession we might acquire can reduce the toll imposed by the fragility of existence, since every asset is always precarious, relational assets, while they do bring value to life, at the same time increase its level of vulnerability, and this is a sign that human beings will never find a shelter for their weakness.

There is a pain that we experience when we have to put up with evil, the evil that strikes the flesh or wounds the soul, which comes from the behavior of others or which we produce ourselves because we lack wisdom of things human. But there is also another kind of pain, it is what we experience when good is missing. This is a strange pain: it is not caused by something that strikes us, but it comes after the feeling that something essential is falling apart, something fundamental that makes life worth living. Since only good gives value to life, when it is lacking, we feel deprived of the essential, we feel we are left without a true sense of being-there.

The difficult part of the human condition is to have to commit oneself to where the highest risk of vulnerability lies. For this reason, it is the continuous search for a difficult balance between starting and maintaining relationships with others which characterizes existence, together with the attempt to avoid suffering and the danger that those relationships might imply. On the pediment of the temple in Delphi, there were three sentences. One of these stated: "Do not become too attached". It is clear that the flourishing of our being is subject to events and decisions of others that are beyond our will. But if it is true that the quality of our existence is jeopardized by our vulnerability, at the same time it makes our vulnerability necessary, since our development is closely connected to it. To be open, receptive, flexible and tender, to be emotionally invested in relationships or engaged in supporting them, to be able to nurture and be nurtured with love are ways of being necessary for accomplishing some of the most important goods of human life (Carse 2006, p. 35).

In order to avoid the pain that follows the loss of our relational assets, we could be tempted to direct our existence toward seeking forms of self-sufficiency. But besides being impossible, a completely self-sufficient life is not truly human, for the very reason that we are relational beings. To contradict certain theories of his time, Aristotle affirms that is absurd to think that people who live in solitude can be happy, because nobody can find happiness within himself, but needs friends (*Nicomachean Ethic*, IX, 9, 1169b 18–22). Therefore, not only do we need to take care of our relationships, but it is within those relationships that human excellence finds its possibility of actualization. Vulnerability, then, is inevitable, it is a structural quality of existence.[8]

Fragility

Even if we were not dependent on others, but could be self-sufficient, we would still lack something, we would always be at the risk of not being. Not only are we vulnerable because we are exposed to the blows of the world, the blows that we ourselves strike and those we receive from others, but we also suffer from an inner fragility: we are fragile because we come into being independently of our own will, once in the world we find ourselves part of the flow of time, and this being in time is not under our control.

Since we come into being without being able to decide whether we want to or not, but find ourselves already within existence, and then for the rest of our life we are in the power of that same existence, the innermost quality of the human condition is inconsistency. Our being-there does not derive from itself, but it comes from elsewhere and it occurs as if it is being prolonged moment by moment thanks to decisions that have nothing to do with us. In point of fact it is precisely our percep-

---

[8] The Aristotelian argument developed in *Politics* is the following: If X is part of C, then no description of the purposes of C's life can omit X; if following this reasoning (Nussbaum 1986, p. 351) we take it as valid, then, since relatedness is part of the human being, we cannot exclude relationships from his life. But this argument is not enough to prove the amount that should be invested in relationships. To take this step, we must resume the theme of the search for good: if as a quality of our being we are relational beings and when we seek, we seek for good, then good has a relational essence, consequently excellence must be sought in a relational experience. Good is something shared, that is, it concerns us as beings-with-others.

tion of our own state of being from one instant to the next, rather like autumn leaves on trees, that makes us so fragile. Discovering that I do not depend on myself, and that I am nothing by myself makes me realize how fragile and inconsistent my actual being is.

The fragility of our being is made more evident by the fact that our origin and our end are enigmatic, by the emptiness of a past unknown by us and by the impossibility of accomplishing all we desire. In Heidegger's words, we are beings who have been thrown into the world, and simply because this is the human condition, we are not given sovereignty over what determines the realization of our essential task, which is to develop our own being-there. We are in constant development, and the *logos* remains transcendent in relation to our possibilities. The abyss of nothingness can open at any moment, without our being able to avoid it. Since our weakness originates in the foundation of our being, fragility is our ontological quality.

The generative matrix of life abandons living beings to the hazardous condition of becoming, without providing any protection. However, human beings, as different from the vegetables and animals, are more open to risk (Rilke 2000, p. 529). Because we are not simply thrown into the world, like any other object, but as different from the other living beings that bring with them the form of their development, we face the task of inventing the shape of our own being-there quite alone. The cherry tree knows how to flower and the bee how to find nectar, in our case we have to invent the moves of our existence. In this task of life, we lack foundation, since we also lack the primary power on which our being-there depends; we always depend on other things. In this sense, living is daring; in this process of daring we are left alone with no shelter. As is recounted in the myth of Chronus human beings are abandoned in the world with the burden to care themselves from themselves (Plato, *Politicus*).

In our culture, we soon learn that the greatest good is freedom; and for our entire lifetime we seek ways of being that are the phenomenal concretion of a free spirit; but in this search, the paradoxical and dramatic quality of the human condition is evident, because it is an entity in the midst of its existence that seeks its liberty, and does this without having decided it, with a project which constantly has to deal with the limits imposed by reality, for instance other people's intentions and plans. Existence starts on the basis of a non-free decision, since it does not derive from us, but then for its entire lifetime the soul will feel the relentless longing for freedom. It is, one may say, as if at the very moment of initiating the being-there of each of us and conditioning us to become, the free core of being from which the becoming of everything originates has left in the soul the seed of its own quality of freedom.

Moments of freedom are privileged ones for being-there because they nurture the soul with that vital energy that makes the work of life more bearable; but these moments, when we feel truly alive, make the contrast with the other aspect of human condition even sharper: evincing the fact that we are always and forever compelled to deal with events and decisions that are beyond our control and that the quality of human life is totally *conditioned* by this.

Human beings are indeed conditioned entities: not only because when their existence begins it depends on a decision that comes from elsewhere, but also because everything they come in contact with becomes a condition of their experience (Arendt 1958, p. 9). Not only does the natural world influence us, but also the artifacts of human work, since once we are part of a dwelt-in space these things condition the ways of our existence, as do other people's actions towards us, be they intentional or not.

We have no control over the necessary provisions for the safe realization of the existential ontological task of developing our own being, because the human condition embodies a constant mix between what depends on us and what comes from the world. This is the sense in which our condition may be interpreted as one of being thrown. Since in the ground our being we are powerless, our ontological quality is *fragility*.

The condition of fragility also depends on the temporal substance of being-there. The expression "I am" does not indicate something that is solid, but a fluid substance: what I am is constantly changing with time, since our being is always a becoming. When we reflect on ourselves, we find that what we were an instant ago, now does not belong to us anymore, and the future instant is not actual yet. Because of our inexorable flowing our being is prolonged moment by moment. That reveals our ontological fragility.[9]

---

[9] The dimension of time is so important that the human being leaves the state of animality and rises to humanity when he/she manages to assign order to the flow of things in time. Prometheus, in facts, explains that: "First of all, though they had eyes to see, they saw to no avail; they had ears, but they did not understand; but just as shapes in dreams: throughout their length of days, without purpose they wrought all things in confusion. They had neither knowledge of houses built of bricks and turned to face the sun nor yet of work in wood; but dwelt beneath the ground like swarming ants, in sunless caves. They had no sign either of winter or of flowery spring or of fruitful summer, on which they could depend but managed everything without judgment, until I taught them to discern the risings of the stars and their settings, which are difficult to distinguish" (Aeschylus, *Prometheus*, ll. 447–458). So the first fundamental acquisition of knowledge consists in creating an idea of the passage of time, and to elaborate this vision means to enter the reality of the human condition.

It is this possibility of becoming our own being that makes the work of existing possible. It consists in trying to create our best form. This becoming, though, is not an event which occurs while following an intrinsic direction, but a duty to become our potential-for-being. The hard work to give shape to this is paradoxically the most delicate task we could undertake: it is a constant construction of ways of being-there that while responding to the compulsion to transcend every already achieved state so as to project itself further takes on a certain form, but this is always temporary and always to be exceeded. Even the most solid form that we can invent is always subject to a ceaseless ontological diminishing. The experience of existing, that we plan day after day, even in the best form and most stable appearance that can be created, always makes us feel like snowmen about to melt in the first rays of the sun.

We have to become our potential-for-being, and this process constitutes the work of existing. But just as the effort with which we preserve life must always be reiterated, because the result of this labor does not possess the quality of durability, so must the work of implementing our own being, because much of what we think has been acquired is always in danger of being lost. We are called on to find ways to preserve life and to invent a way to be-there that can give a meaning to our existence, but what we have created can easily disappear like dew in the warmth of the morning sun. Even our finest action will only last for a short time and is destined to slip away into the non-governability of becoming that overwhelms everything. It is as if existence is exposed to an eternal wind that shatters the path of experience, so even the most solid constructions end up surrendering to the blows of reality.

We work to develop expertise, but if this is not utilized we tend to forget it; we cultivate habits of the soul, but those too are never durable: they are fragile, they become inactive very easily; we can dedicate days and days to developing a manual ability, for instance that of being able to play the guitar, but an unexpected event could easily frustrate all our work. Anyone who conscientiously interprets the task of forging her/his own experience, devoting considerable time and energy to shaping her/his own being and to developing cognitive, affective and ethical stances. But however intensely we devote ourselves to cultivating this "technique for living", nothing of what we acquire has the slightest guarantee of permanence; we find ourselves having to deal with the inevitability of starting all over again so often, to the point that our most determined and passionate commitment feels futile. The awareness of our ontological fragility resonates in the words pronounced by Talthybius: Those with a reputation for wisdom are not a bit better than the insignificant (Euripides, *The Trojan Women* ll. 411–412). Our tragic ontological quality is that we are simply a breath of air. We busy ourselves structuring meaning, that then may be made to vanish with little effort. Kohelet painfully affirms that "behold, all was vanity and vexation of spirit, and there was no profit under the sun" (Ecclesiastes 2,11).

We could hypothetically unite our strength and realize an ideal world in which there is full agreement about the fact that vulnerability must no longer be possible by realizing a community where the vulnerability disappears because of the realization of perfect ethical relationships. But our fragility caused by the fact that we originate from an intention that is not ours and are going towards an end which is independent of our will, of our finding ourselves situated in being when for the entire time we can only actually exist in the present moment, with a past that is no longer here but may still influence a future that could be different from what we imagine, renders human life a tangle, enmeshed among forces that it cannot govern. Existence is a punctiform phenomenon of the actualization in the present of our potential-for-being; only in the present can we get in touch with being, and everything depends on what happens in the brief duration of moments ceaselessly following one another. Temporal being is something that is immediately transformed into non-being. As soon as we are in the present in which we happen to find ourselves and a point of being materializes, the former point is no longer there and almost immediately the present one too will slip into the past.

Awareness that our being-there is limited to the present and that neither past nor future are in our possession makes us acknowledge the fragility of our being and its instantaneity. This awareness suggests that is beyond the capabilities of any human being to take upon her/himself the whole duration of time. It is an unbearable burden to agonize over the entire length of our being since it is not in our control. This is what the Gospel means, when it reminds us: "Take therefore no thought for the morrow, for the morrow shall take thought for the things of itself. Sufficient unto the day is the evil thereof" (Matt. 6,34). To stay in the present, therefore, does not mean to be irresponsible, but to accept the quality of our being.

Simply because our being is a constant flow of moments of presence that one after the other slip into the irretrievable past and are leaning towards an unpredictable future, means that the ontological quality of the human being is a constant fluctuation between being and nothingness. This ontological quality of being always between being and nothing, that the mind cannot help perceiving, indicates that our being is intrinsically mixed with non-being. Our condition is that of a becoming that is never fully actualized, since the time to which our being belongs is nothing but a flux of moments. Its enduring anchorage is the flowing present (Stein 2002, I Vol, p. 40). It is our temporal substance that makes true possession of existence impossible, just as impossible as the control over life to which the soul, though realizing this impossibility, inevitably aspires.

Our being has its duration, but it is not actual for the entire time, its actualization dwells in the moment at which something potential of its being becomes real. When joy allows our soul to breathe, our being takes on a new quality, one it did not possess before; however, when this joy disappears, the soul is not fully alive any longer and our being takes on different nuances, or in other words, it changes its mode of actualizing itself. The actualization of being is therefore in continual development, and nothing can be taken for granted.

This punctiform being-there moment by moment has nonetheless the characteristic of continuity, in the sense that the already-been being leaves something of itself in the present and the not-yet of the future is already here as an anticipation that can influence the current being. Suffering that has already been experienced and replaced by other actualizations of being is only apparently nothing, since even if it is not fully alive any longer, it still remains imprinted in the soul, ready to revive again unexpectedly and able to alter even the most arduously conquered balance. As time goes by, being is congested with past events which, even if no longer relevant, dwells in between the folds of the skin of the soul, ready to come back to life when they collide with experience.

It is precisely the rekindling in the mind of ways of being that are already in the past, and that are no longer really under the conscious control of reason which render us fragile regarding experience. The fact that what was fully alive in the past and is now no longer so, still has the potential to become in its way of being-present, renders the past always potentially current. If this stratification of being is from one point of view what makes the richness of our own becoming, from another it renders life an unpredictable and manifold happening requiring a consistent investment of vital energy when it must be dealt with. Our being-there, prolonged from moment to moment in a punctiform actuality, takes no account of the lightness of living immersed in the present moment, since every moment potentially contains the entire phenomenological extension of existence: in every moment the past can be revived to contaminate the present and in every moment the making-present of the future colors the present moment in which we find ourselves with possibility that still does not exist. In this sense our flowing from moment to moment evinces at the same time both the ontological weakness of being and the weight of our becoming, which is an accumulation of past layers that only in privileged moments of being experiences the quality of lightness. It is evident that our ontological weakness, its lack of a fully actual being, is not the same as lightness when we consider that everything in us is potential, and because of this it can transform into actuality. Even its actual becoming is not certain, still "it is not not-being" (Stein 2002, I Vol, p. 39). In our punctiform actuality we are caught within the phenomenical extension of the temporality of existence: in this is concentrated all the ontological difficulty of our temporal substance.

In order to make our fragility tolerable, we count a great deal on thought: an activity human beings would like to think is exclusively theirs. We rely on reason—on its capacity to deliberate and choose, to make a plan and to decide what has value—in order to reduce the level of fragility and precariousness of human life (Nussbaum 1986, pp. 1–2). We acquired the notion of the value of reason at the very beginning of western culture and time shows that it is thanks to the use of reason we have evolved techniques which have permitted us to improve the quality of life.

It is true that thought can do much: through its use we have learned to understand the complex relationships of an ecosystem, to reconstruct the positions of the hanging stars from the hidden sky, to penetrate the most recondite secrets of matter and exploit this to build new worlds, plan cities, create poems where feeling finds words express itself, and last but not least comprehend the quality of someone else's lived experience and to seek with him/her ways of mutual understanding. Thought has the strength and the power to do this, and we can nurture it, direct it, bend it to our will; but we have no sovereignty over thought, either, even if we tend to identify our essence with it and we trust in its strength to help us cope life.

Not only has thought limits and can cause us to make mistakes, but suddenly this arduously conquered rationality can disappear and leave us to the mercy of the other irrational parts of our being. It is easy to experience the fundamental transience of the forms of being, even of those mastered through great effort. Without warning we realize that the mind is following unwanted and unexpected thoughts, and we can do nothing to stop this involuntary mental urge but only let it happen. Even reason, on which we have always relied to achieve sovereignty over experience, is in its turn in the control of life. Indeed, when the mind seeks quietness, a pause from thinking, it continues to feel the inexhaustible flow of ideas and emotions that nothing can stop. As if the life of our mind were nothing but a moment in a greater flow over which we have no power and that it resonates within it. If our essence consists in the life of the mind and if the quality of our being is fragility, then reason itself can only be fragile. We should remember that in Greek the word for the soul, *psyche*, also means *butterfly*, a metaphor for what is most delicate and fragile.

Granted, therefore, that the human being lacks a finite form and because of this he/she is burdened by the call to give shape to its being-there, if possible a good shape where the soul can reach moments of fullness and is characteristic of its becoming, we cannot avoid making projects for the development of our possible being. However, any project needs mastery over the conditions to be realized: we instead have only the present and this present, although it contains possibilities, does not guarantee any control over them. Ontological fragility consists in the hopelessness of solving the enigma of our origin and also in the impossibility of filling every single moment of our time with meaning, of calling into being everything we want and of nullifying everything else.

There has been evidence of a keen awareness of our lack of control over existence and of its subjection to external forces that subvert our projects from the literature of Ancient Greece onwards. So, at the conclusion of Euripides tragedy *Helen*, the Chorus announces: Many are the forms of divinities, and many things the gods bring to pass unhoped for. And what was expected has not been fulfilled; for what was not expected, a god finds a way (ll. 1688–1691). Occasionally, our lack of sovereignty over the project of existence is made so evident that it makes us feel at the mercy of events. In the texts of the great Greek tragedians there are many reflections on the impact that events out of our control have over our existence and on being subject to a destiny in which we can scarcely intervene: such is the power of these ungovernable forces that we could find ourselves "A life that's no life at all was your lot" (Euripides, *Helen*, l. 210). Some suffering cannot be avoided, but we can only learn how to bear it, to carry the burden without letting ourselves be overwhelmed. The perception of our own ontological weakness can be very severe, so much so that it can make us think that we have no longer the slightest control over our life and that even the last possible comfort—the hope that eventually things will change—has vanished. At this point it is inevitable to ask oneself: "So why do I go on living? What's left for me?" (Euripides, *Helen*, l. 290), questions which have the effect of intensifying one's sense of existential disorientation.

When we have in mind a distinct perception of our own undeniable fragility, according to which living corresponds to losing the possibility of life moment by moment, ontological suffering can expand in the soul and it is here, during moments of lacerating pain, that we come to realize the good that derives from the care that we can receive from others. Just one word can be enough to dispel the cramps of the soul, a single caress can make you feel the shards of your being come together, the tenderness of a hug can rekindle the life force. The experience, even if brief, of the good that you can derive from a caring gesture remains in the soul to nurture it with faith in the possible: the only thing that helps us in our search for the necessary energy to sustain the work of existing.

Ontological Weakness

Fragility and vulnerability cause ontological weakness.

We experience the fragility and vulnerability of our being all the time: to go on living we have to build a world where we can implement our possibilities, but any human artifact has a fragile and vulnerable consistency, either because it is exposed to the forces of the world, or because it must endure the ontological limits of our being-there. This is true not only of material artifacts, but also of spiritual ones.

There is a both a vulnerability and fragility of the body and also of the soul. Not only can bodily suffering drastically compromise the development of our being and threaten our faith in the possible, but also past difficulty—anxiety, anguish, fear of living—can gradually or abruptly penetrate the soul and exhaust vital energies. Our immaterial substance is made up of thoughts and emotions. When these are positive they nurture the mind, but when they are negative they cause suffering both to the flesh and to the spirit. With words we can construct worlds where we can experience the pleasure of being-there: where we can discover areas of meaning that expand the possibilities of life, emotional spaces, aesthetic openings, original ways in which to relate to other people and to things. But words do not always work in a positive way; even though they are incorporeal they can wound: they can destroy a dream, hurt the soul, break a relationship. In a fragment attributed to Parmenides it is said that words and thoughts structure the being (frag. 6) and if we assume that thoughts have the same power as actions, then we can say that uttering words to ourselves and to others has an ontogenetic power that should not be underestimated. In the tragedy that tells the story of Helen, Euripides explains that a ghost "Of thin air" created by an irate god was enough to cause war between two nations (Euripides, *Helen*, l. 35); and that an invention of the mind can be powerful enough to bring "So much grief" (Euripides, *Helen*, l. 195).

Expressing our ontological weakness in Aeschylus' *Prometheus*, the Chorus sings: "Do you see how weak [human beings] are, made from nothing, like a dream in which the blind race of Man sleeps forever" (ll. 547–550). Ontological weakness is a consequence of the fact that we are conditioned beings, since not only every natural things, but also everything that we build with our work inevitably become something that influences our existence (Arendt 1958, p. 9). In this sense freedom remains a dream.

Precisely because being-there is always a feeling, the awareness of our weakness is revealed in specific affective states that accompany experience. Our awareness of the fact that we are beings subjected continually to our transcendence, since we are constantly called to go beyond the present form of being in order to conceive and actualize other possible forms of existence, finds its expression in apprehension. The realization of the difficulties and unpredictability accompanying the effort of existing cannot help generating apprehension. Simply because the weaving of forms of existence is ceaseless, apprehension is an affective tonality typical of life. It can become a negatively problematic tonality, as is the case in moments of crisis, when it becomes excessive and jeopardizes the soul. But it is not necessarily a negative feeling; indeed, it carries out the essential function of accentuating being-there, rendering it open to the call for something further; in this sense it is the key-feeling of existence.

But at the very moment when we become aware that we can never fully actualize our potentiality-for-being, and that every instant something that nullifies what we built up can come to pass, another feeling may take possession of the soul: the anguish that we may not develop our being the way we want. Since we know that we shall not be able to actualize fully our potentiality-of-being, it is easy to be overwhelmed by anxiety. Lévinas, who devotes a significant part of his work to emphasizing the importance of the feeling that accompanies the awareness of their ontological status in all human beings, finds this to be anguish when faced with being (Lévinas 2001), as different from Heidegger, who maintains that anguish is the feeling that overcomes the spirit at the thought of death. Lévinas thinks that we experience anguish when we become aware that we are part of a reality that becomes regardless of our projects, as if insensible of our compulsions.

The mind is trapped by anguish when it perceive our being-there is trapped in that anonymous web of being that by Lévinas is named il-y-a, to indicate something that is there and it is there independently of me and that from this being there is no possibility of escape. The anonymous and undifferentiated il-y-a where we happen to exist and regarding which only when we decide to exist are we able to stand out with our own singularity, constitutes, nonetheless, a limitless germination of forms of being. It is not possible to escape from the bonds of the dense and unpredictable web of connections that ties us to the world as "il-y-a", that is as the anonymous state of being (Lévinas 2001). It is this awareness of being tethered to the network of things, within the tissue of reality, the dwelling of an endless uncontrollable tremor, which generates anguish.

We cannot experience being-there without feeling; feeling moves and orientates our own becoming. For this reason, it is necessary to take care of our emotional life, and as it expands in the soul, to prevent its negative tonalities from becoming an obstacle to the work of giving the best shape to our existence. In critical moments anxiety could become frenzy and anguish could become excessive and directly threaten the life of the soul. So, it becomes necessary to train ourselves in curtailing the risk of being consumed by negative feeling. Learning to slow down tensional dynamism and stay within the little presence we possess: this is the means towards accepting our condition of lack, the impossibility of becoming everything we would like to be. It is this that calms the soul and allows it to breathe in life through time.

If anxiety is something that we happen to experience involuntarily and anguish suddenly invades the soul like an avalanche when we unexpectedly realize we are lacking-beings instead, when we intentionally meditate on our weakness in detail, another feeling is generated, a sort of sentiment we can define as ontological pain. It is not an elusive feeling that, like apprehension, accompanies our becoming almost without our realizing it; nor is it an upheaval in the soul, like anguish, due to the discovery that we are faced by an apparently unbearable reality; but it is a thought that develops gradually during those periods when the mind pauses to meditate on being-there and becomes profoundly aware of the intensity of our ontological weakness. In comparison to apprehension and anxiety that are feelings that we are subjected to, we experience ontological pain when we investigate the quality of our condition in greater detail. For this reason, knowing is suffering (Aeschylus, *Prometheus*), since knowing means to learn how to see things for what they are, to see them from all points of view and to feel the quality of reality in the innermost layer of their substantiality.

To face with the difficulty of dealing with the acceptance of the quality of our being-there is, paradoxically, one of the limits of human reason: the tendency to sometimes absent oneself from the real and evade the necessity for a deep investigation of problems. If we spent whole our time thinking constantly about the inescapable importance of our inner weakness, the ontological pain could become so intolerable as to absorb all the energy that nurtures life. The mind possesses a sort of trick mechanism that prevents us from realizing our hidden impotence. In fragment 29 Semonides, remembering the sentence that he himself defines as very beautiful in the essay by Chios, where he writes "As leaves on the boughs are the destinies of mortal human being", and then continues: "Few are those who after listening to her/keep her in their hearts: but in everyone dwells hope/innate in the youthful soul".

Awareness of life emerges in an individual after a disruption, an interruption of his/her dwelling in the openness of being, in the immediacy of the becoming of things. When we become aware of our own ontological quality, we feel torn away from the substance of existence, irremediably far from the simple being of sensitive things; It is this feeling of alienation from natural order that causes Zambrano[10] to say that human beings "lack pure and simple reality" (Zambrano 2020, p. 60). We lack the immediate reciprocal giving of things. We find ourselves called to the work of living and of having to bear alone the duty of constantly transcending the being-there that we are for a further being-there.

The awareness of our ontological weakness is something hard to put up with, it is like an unbearably heavy burden and thought tries to escape this burden in every way possible, so we invent a soul that goes to heaven: "and when, after having

---

[10] Please note that all the translations from the Spanish of Maria Zambrano's works are made by the author herself.

freed yourself from your mortal body, you go to heaven, you will be like a god, /no longer mortal but immortal, incorruptible", said Pythagoras (The golden verses). Or else we find consolation in the impermanence of our being remembering that "death looms over everybody: /equally divided/between good and evil" (Semonides, frag. 9).

Finding ourselves conditioned by the fragile quality of our being and by our vulnerability to the physical and relational forces that operate in the world challenges the human spirit to the extent that the greater part of ancient philosophy devotes itself to finding ways of rendering this condition tolerable. In Plutarch's opinion, the capacity to accept what befalls us epitomizes the most favourable predisposition towards the attainment of the greatest good a human being can aspire to: a serene soul. Since we have no sovereignty over life, wisdom asks us to accept what happens as necessary, and from this necessary occurrence we should try to identify whatever good, whatever advantage, this may bring us (Plutarch, *On tranquillity of mind*, 466e). To encourage the feeling of opposing the necessary order of things is not just useless but also harmful, because it just adds pain to pain: "So must I bear as lightly as I can, that destiny that fate has given me, for I know well against necessity, against its strength, no one can fight" (Aeschylus, *Prometheus*, ll. 103–105).

Knowing how to accept the quality of our own being has nothing to do with resignation. Pain, negativity, finding ourselves conditioned by what we cannot control are an inevitable part of existence. To accept the quality of the human condition simply means to know what we are in order to project our being-there within its limits, not to abandon every single desire of further being. Every human being, since s/he is unique, comes into the world to begin her/his own beginning, and because of that s/he has within her/himself the capacity to act both physically and mentally to initiate a new occasion of being. Since this beginning happens in a world whose dynamics are unpredictable for us, we cannot delude ourselves that it is possible to avoid experiences of apprehension. But knowing that anxiety is typical of the human condition, does not signify giving up the search for moments of quietness, because even if it is true that suffering teaches us to look at things differently, it is also true that the modicum of truth available to us can only be apprehended when the soul is at peace.

Sustaining the work of life and dedicating vital energy to the cultivation of the art of existing requires the knowledge of how to endure *ontological pain*. Not the sort of endurance that that is defiance, but a forbearance that comes from understanding how to accept in full the dramatic quality of our immanence, and this, moreover, while husbanding the desire for transcendence. Knowing how to accept is not to be intended in the sense of giving up, but of embracing the quality of the real because abiding by our perception of what we are is essential for us to be able discern the tiny window of opportunity making accessible our actualization. In other words, to accept while continuing to foster our own desire, the desire of good, of *eudaimonia*.

So, if we are lacking beings, non-finite in the form of our being-there, and, owing to this, we are called on to become our own potentiality-of-being-there, and if this work of becoming has to deal with our intimate fragility and deep vulnerability, if this development is entwined with that of others who lack and need what fosters life just as we do, then after having defined care as the action that preserves, shelters and protects being, we may affirm that, on the basis of what can be defined as *ontological evidence*, that we all need care: care is the ground of our being.

To arrive at this thesis, a basic but essential analysis of the human condition has been developed; this analysis is indispensable to the task of drawing a theory of care. Indeed, when attempting to determine if care may be considered as a proper component of being-there, in its relating to others and its dwelling in the world, we need a vision of the human condition that is as clear and rigorous as possible. An effective theory of human experience must be able to comprehend the essential quality of our being.

The Paradigmatic Horizon

The act of thinking is essentially the formulation of concepts. The dawn of an idea is a wonderful moment, but it may remain unrealized, however long we ponder and refine upon it, as the problem lies in finding ideas that are able to express the *essential part* of a phenomenon. In order to permit these artifacts of the mind to carry out their required function of illuminating experience, they must be examined, tested against reality, reformulated over and over again. We must care for the work of thought as it is the essential work of being-there. Considering how complex reality is, we must always bear in mind how incomplete the products of our thinking are. Accepting uncertainty, the non-finite, means staying within the bounds of reality.

Considering that every product of the mind takes shape within a precise horizon of thoughts and therefore is inevitably situated inside specific cultural boundaries, it is a principle of epistemological ethics to define this horizon as clearly as possible. Phenomenological philosophy is the essential reference for the development of the discourse that we are elaborating here, both based on its specific ground and on thinkers who are close to this particular philosophical theory, not only because it is in the phenomenological field that the theory of care takes shape in contemporary thought, but also owing to the method of thinking that phenomenology demonstrates. Then, because philosophy, as it always has, inevitably returns to its origins, the fundamental reference is to ancient Greek thought, where the concept of care, and with it the idea of being-there, has its beginning.

Before I start to define my argument, it should be specified that a constant reference for the elaboration of the descriptive theory of care is the analysis of data that I have collected during the course of time on the thoughts and the sentiments of those who work as care providers. An empirical phenomenological research, which deals with the comprehension of a phenomenon through the analysis of the world of meanings elaborated by people who have direct experience of this phenomenon, must immediately identify those defined as "privileged witnesses". In this case we consider them to be those who are designated by other care professionals in the community they belong to as examples of good care practice. If care is the primary human activity, in order to understand its very essence we cannot analyze mediocre conduct, but experience that people who lived them indicated as examples of good practice of care for everybody.

To derive our reflections from practical data keeps theory in touch with reality. In many cases philosophy prefers to discuss reasoning rather experience (Murdoch 1997, p. 369), but while doing so it loses its depth, it loses touch with the reality that alone can lend perspective to the act of thinking. Being anchored to experience, rather than to an analysis based on critical jargon, can give the impression of articulating thoughts which are too simplistic, almost banal; but thoughts faithful to reality, leading to where the meaning of things resides, are often just the simplest ones.

Bibliography

Arendt, H. (1958). *The Human Condition*. Chicago (Il.). The University of Chicago.
Aristotle in 23 Volumes, translated by J. H. Freese. Aristotle. Cambridge and London. Harvard University Press; William Heinemann Ltd. 1926.
Aristotle, R. W., Ackrill, J., & Urmson, J. (1909). *Nicomachean Ethics*. University Press.
Benner, Patricia and Wrubel, Judith (1989). *The Primacy of Caring*. Menlo Park-CA: Addison-Wesley Publishing Company.
Bowlby, S.A. (1969). *Attachment and loss, vol I, Attachment*. London: Hogarth Press.
Bubeck, G. Diemut (2002). *Justice and the Labor of Care* (pp. 160-185). In E.F. Kittay and E.K. Feder (Eds.). *The Subject of Care. Feminist Perspectives on Dependency*. Boston: Rowman & Littlefield Publishers.
Burian, P., & Shapiro, A. (2011). *The Complete Euripides*. Oxford University Press.

Carse, A.L. (2006), "Vulnerability, agency, and human flourishing". In Taylor, C., Dell'oro, R. (a cura di), *Health and Human Flourishing*. Georgetown University Press, Washington DC, pp. 33-52.

Cicero. M. T. De Officiis. With An English Translation. Walter Miller. Cambridge. Harvard University Press; Cambridge, Mass., London, England. 1913.

Colli, G, (1993), *La sapienza greca*. III Eraclito. Milano: Adelphi.

Euripides, Morwood, J., & Hall, E. (2001). *Hecuba; The trojan women; Andromache*. Oxford University Press.

Euripides. The Complete Greek Drama, edited by Whitney J. Oates and Eugene O'Neill, Jr. in two volumes. 2. Helen, translated by E. P. Coleridge. New York. Random House. 1938.

Harré, R. e Gillet, G. (1994). *The Discursive Mind*. Thousand Oaks, CA: Sage.

Harré R, Gillet G. (1996). *La mente discorsiva*. Milano: Cortina (Trd. Italiana).

Harreé and Gillet 1996, La mente discorsiva.

Heidegger, Martin (1962). *Being and Time*. Translated by John Macquarrie and Edward Robinson. New York (NY): Harper Collins Publishers.

Heidegger, M. (1988). *The basic problems of Phenomenology*. Translation, Introduction, and Lexicon by Albert Hofstadter. Bloomington & Indianapolis: Indiana University Press.

Heidegger, M. (1992). *History of the Concept of Time: Prolegomena*. (Translated from German by Theodore Kisiel) Bloomington, In: Indiana University Press.

Kittay, Eva (1999). *Love's labor. Essays on Women, Equality, and Dependency*. New York and London: Routledge.

Lévinas, E., (1987). *Time and the Other* (translated by Richard A. Cohen). Pittsburgh, Pa: Duquesne University Press. Originally published as Le temps et l'autre. Grenoble-Paris: Arthaud, 1947.

Lévinas, E. (2001). *Existence and Existents*, Translated by Alphonso Lingis, Pittsburgh, Pa: Duquesne University Press.

Mitchell, S.A. (1988). *Relational concepts in psychoanalysis. An integration*. Cambridge – Mass: Harvard University Press.

Murdoch, I. (1970). *The sovereignity of good*. London: Routledge.

Murdoch, Iris (1997). *Existentialists and Mystics*. London: Chatto & Windus.

Nancy, J-L, (1996), *Etre singulier pluriel*. Paris: Galilée.

Noddings, Nel (2002), *Starting at Home*. Los Angeles: University of California Press.

Nussbaum, M. (1986). *The Fragility of Goodness. Luck and Ethics in Greek Tragedy and Philosophy*. Cambridge: Cambridge University Press.

Nussbaum, M. (1994). *The Therapy of Desire. Theory and Practice in Hellenistic Ethics*. Princeton: Princeton University Press.

Nussbaum, M. (2001). *Upheavals of Thought: The intelligence of emotions*. Cambridge: Cambridge University Press.

Plato (1952). *Plato in Twelve Volumes*, translated by Harold N. Fowler. Cambridge, MA, Harvard University Press; London, William Heinemann Ltd.

Plutarch (1970). *The Tranquillity of Mind*. In Moralia. VI. (translated from Greek by W.C. Helmbold. Cambridge: Loeb Classical Library.

Ricoueur, P. (2007). *Etica e morale*. Brescia: Morcelliana.

Rilke, R. M., (2000) *Poesie* 1907-1926, (translated into Italian) Torino: Einaudi.

Seneca L. A., *Minor Dialogs Together with the Dialog "On Clemency"*; Translated by Aubrey Stewart, pp. 162-203. Bohn's Classical Library Edition; London, George Bell and Sons, 1900.

Stein, E. (2002). *Finite and Eternal Being: An Attempt at an Ascent to the Meaning of Being*, translated by (Vol. I). Washington: Ics Publications.

Stein, E. (2002). *Finite and Eternal Being: An Attempt at an Ascent to the Meaning of Being* (Vol. II). Washington: Ics Publications.

Stolorow, R.D. and Atwood, G. (1992). *Contexts of being. The intersubjective foundations of psychological life*. Hillsdale, NJ: The Analytic Press.

Stolorow, R. D., and Atwood, G. E., (1995). *I contesti dell'essere. Le basi intersoggettive della vita psichica*. Traduzione di E. Griseri.Torino: Boringhieri.

Weil, S. (1970). *First and last notebooks, translated by Richard Rees*. London: Oxford University Press.

Weil, S., Waiting for God (1973). Introduction by Leslie E. Fiedler. New York, NY: Putnam's Sons -Harper Colophon.

Winnicott, D. W. (1987). *Babies and Thei Mothers*, The Winnicott trust, Addison-Wesley Publishing.

Zambrano, M. (1996). *Persona y democrazia. La historia sacrificial*. Madrid: Siruela.

Zambrano M., (2020). *El hombre y lo divino*, Madrid: Alianza Editorial, 2020.

The Essence of Good Care

2

The heuristic aim underlying this work is that of defining a rigorous philosophy of care, one that identifies the essential qualities of this primary subject. The epistemic assumption that serves as a horizon for the study is that the phenomenological method embodies the approach most likely to yield the paradigms leading to a rigorous theory of care. The adoption of this method entails investigating what specifically constitutes the essence of care. A phenomenology of care is not limited to providing a description of caring acts, but directs the inquiry towards identifying the exact meaning and significance of this term. Using the above generative research issue as a starting point, the study hopes to provide a descriptive theory whose focus is the essence of care.

Questions of Method

In Search of the *General Essence*

The main purpose of this study is that of deploying an argument that may be of use to people who deal with care so as to improve and guide their actions. Indeed, to do the right thing in the right way it is necessary first of all to know what one is dealing with. As Socrates states, there is only one principle for those who intend to decide well: we need to know what the decision is about, otherwise an utter mistake is inevitable and to know this means to know the essence of a thing (Plato, *Phaedrus*, 237c). When the essence of what we are talking about has been clearly defined, then the rest must be said with this definition firmly in mind (*Phaedrus*, 237d).

One of the principal tenets of phenomenology is that the first stage in a deliberately rigorous theorization of any branch of knowledge consists in determining the essence of the subject under discussion, that is, identifying its essential qualities. The term "essence" refers to the core structure of something, which is made up of the series of essential qualities that necessarily define it, since without them it could not be: «Everything belonging to the essence of the individuum another individuum can have too» (Husserl 1982, p. 8). Husserlian phenomenological theory maintains that every object of thought has an essence, and this essence is the fullness of specificity that constitutes it. Husserl distinguishes between eidetic and experiencing intuition: the experiencing intuition has an empirical object while the datum of eidetic intuition is a pure essence (Husserl 1982, p. 9). For comprehending the essence of care we put in act the experiencing intuition which has to be applied to each phenomenon of care, in order to grasp the essential properties that constitute it, and without which it ceases to be care at all.

The recurring events of daily life make us realize that the possibility of care comes in many guises. Each one differs according to the subject that puts it into practice, when and where it is carried out, the feeling that accompanies the experience, and so on. But even if the practical instances of care are many and various, the essence of care is unique, and is always implemented whenever and wherever one acts with care. The essence is the factor that "is there" in every variation of any kind of phenomenon. This same factor represents the essential properties of a phenomenal field, that is, it manifests its specific identity.

Essence can be defined as the characteristic core without which any reality would be no such thing. When the essence of a thing is put in words, others who have not had direct experience of it can intuitively grasp its essential qualities, which according to a radical phenomenological vision are universal and necessary qualities of all things of this type. Husserl states that the essence is an invariant, that is "the *necessary general* form, without which an object such as this thing, as an example of its kind, would not be thinkable at all" (1973, p. 341). This "invariable factor", which identifies all the variations of a phenomenon, is the "universal essence".

Such cognitive balancing acts necessitated by the search for the essence of a phenomenon may seem futile. Nonetheless, the eidetic operation of identifying essence, understood as the general property of a class of phenomena, is fundamental to the construction of a strictly grounded discourse, since only when the essence of care has been defined is it possible to identify among all the phenomena we experience those that can be referred to as "care". For a phenomenon to be defined as "care" all the qualities that structure the essence of care must present. An eidetic analysis aims at a formal and general definition of care, since it indicates the qualities that a phenomenon in general must possess in order to be defined as care.

Thought which searches for essence as such is essential, can be defined a form of action since it draws fields of reality (Heidegger 1998, p. 236).

The Essence of Concreteness

The essence of care can be summed up in a concept that must then apply to every experience of care. It is like the empty form of everything, so it can be defined as a *general-formal essence*, "it is precisely this essentiality of essence that phenomenology is looking for".

In concrete reality, however, we do not encounter pure general essences, but particular actualizations of essences. I encounter joy inasmuch as I experience it, not joy itself as an idea. Joy itself is a conquest of the mind, not an individual lived experience. In the same way, I experience care as I receive it or in the way I perform it in my being here and now, not in its general essence. The examination of single events, even though they are always diversified by experience, is therefore absolutely necessary if we want to recognize reality. Exact knowledge is based on data, on what Aristotle defines "τὸὄτι" (Aristotle, *Nicomachean Ethics*, I, 4, 1095b 6). Referring to data means offering a phenomenological analysis of concreteness.

If we agree to consider essence as something that cannot be changed or deprived of one single thing, since it categorically constitutes its own reality, then it is possible to speak of essence even in the contingent world of becoming, in which phenomena vary continuously. In actual fact, every phenomenon exhibits specific qualities, which even if they are not part of essence in general, contribute to defining their particular essence, their essence as *individuum*. Starting from this assertion it is legitimate to speak of an *essence of the concrete*, which is *contingent and situated*, since it consists of those *concretely essential* qualities that qualify a specific event of experience.

The peculiar phenomenal concretion of an essence (Heidegger 1992, p. 257), in addition to embodying some essential qualities, also highlights other properties that depend on the specific way of its happening; these are not part of essence in general, but combine to define its singular essence, which is a particular concretion of general essence. In fact, everything has its own essence as an *individuum*. Expressing the essence of care as such is something other than indicating the essence of a particular care experience: to be able to talk about "cats" it is essential to identify the essence of cat-ness; all entities that show the essential properties of cats are cats; but then a cat can be brown, soft or cuddly. The set of qualities that specify an entity as an individual constitute its particular essence. For this reason we speak of *essence of the concrete* as distinguished from *eidetic essence* which is the essence in general of a series of phenomena.

General essence is an object that can be experienced through thought, while particular essences are embodied in phenomena that are part of the real world, so we experience these in flesh and blood. While phenomenological philosophy as an eidetic science is concerned with general essence understood as a set of universal and necessary qualities, a philosophy of experience whose field of interest is the everyday world, where care occurs in a multiplicity of different phenomena, is interested in conceptualizing the essence of a concrete phenomenon in a description which is also able to express the changing and changeable qualities of experience is therefore crucial. To understand the qualities of reality it is necessary to deal with individual acts of care: the care that a mother shows for one specific newborn in one specific situation; the care a teacher puts into facilitating a student's learning process; the care that a nurse dedicates to a specific patient in a specific situation within a particular healthcare environment; the care that a social worker dedicates to a child in foster care with his/her own unique experience. If we assume that every object of thought has an essence, and this essence is the fullness of particular specificities (Stein 2002, I Vol, p. 70), then it should be possible to discover the essence of every single concrete actualization of care.

The search for general-formal essence should be understood as having a significant relationship with the search for singular-concrete essences. General-formal essence must be thought of as a framework that is filled with concrete elements in relation to the single determinations that give shape to the actual occurrence of things. If we accept the idea that there is a necessary relation between the multitude of general ideas and individual concretions, then the construction of a philosophy of care should develop a descriptive theory of care that should reveal both the general essence of care and the concrete essences of the lived experience of care.

If solving the problem of general-formal essence also satisfies the urge to find a stringently exclusive core for discourse, it nonetheless confines thought to a plane that seems far removed from the concrete happening of things. On the other hand, attention to the essence of the singular-concrete, though it places thought within the concrete happening of reality, still keeps it dispersed among individual phenomena. To construct a rigorous theory of care it is not sufficient to define the general essence of care and furthermore to analyze singular phenomena, but it is necessary to identify a middle ground of analysis between the general and the individual plane; that means distinguishing different *phenomenic areas of care*, and then to identify their essence. Indeed care is actualized in different *phenomenic areas*, that can be defined *regional phenomena*, which depend on the context in which it occurs: in education, in family life, in health care, in relations between peers, etc. A regional area includes all concrete acts of care sharing a set of qualities: maternal care, friendship care, educational care, health care ... To understand the concrete reality of care, it is necessary to conduct an analysis that captures the specificities of each phenomenic area. Given that there exists a *universal essence* (Husserl 1973, p. 341), a *regional essence* and a *singular essence*, then a research genuinely interested in the truth of experience should deal with the general eidos of care, with ideas of various regions of care (educational, maternal, nursing, social), and also with the essence of the individual concrete acts of care.

Seeds of Method

Phenomenology, conceived as an eidetic science concerned with the essential and general qualities that define the core of a phenomenal universe, is not concerned with the contingent qualities and particulars which characterize a phenomenon in its singularity, because, being non general, they are considered invalid for the purpose of constructing foundational knowledge. Nonetheless, to a philosophy of experience, intended to embrace the qualities of phenomena that are met with in ordinary life, even the contingent qualities that belong to a specific phenomenon are important. Human experience, as well as the biophysical world, in its continuous variation cannot be grasped in its true essence if it seeks only the universal and necessary forms, disregarding its happening in the concrete, specifically located and contingent forms of daily becoming.

From the point when the difference between general and concrete essence begins to emerge, either in its singular or regional manifestation, it would seem appropriate to hypothesize a strict distinction between theoretical and empirical thought, and then consider general essence as an object of the theoretical investigation and concrete essence as an object of empirical research. Empirical research, in the field, concentrates on situations in which people implement caring actions; theoretical analysis, getting down to brass tacks as it were, so defined because it considers the products of thought as data, tries to identify the essential qualities of care independently from the single situations in which it can happen.

Keeping the investigation levels of the theoretic and empirical investigation separate, however, does not have any epistemological legitimacy if we mean to arrive at a descriptive theory as faithful as possible to the essence of things. The investigation that aspires to construct a true knowledge does not recognize any separation between hypothetically different sets of reality; if we examine the life of the mind from a phenomenological perspective, we see that theoretical thought cannot

exist without reference to experience, just as the heuristic process that has concreteness as its object always has a general idea as a criterion for its investigation.

When Husserl hypothesizes that essences are objects of an intuitive action, he
evokes the platonic vision of ideas and the pre-discursive thought that could grasp
these intangible noetic objects, through a sort of intellectual perception. Taking a
step back from Husserlian idealism, we should not consider the essence of care as
a pure idea or an intuitive recognition, which is free from any experiential reference; as ever, essence is the fruit of a train of thought that slowly builds up an idea
starting from the constant, if not evident, reference to experience; just as the single
and contingent phenomenology of care cannot be considered as an experiential
discipline if the mind does not possess at least a germinal level of general eidetic
knowledge of care.

Essence, and this is generally true of many other things, can only be apprehended
through the method of a comparative consideration (Heidegger 1949, p. 294) of
many elements. If we must access and analyze the greatest possible variety of poems in order to appreciate the core of poetry (Heidegger 1949, p. 294), we need to
examine many different experiences of care to enable us to discern its essence.
These, however, may be considered as phenomena of care only if we have in mind
an idea of care that does not already possess a definite connotation but is sufficiently
abstract or, in other words, is disconnected from the particular, so that we can identify and therefore classify determined phenomena as being actions of care.

This goes to show that there is in fact a circularity between two different planes
of thinking which is difficult to pin down: the plane of thinking which is immersed
in the facts of concrete experiential happening while attempting to distinguish the
essential qualities of these facts, and the plane of thinking which is theoretically
working on a more abstract level and trying to discover the innermost and at the
same time more general interweaving of things so as to establish this as a condition
for the ordering of experience.

Husserlian eidetic phenomenology establishes as an objective of its investigation the search for the essence of a phenomenon that must be apprehended in its
purity. We know this to be an unreachable target, since knowledge is always situated: during field research, we find actualizations of care which are always influenced by context and which are able to realize only certain aspects of care. Even if
our theoretical research starts from the general question "what is care?"; in reality,
during the stage of analysis, we are inevitably conditioned by the perspectives of
the studies we encounter and utilize, which are always situational and therefore
partial. There are of course inevitable limits to the process of cognitive actions towards the ideal of a knowledge that is capable of containing the universal essence
(universal as far as the cultural context in which we act is concerned, not, of course,

valid for any possible cultural world). But although these limits are quite clear from the outset, we cannot give up the search for a heuristic process that allows the most complete and rigorous access to the essence of care.

Reasoning from a phenomenological point of view, though this is indispensable to the establishment of guidelines for a rigorously developed analysis, nonetheless entails distancing oneself from realism. To be realistic means to believe that knowledge of a given reality consists in recognizing the qualities of this reality, while to be constructivist means to states that direct access to a reality presented in objective terms does not exist, since the discerning subject always intervenes in the real. Therefore, when searching for the essence of care, I must realize that I do so by first defining the limits of the phenomenon and this anticipatory definition is possible because I have constructed my ideas on the basis of experience. This enactive vision of knowledge underlines the impossibility either of separating the cognitive levels or of dividing up the elements of the process by clearly identifying the original point of the elaboration of an idea.

According to Husserl, the cognitive act that is able to grasp generality is intuition, specifically the intuition of essence. From the moment at which Husserl affirms that "originally presentive intuition" is the source of the knowledge of essence (1982, p. 36), he confers the quality of a science to eidetic knowledge. With this epistemological thesis, Husserl determines the difference between eidetic science and experiential science, and in so doing he locates the rigorous scientific thought far from experience, since experiential thought captures only singularities and no universalities (1982, p. 37).

I built up and developed the research on care by taking some steps away from Husserlian theory. In order to describe the essence of lived reality, I think there is no definite separation between eidetic and empirical science, since there is no impure knowledge of the experiential data and pure knowledge of eidetic intuition. We are permanently in touch with concrete things in the world and the knowledge of essence must inevitably be blended with experiential knowledge. This means that when I look for general essence I am obliged to refer to my concrete experience, even if the tension that directs thought is about pinning down that essence of the thing that is not tangible although it is fully real in every aspect. It is therefore impossible, as Husserl nevertheless asserts (1982, p. 37), to replace experience with something more general, that is, intuition and from this to theorize a discontinuity between a science that develops at the level of general ideas and an empirical science which takes attention to the singular phenomenon.

In an era marked by constructivism it is difficult to accept, as Husserl does, the platonic vision according to which data founded on intuition are primary factors and therefore starting from intuition means "we take our start from what lies prior to all standpoints: from the total realm of whatever is itself given intuitionally and prior to all theorizing, from everything that one can immediately see and seize upon" (Husserl 1982, p. 38). There is no thinking without experience, but we certainly have different kinds of thought: the more experiential type and that which becomes progressively more abstract. Any investigation that searches for general essence is bound to take into account that this is always relative to the concrete phenomena of experience, therefore the search for the general cannot be thought of as separate from the analysis of the particular. It is not therefore an intuitive action that recognizes the essence directly but one that returns to the definition of the concept of essence through an analysis of specific cases until it is possible to find those qualities that they all share.

A philosophy of care that intends to establish itself as rigorously founded knowledge must therefore necessarily develop the two different levels of the investigation. It must aim at defining the general essence while never losing sight of the concrete; it must examine the manifold aspects of concrete phenomenicity by constantly evaluating the results of those cognitive actions which analyze experience through the idea of general essence that is taking shape in the mind. A dialogic and recursive movement between different planes of the life of the mind is the specific trait of an interpretation of the phenomenological method that unites the principle of faithfulness to reality in its concrete happening with the necessity of a theory as generic as possible.

This study represents the last stage of a series of research where I alternated the analysis of literature, the research of a general knowledge of care and a series of empirical investigations in experiential worlds where care is carried out. In this interlacing of critical, theoretical and empirical investigations, the research of the general-formal essence is developed together with the attention to single cases of care actions and with them the research of the regional essence of care as it is actualized in different areas of experience: the informal maternal relation and friendly relationship (Mortari 2006), the formal education (Mortari 2013) and nursing relationship (Mortari and Saiani 2013). However, it is only at this point that a descriptive theory of care in search of the *eidos*, that is to say its essential general qualities, is beginning to take shape. At the same time it is managing to salvage the concrete phenomena, or in other words the qualities of the phenomenic happening of care.

Before starting the real job of outlining the essence of care, we should bear in mind one important idea. According to Arendt, the human mind is capable of recognizing the essence of things that surround us, of everything we are not, while it would not be able to understand the essence of human nature (1958, p. 10), since what intimately constitutes us can only be understood by another entity that does not share our condition, and can therefore think from another ontological perspective. It is true that to seek for the essence of care is not the same as to seek to understand human nature. Precisely because care is something that gives a shape to our bèing, it is not easy to talk about it, as is the case for things that are outside us. Any discussion about the essence of care requires both a degree of caution and the ability to accept its inevitable non-definiteness. A philosophy that searches for the essential knows its own non-completeness, since essence is something destined never to be captured in any definite way, and for this reason it pays attention to every sign that comes from the phenomena under investigation. Whoever is in search of the essence should cultivate a mood of "simple insistence" (Heidegger 2001, p. 84).

The General-Formal Essence of Care

Epistemological Boundaries

In literature, we encounter many definitions of care, but they are not very often exact ones (Held 2006, p. 29). The phenomenological method proves to be the most suitable for the objective which has been established here, that of finding more easily understandable formulations, since it provides guidelines for a rigorous analysis of the phenomenon that functions as a solid foundation for further investigation. A descriptive analysis and conceptual clarification must be arrived at, exempt from value judgments, since in phenomenological terms a similar analysis constitutes a stable basis for any other possible research, either theoretic or empirical.

General essence is available to theoretical thought, while particular essences are embodied in objects that are part of the real world. Dealing with the definition of the essences can be seen as something that only involves an abstruse meditations of a thinker who is totally estranged from ordinary experience; instead the apperception of essence constitutes the precondition of any accurate discussion of matters relating to daily life. Heidegger (1992, p. 256) explains that the definition of a phenomenon and its essential structure is necessarily preliminary to the description of that phenomenon in the ways it occurs in the particular. Defining the general essence of care is essential to finding a solid basis for the construction of a philosophy of care.

When we examine the literature available on the subject, the definitions of care that we find seem at first glance to have a general significance. After a more stringent analysis, however, they often appear to be formulated starting from a definite point of view that ends up by restricting the field of implementation of the concept articulated. When, for instance, Mayeroff defines care as an action to "help him grow and actualize himself" (1990, p. 1) is clear that he is thinking of care starting from the presupposition of a relationship which develops over a long period, as it does in the practice of education. However there are also caring activities that have no need of a long term project, but are implemented in the short space of a meeting; just as there are procedures that are not possible in an extended program, for instance those which facilitate the process of an individual's development, but that are meant as aid in a situation of potential emergency. A general definition of care, that emerges from an eidetic analysis, should identify the characteristics that are true for any caring action and therefore that any phenomenon needs to possess in order to be defined as care.

A philosophy of care is here intended as a philosophy of experience. Therefore, while still taking into account previous methodological observations, we should distance ourselves somewhat from the platonic nucleus of Husserlian epistemology, according to which eidetic research replaces experience with intuition, and in this way causing a split between eidetic and empirical science (Husserl 1982, pp. 37–38). If eidetic science, understood in its idealistic purity, relies on intuition, or in other words on an ante-predicative action, a philosophy of experience that is phenomenologically oriented cannot but consider that thought is always a discourse, and that a rigorous discourse is constructed while moving upon many levels.

If, following constructivist epistemology, we take into account the impossibility of developing eidetic research at an ante-predicative level and bear in mind that inevitably the acquisition of an idea always happens through questioning and examining things from different perspectives, it becomes obvious that in order to develop an analysis that captures the essence of care it is necessary to fine-tune a paradigm of investigation that constitutes the framework of the research.

First of all, since care is something that deals with human experience we should specify what kind of experience this is: intimate or relational; noetic, affective or practical. Once we find the typology of the phenomenon, we can define the horizon of observation points, or in other words answer the following question: where does it happen? How long does it take? What activates it? What is its object? Where is it heading?

Unlike the classical approach of analytical discourse, that requires the analysis of each and every point before formulating a synthesis of the resulting discursive nuclei, I shall first give a brief summary of what constitutes the *eidos* of care and then treat the various most relevant questions in greater detail. The first things that need saying are that the essence of care consists in practice, that it occurs in relation to others and that its duration is variable. Moreover, it is motivated by interest in other people, it is oriented towards nurturing their well-being, and it therefore deals with something essential for others.

The Essential Quality

Care is not an entity of the biophysical world, but it is part of the human experience; for this reason, it could consist of a thought, an emotion or a gesture. We define care as a practice: it is not a simple feeling, it is not just an idea, but it is something that we do in the world in relation to others. If it is true that human beings "are what they do" (Heidegger 1962, p. 163) and that an essential fact is the practice of care, then we can say that the way we implement care is the way we are, is indeed who we are.

Joan Tronto sees care as "engagement" that requires a form of action (1993, p. 102) and she considers it both a practice and a disposition (1993, p. 104). Virginia Held also recognizes that care is a practice, although she prefers to affirm that it is at the same time a value. Instead, in Michel Slote's opinion care is a "motivational attitude" (2001, p. 30), while for Lawrence Blum (1994) it is more of a virtue.

In the fable of Care referred to by Heidegger (1962, p. 242), Care is a person who is moulding clay, she takes action, she does something, she gives a shape to being. If we assume that care is a practice, we can say that we are in the presence of a phenomenon of care only when we find a person who takes action: with gestures and/or with words. Of course, there are thoughts and feelings that can be defined as care, since they are fundamental towards implementing an action of care, but until an intention, a desire, a project is translated into a perceptible action causing the person on the receiving end to feel that they are an object of care, it cannot yet be called care.

Noddings separates "natural caring" from "ethical caring" (2002, p. 29). When she speaks of "natural caring" she affirms that a form of caring "arises more or less spontaneously out of affection or inclination" (2002, p. 29); this should not require any particular ethical deliberation, since it manifests itself as an immediate response to the needs of whoever receives care. She also points out that while formulating a "natural" caring, she does not mean with this that the capacity to take care does not need to be nurtured. It is actually the opposite since care requires a constant and sensitive dedication. "Natural caring" should be an action that emerges spontaneously from our perception of another person's need.

According to Noddings situations may arise where the caring actions are the result of a pragmatic deliberation determined by the sense of responsibility towards an imperative that the mind considers as inevitable. In other words, there is an "I have to" that does not emerge spontaneously. Noddings (2002, p. 30) also opines that whoever implements a work of care carries out "ethical caring", possessing characteristics of acts motivated by a sense of duty similar to the ethical attitude of Kant. In this way, Noddings qualifies the ethical dimension of care in Kantian terms, and even when she argues the opposite by affirming that "ethical caring" maintains a significant distance from the theory of Kant, her argument that a person who needs care does not rely on the logic of a categorical imperative, but on ethically modelled characteristics, is not sufficiently convincing (2002, p. 30).

The introduction of distinctions helps in understanding the phenomena, but in some cases, it creates simplistic shortcuts. Considering that our being there, since our birth and for our entire life, belongs to a cultural context, the distinction between "natural" and "ethical caring" sounds far-fetched, since not only does it supposes something outside culture but it explicitly entails "natural care" with an un-ethical dimension.

Where Care Takes Place

Caring usually *takes place in a relationship* between one person who-cares-for and another who–receives-care. Relationships can be informal (maternal, parental, friendly, etc.) or formal (in educational, therapeutic, welfare, healthcare contexts), with a specific identification of the person in charge of care and the person receiving it. Generally, even if not always, the relation of care is asymmetrical, that is one extreme of the relationship is responsible for the situation of the other, and the other falls into Peirce's category of secondness, since he/she needs care. For this reason, typical of care, there is an ethical problem.

Since relationships can be either formal, in the sense that they are not experienced directly (as in that between a governor and a citizen) or concrete, in other words immediately experienced in flesh and blood during daily life (as teacher and pupil, nurse and patient), it is a question of deciding whether both types of relationship can be defined as care.

Regarding this last point, we come across many different points of view in literature: there are some who think care requires a face-to-face relationship (Bubeck 1994; Sevenhuijsen 1998) since it is "always specific and relational" (Benner and Wrubel 1989, p. 3); others on the other hand maintain that even from a distance there might be caring actions, but that in this case we are dealing with a type of care that is different in quality, and they distinguish between direct caring, "caring for", and caring at a distance, "caring about" (Noddings 1984, 2002). Joan Tronto shares the aptness of this distinction, but thinks that we have to give a different name to the direct involvement in the relation of care that she defines as "care-giving" and the organization of conditions necessary to implement acts of care, which she names "taking-care-of" (1994, pp. 106–107). For example, establishing a field hospital in a war zone is considered as an act of "taking care of" (Tronto) or of "caring about" (Noddings), while the operations in hospital to treat sick people directly is defined as "care giving" (Tronto) and "caring for" (Noddings).

There are also those (Bowden 1997; Held 2006) who assert that it is possible to implement from a distance a form of care that is qualitatively identical to the direct one, since it is possible to activate attention, responsiveness and understanding for the other's situation from a distance, too (Held 2006, p. 18). Slote (2007, p. 11), who agrees with Held, distinguishes between "communitarian care" performed from a distance and "personal care" which is implemented on the spot. The thesis according to which care is also possible from a distance is considered by these philosophers as a necessary ground from which to develop a theory that considers care as a form of ethics also capable of establishing political relationships.

In Noddings' opinion direct care and care from a distance are qualitatively different, not only because "*caring about*" presents its own qualities, inherent in this activity, which are inspired by the principle of justice (2002, pp. 3, 22), but also because care that is provided in a real relationship should have an experiential primacy: implementing an indirect form of care addressed to distant subjects is considered possible only if it is based on direct experience of care, involving relationships undergone at first hand (Noddings 2002, p. 22). Even if the opposite can be true, and actions of "*caring-about*" that are inspired by a sense of justice are functional in establishing conditions that make actions of *caring-for* possible, for Noddings it is fundamental to operate according to the rubric of "*caring-for*", since "*caring-about*" is always useless if it does not culminate in caring actions (2002, p. 24). However, it would be a mistake to consider "*caring-for*" possible without the actions of "*caring-about*", which are geared to work in a world where it is possible to act well, in other words for a world in which taking responsibility for acts of care does not imply making too much of an effort in our own life (Noddings 2002, p. 48).

Noddings' view is that, given the profound interrelation between direct and indirect care, the best thing that each individual can do is to get involved in both sides of the action: taking direct care of anyone we meet who may request it, and taking indirect care of all the others by trying to realize those conditions of context in which care can prosper.

For the very reason that, as Noddings says (2002, p. 49), we must not fall into the error of considering these two methods of care as identical actions, the thesis that we intend to support here is that any caring relationship is a direct relationship or, if not direct, yet still with people with whom there is a possibility of such a relationship. In this perspective, even the far-away friend with whom we have a long-distance contact can be an object of care that is carried out just by talking and listening. Consequently, the assumption that care is an embodied practice (Hamington 2004) for all those actions finalized towards constructing contexts where care is possible and made easy but without a direct action between whoever takes-care and whoever receives-care, we should only talk about sustaining policies for acts of care, not about care itself.

Establishing that the practicalities of care are possible within a concretely experienced space of direct relations does not mean excluding formal relations, those that do not happen face-to-face but take place at a distance. For example, the relationship between a citizen and the large political community to which he/she belongs is not necessarily extraneous to the culture of care; we can actually hypothesize that the philosophy of care may also constitute a paradigm of political life in its broadest sense. This hypothesis, however, can be validated only after an analytical examination of the practice of care that allows us to determine if and by what means it can effectively inform political life. Such an examination takes place when, after identifying the behavioral indicators of caring actions, we can determine if they also have a phenomenal concretion in indirect relations and what kind of concretion is possible of the modes of care in an indirect relationship. If we answer this question in the affirmative, then we could hypothesize a second type of caring relationships, those that are not experienced in a direct way, and we could also talk about care in public or political contexts. If the conceptual action to limit the practice of care to the field of direct relationships seem to reduce the value of care meant as fundamental practice for life, the decision to verify if remote relationships can be qualified according to the indicators of the direct relations of care sanctions the possibility of a broader definition of the reality of care, that authorizes us to mention care in a political context too.

The thesis put forward here, which states that we can talk about care only in the case of relations between persons who are in direct contact, not only seems to reduce the value of care but also distances itself from Platonic discourse, one of the fundamental references for the argumentations expressed in this study. In the *Republic*, when Plato talks about the art of governing the city well, he uses the word "*epimeleia*" and mentions "care for the city" (*Republic*, VI, 770b). In reality, the hypothesis of a distance between the thesis maintained here and the Platonic paradigm of care is not valid, since here the intention is not that of eliminating the value of care in political life, but rather of defining the difference between care as a practice among persons in a direct relationship and care as a paradigm of action:

the first type of care can be implemented only in experienced relationships, whereas the second type informs the philosophy of political life.[1]

Another element of Noddings' theory that gives food for thought is the fact that it does not merely concern the *"caring for"* that takes place among people who belong to the micro-system that has been experienced directly as a prerequisite towards implementing the *"caring about"* distant people, but also because it makes the capacity for taking care of another (*"caring for"*) dependent on the object of care. In point of fact she affirms that "learning to care about depends on learning to care for, and that in turn depends on having been cared for oneself" (Noddings 2002, p. 31). In this thesis, there are two aspects that need to be considered. First of all, the idea that we learn the value of care only through direct experience. If this were so, it would mean excluding from this dimension of being-there anybody lacking experience of care. In actual fact, it is just as possible to learn things simply because we are lacking them: being spectators of caring actions and being able to understand what implications the experience of care has in the life of other people allows us to understand the value of care and the lack of it in our own experience. The lack of something valuable can generate stirrings of being that can be equally fruitful, in terms of learning, as having had direct experience of something, because feeling and knowing that we have missed something can ignite the passion to search for this very thing.

Secondly, the primary importance given to the first care that a baby receives from its family, corroborated by the results of psychological and anthropological research, corresponds to a precise political intention: "we have launched a project that reverses traditional philosophical procedure. Instead of starting with an ideal state or republic, we will start with an ideal home and move outward" (Noddings 2002, p. 31). Although by focusing on family life we allow ourselves to reflect on the primary value of the quality of experiences in private spaces, we must make clear that putting the family environment at the center of the question, in order to forward a political design for existence, risks returning care to the confines of an intimate and family related interpretation, that lessens its power of changing the culture of the community it seeks to care for.

Joan Tronto in particular takes the opposite position regarding the centrality that Noddings attributes to the mother-child relationship. She argues against the dyadic conceptualization of the caring relationship, because it risks overemphasizing an

---

[1] In order to support the thesis of a distinction between direct and indirect care, it is necessary to identify clearly the essential characteristics of both. This is something that we do not find in the work of those describing the two forms of care. Noddings herself does not identify the qualities that specifically characterize indirect care.

individualistic interpretation (1994, p. 103) that would prevent care from being a paradigm of public life.

The belief that we can talk about care in relation to actions towards a non-human world: animals, plants and a built environment should also be born in mind. Berenice Fisher and Joan Tronto define care as:

> everything we do to carry on, repair, and maintain ourselves so that we can live in the world as well as possible. That world includes our bodies, ourselves, and our environment, all of which we seek to interweave in a complex, life-sustaining web. (Fisher and Tronto 1991, p. 40)

Regarding this, we should not forget the distinction that Heidegger establishes between "concern" and "solicitude": "concern with the world" and "solicitude for others" (1962, p. 183). Concern is our circumspective dealings with entities encountered within the world which are ready-to-hand, solicitude is towards the other beings with whom we share the call to care for life (1962, p. 157). If we agree with the Heideggerian perspective, according to which the other human beings are "are not objects of concern, but rather of solicitude" (1962, p. 157), then, since care is a relational activity where the other does not appertain to the mode of being of the merely functional, the appropriate linguistic expression to define the action of care towards other people is therefore to *care for*. Instead if we were to talk about concern for entities ready-to hand we should use the expression *taking care*.

Temporal Duration

Care is something that regards life, and since life is developed within time, care also has a temporal quality. The action of care could require a long time, as in the case of facilitating the weaning of a child or the implementing of sound educational practices, but it can also require a relatively short time, such as that needed by a nurse to explain the reason for a particular therapy to a patient and to reassure him/her, or the time a teacher might need to encourage a student in an especially difficult moment in the process of learning, or a social care provider during the integration of a difficult subject in a new environment. For the very reason that care, just like any other experiential phenomenon, needs time, we can also talk about care as accompaniment.

As far as the temporal dimension of care is concerned, there are caring gestures that may just last a few moments, but which have the same depth and value as gestures that require more time, for example when the intention of care is manifested through a glance, a caress or a word offered at the right moment. A word that expresses awareness of the situation experienced by another can be strong enough to bring unexpected relief; a caress can demonstrate a conscious and sensitive closeness, which, by communicating to the other that our attention is focused on him/her, generates a feeling of being welcome and cherished.

The Generative Matrix

It is *interest in the other* that sparks off a caring act. By interest we do not merely intend simple curiosity, but the inter-being, or in other words regarding the other motivated by a feeling of connection with him/her. To feel an inter-being for another means to be concerned about his/her condition. Annette Baier talks about a "strong concern for the good of others and for our kinship with them" (1987, p. 43).

Interest or concern for the other is stimulated by our realization of his/her state of necessity. Each of us always needs someone else, since nobody has full sovereignty over being and because human being-there is always vulnerable. We feel a pressing need to care-for when we perceive the other in need of something that he/she cannot find by him/herself. Others need care when they are in the phase of developing their identity and therefore want someone to support them and to guide them in their becoming; or when they are experiencing a phase of life that is extremely vulnerable (newborn baby, elderly person), or because they have been hurt in their physical or spiritual being (illness).

Concern for the other is expressed with different degrees of intensity: from simple availability to respond to requests that are expressed by the other (the level of interest that does not affect us deeply), to taking things to heart, where the situation of the other is at the center of our thoughts (it is a kind of interest that affects us deeply. Taking something or someone to heart is also manifested with different levels of intensity, that go from *solicitude* and *consideration* to *devotion*.

The word "devotion" recurs quite frequently in care culture; we may recall that Winnicott (1987, p. 1) talks about a mother who is "ordinarily devoted" meaning the mother capable of good care; Eva Kittay, when defining the specific features of caring work, talks about "devotion to the well-being of another" (1999, p. 39). However, considering the strong religious semantic weight of the lexeme "devotion" which is typical of our culture, it is necessary to examine if and how the way of being that expresses the meaning of the word can find its place in the practice of care and specifically in its essence.

The poet Rilke (1997) wisely describes this devotion in the third duino elegy, in which a mother is aware of her child's every breath, watching over him the whole night and immediately conscious of anything that might disturb the baby's peace. While describing a mother's way of caring, he speaks of simple, ordinary gestures that notwithstanding their simplicity reveal the power of the practice of care, the power to defend and protect existence.

Devotion denotes an attitude of profound dedication to another. In the religious sphere, it signifies the state of being intensely dedicated to something. The essential reason for the decision to dedicate oneself intensely to someone/thing is to be found in our judgement of the other as a worthy entity. When we see in the other the source of inviolable value, requiring deep dedication to protect and safeguard it, then devotion is called into being. Devotion is an attitude of intense attention that renders us constantly and receptively concentrated on the other, totally present and swift to react to his/her needs and appeals. In a relationship of devotion, a part of ourselves is totally dedicated to the other: this happens in the maternal relationship, when a mother focuses her attention on her baby, and in the love relationship where a lover is capable of an intense dedication towards the other and finds joy in experiencing the other's wellbeing.

In this sense, the attitude of devotion cannot be considered, as Mayeroff believes (1990, p. 5), as an essential ingredient of caring actions to the point that if "devotion breaks down, caring breaks down", since if this were true, care would only be possible in rare, discretionary or facilitated relational situations. Nevertheless, certain contextual situations are often to be met with which are implemented through the mode of devotion and in these cases we are witnessing an intensive form of caring actions. If care is definable as an opportunity to respond to another's appeal to help him/her to achieve the realization of what is essential for him/her to exist (Mayeroff 1990; Noddings 1984), then the way of devotion or dedication is the right way for people who understand life as "a favorable response" to what they perceive is necessary to the other (Noddings 2002, p. 51).

Dedication is something "more" that can characterize those situations where whoever-cares-for offers an exceptional availability; devotion can occur, for example, when doctors and nurses, once they find out a patient's particular necessity, make themselves constantly available until the critical situation is over; or when a teacher dedicates thoughts and concrete presence to the student beyond a set time: in his/her free time, he/she thinks about the educational need of that particular student and he/she prepares learning situations that are helpful for the student's requirements, being motivated by the desire to enable the expression of his/her student's uniqueness. In this sense, devotion is a way of being of the work of caring that requires from whoever cares-for a distinct aptitude for exceptional dedication. Since this is rarely met-with, it cannot be included in the list of essential qualities of caring work, because these specify the necessary features without which a phenomenon cannot be classified as care; devotion on the other hand can only be identified as one possible, very intense form of taking the other to heart.[2]

Interest in others, either in the form of momentary concern or of long-term consideration, should be taken into account, since it opens up a problematic area. The desire for the other's good makes me lean towards him/her, it puts me in the position of getting closer to him/her. Care means wishing for someone's good and this desire leads us to move towards the other. A caring relation implies a tension that makes us lean towards one another, and the stronger the impulse to care, the stronger the inclination. Rollo May suggests a connection between inclination and care when he puts care and tension in relation with each other: "Tending means a tendency, an inclination, a throwing of one's weight on a given side, a movement; and also to mind, to attend, to await, to show solicitude for. In this sense, it is the source of both love and will" (1969, pp. 292–293).

There are, however, both dangerous and appropriate inclinations: the dangerous ones, that jeopardize the self and the other, are those where we exceed the limits of our inclination and risk overbalancing, which in turn compromises the possibility of our freely resuming other forms of inclination; the appropriate ones, on the other hand, include those disposition towards the other which can be achieved without losing balance, without missing the point of contact with ourselves. There can be no relationship if there is no inclination towards the other, but—speaking in geometrical terms—the inclination should not exceed "forty-five degrees". In other words, it should never become a leaning towards the other that makes him/her feel our presence as excessive and that makes him/her lose balance. The problem is always to find the correct degree of our position towards the other. At this point is

---

[2] The distinction between the *different levels of intensity* of caring work is useful in focusing on a problem that characterizes care-related jobs. Here the objects of our consideration are those actions that prove who-cares-for is someone who looks after others. We usually measure the level of competence with which they are implemented; whereas the way of being-there and of feeling concerned, which is an index of personal involvement, is located on the horizon of *non-determinable possible*. The problematic act of worrying, about oneself or about another, constitutes the qualifying element of a caring activity. In the case of a teacher, we can measure his/her capability to establish and develop a positive teaching practice following accredited didactic principles, but the readiness to listen to a student in difficulty or the ability to maintain a firm position of resistance towards problematic behavior are not accountable for; in a nurse we can document his/her technical preparation when administering a particular pharmacological therapy, but the therapy of the soul that s/he implements with gestures and thoughts of care is not included in the categories of behaviour that are evaluated when judging her/his performance. The necessity to develop different forms of thinking of and treating phenomena of being-there evinces that what is essential to the quality of life has no importance in conventional ways of assessment.

evinced the importance for care-givers of developing a critically reflexive posture with regard both to their relationship with others and to the effects of their own actions.

The Object of Care

We care for when we deal with something essential for the other (the preservation and protection of life, the opening of existence to something further, the healing of injuries) that the other is not capable of finding for him/herself, otherwise it would be conceptualized as a service. Dealing with what is essential for the other means getting into close contact with the core of reality.

Dealing with the essential means to "identify and respond to needs" (Noddings 2002, p. 53). Caring for the other is essentially a receptive and responsive attention to the other's essential needs. The educational relationship is not only about satisfying the needs that the other is not autonomously able to achieve, but at the same time is about putting the other in the condition of learning how to satisfy them independently. Instead, the aim of therapy is usually that whoever cares for has to assume on oneself total responsibility him/herself for all the actions necessary towards satisfying the needs of the patient. One of the problems that whoever is responsible for providing care has to deal with is the actual identification of the needs to be satisfied, the basic needs or "course-of-life needs". Then the next consideration must be which actions to implement in order to satisfy the other's needs without expropriating his/her subjectivity, even in situations of severe dependency. In fact, the boundary between care and paternalism is very fine, just as is the distinction between a necessary and a non-necessary action for the other's wellbeing, since when an action is not necessary not only can it waste the energy of whoever is taking care, but it can also contribute towards concentrating its praxic power, with a consequent weakening of the position of the care receiver.

The identification of essential needs, or in other words of what is necessary for a good life, is not easy. It is easy to identify biological requirements, but these are clearly not the only ones: there are also relational, cognitive, affective, spiritual, aesthetical and political needs. Noddings (2002, p. 57) thinks that only when essential needs have been identified are we able to establish the prerequisites for a real culture of care. The tendency to organize such needs into hierarchical structures is a mistake that should be avoided (Noddings 2002, p. 60), because if we are dealing with "essential needs" they must all be considered as equally necessary.

In this context, Joan Tronto (1993, p. 138) affirms that the meaning of the expression "to meet basic needs adequately" depends on the specific cultural, technological and historical circumstances where the action of care is implemented. Actually, to radically adopt the constructivist vision means ignoring reality, because if it is true that like anything else in the human world even "needs" are socially constructed, it cannot be denied that they are, above all, demonstrable facts: unquestionable needs are those that exist "independently from anything else", and what make the difference are the many possible and varied cultural interpretations. That everybody needs enough to eat is an objective fact, the cultural dimension intervenes in the interpretation of which type of food is perceived as fundamental for each of us. The need for relationships is an ontological human data, the mode of understanding the relational life is a socially constructed tenet. Precisely in order to identify essential needs and the conditions to satisfy them in an adequate manner, a philosophy of experience should be developed and continually updated in order to analyze different life contexts.

The question of necessities is not, however, simply a matter of distinguishing between primary and secondary needs, but also of understanding exactly when and how we can implement an authentic action of care for another. Since there is no doubt that the availability of food, water and physical and relational spaces in which to find shelter and protection are essential needs, the method whoever cares-for employs to satisfy these necessities may have radically different implications for the person who is receiving care. There is in fact a way in which to gratify needs that simultaneously alleviates a sense of lack within the other and also encourages a transformation of his/her being and puts him/her in the right condition to become more and more autonomous in the satisfaction of his/her own needs. However there also exists a way of caring for that focuses completely on the person who cares for, so causing a constant weakening and objectivizing of the other; in this second case the impression of care is deceptive.

It is hard to find a geometrically precise criterion to accommodate the practice of care, since we are always bound to a contextual evaluation; in all events, we can hypothesize that once we are sure that we are dealing with an undeniable necessity, we must evaluate if and to what degree it is possible to involve the person receiving care, or in other words, which part of the action of taking care has to be in the form of direct intervention to satisfy needs and which part has to be an indirect enablement for the other so that s/he is put in the condition of providing what s/he needs for her/himself. Only thus can we talk about caring for the other and not simply taking care of another.

Hierarchical and absolutist interpretations of needs that respond to a simplistic logic should be avoided because they cause actions that disregard the other person's past. The assumption that the necessity of food is "more fundamental" than the need of a comforting word can trigger the misapprehension of the caring action as a sequence of separate interventions—food first, then we find time to talk—when instead the other person's past might be such that a reassuring word could establish a difference in the method of satisfying his/her biological needs.

Noddings distinguishes between needs expressed by the person requiring care and needs inferred by the person caring for (2002, p. 64). It perhaps seems easier to respond to an explicit request of the other, but this is not always true especially when the subject misrepresents something as essential when it is not; in this case who cares-for has to make the other understand that failure to satisfy his/her needs is not due to a lack of consideration, but instead is a caring gesture that is caused by the intention of respecting the truth.

One of the most thorny problems to solve is the issue of the needs determined by who-cares-for, such as, for instance, those that are defined as educational needs. Care in education is not just a case of accommodating and enabling the realization of the so-called "objective" needs, but also one of deciding whether something is a vital need or not and acting accordingly, so as to make the other perceive not only whether the need really exists but also if its fulfilment is absolutely indispensable. The educator in this instance will base the decision on collective theories or world views, but this is not enough to render the action problem-free, because not only is it impossible to be completely sure that the specific educational theory referred to is valid, but it is also not always the case that the decision has been made at the right moment in the other person's life. These problems related to interpretation and decision are modifiable in different ways according to the age of the person receiving care and to degree of his/her autonomy: an educator in playschool is obviously responsible for everything, but as the age of the pupils increases, the shared space of cognizant decision-making becomes greater. Furthermore, no interpretative and deliberative tool can obviate the danger that who-cares-for is able to make decisions of ostensible benefit to the other but which are, or could be coercive. For this reason, if it is true that in general care work can be problematic, educational care is always risky and requires the educator to analyze every one of his/her own decisions with a critical eye so as to avoid his/her action deteriorating to the level of the violation of the rights of the individual.

The Intention Guiding Life

Intention characterizes the actions of human beings and since care is here defined as a practice, as well as a form of action, it is fundamental to identify the intention that moves it in order to find its essence.

The identification of this intentionality requires us to consider being-there ontologically, so as to understand if there is a primary, original intentionality that guides the human being in her/his development; in other words, if there is an original tension that channels the movement of existence. It is essential to develop the direction of this investigation because, if we assume that care is a primary ontological phenomenon, then it inevitably sustains an essential relationship with the primary existential intention, the one that each human being perceives as the undeniable direction of her/his being.

If we accept the Aristotelian principle that the good is that at which all things aim (Aristotle, *Nicomachean Ethics*, I, 1, 1094a), we may then affirm that the drive to exist is motivated by the intention of seeking for the good. Aristotle specifies that the good that the human being is looking for is called *eudaimonia* [εὐδαιμονία μριμνᾶτε] (*Nicomachean Ethics*, I, 7, 1097b), from a philological analysis *eudaimonia* indicates a good [εὐ- δαιμονία] condition of the life of conscience [**daimon**] (*Nicomachean Ethics*, I, 9, 1099b 26).[3] To find oneself in a condition of *eudaimonia* means to live with virtue since that is the condition for having experience of the good.

It is our lack of being, and owing to this, our fragility and vulnerability, that makes us entities that desire and fear: what we desire is the good and what we fear is its disappearance. We have always to deal with the reality, forced to be subjected to it. "Man is peered of the gods" "Everything can be borne" (Sappho, fragm. 3), this is the problem: the heart can bear everything, it doesn't break, it doesn't die. The heart can resist even the most terrible pain. But there is a one kind of pain that is almost impossible to bear: it is the kind that originates not from suffering something bad, but from losing something good that we experienced. Losing something good seems unbearable. When we talk about the human being as a lacking entity, what is missing is not being, but valuable things that are the object of a lifelong search. The first thing the human being lacks is the good.

---

[3] Literally *eudaimonia* means to inhabit a good dimension of the spirit. See the etymological analysis developed by Martha Nussbaum to demonstrate that it is not correct to translate *eudaimonia* with happiness, since this word indicates a feeling in current use; the analysis is motivated by the intention to emphasize the level of action, and precisely of that action that looks for the "flourishing of the human being" (Nussbaum 1986, p. 6).

If care is a primary ontological practice and if the primary pulsion of existence is a search for the good, then it is evident that the practice of care is in an essential relationship with the search for the good. Who-cares-for is seeking for the good. Good care is proactive and protective: it is proactive because it looks for the good and it is protective because it tries to safeguard life, our own and others', from any kind of evil. Good care keeps the being immersed in the good. It is this good that makes up the solid ground of our being, that layer of being that keeps us steady among things and people, and that allows us to experience our presence in the world with pleasure.

The thesis that care is related to the search of what makes life good was developed by Plato in the *Euthyphro*; as Socrates guides his interlocutor towards the identification of the essence of sanctity, he also confronts that of the essence of care and, addressing Euthyphro, he asks: "Now does attention always aim to accomplish the same end? I mean something like this: It aims at some good or benefit to the one to whom it is given, as you see that horses, when attended to by the horseman's art are benefited and made better; or don't you think so?" (13b). Further on, he defines care as the art serving a specific purpose and this purpose is the benefit that the person who is cared for receives.

Given this premise, when someone decides to implement caring actions, s/he should always be able to explain the reasons that are at the origin of these actions and the reasons must convince any interlocutor that the intention to encourage the well-being-there of the person in his/her care is at the basis of his/her decisions regarding this person (Noddings 1984, p. 23). We can therefore say that there is care wherever the action is based on the intention to benefit the other. Since the search for what is good for the other generates spaces of being, we may concur that care is the way to promote a relationship with the other that generates possibilities of experience (Benner and Wrubel 1989, p. 1).

Caring for is a relational practice guided by the intention to give relief to the other. Providing the other with what enables him/her to live a good life includes different types of actions: rendering the necessities for survival available to the other, putting the other in the position to acquire what s/he needs through her/his own efforts, protect her/him from potential injury and violence, making it possible for the other to realize his existential potentialities flourish, healing injuries received and relieving pain, both physical and mental. All these actions make sense if they contribute towards rendering possible the experience of a good quality of life.

If care has a primary ontological dimension and the primary intentionality of being-there is the search for the good, then the intention that guides a good action of care is inevitably the search for what is good for life.

Every individual is searching for the good, or, in other words, for a good life. But, since the ontological web constitutes a whole, the development of each of us is deeply intertwined with that of others, and since my existence is strictly connected with that of other people, it is impossible to conceive of the search for a good quality of life in a solipsistic manner. A singular good does not exist, but a plural good does: consequently the search for the good can only be conceived of as a relational procedure. Caring for being-there is caring for finding threads of good with which to weave the time of existence, and since being-there is being-with-others searching for the good is searching for what constitutes good both for me and for others.

The argument that is being developed here allows us to almost automatically undo—or at least lets us do without the necessity to invent further discursive structures—the idea that we must beware of discussions on care and treat them with caution and detachment, because they encourage attitudes of self-sacrifice since their emphasis is overly centred on the other (Dancy 1992). The prerequisite of this thesis is the antithesis between selfishness and selflessness, and consequently it interprets care as an expression of altruism. According to Elena Pulcini the responsibility typical of acting with care requires "pure altruism" from a subject who understands how to act unselfishly. In contrast to this, the philosophy of care here propounded intends to distance itself from the opposition between altruism and egoism and, therefore, from all the topics that are related to it. The theory developed here shows that care for ourselves is not separate from care for others because one's own good cannot be separated from others' good.

The practice of care is guided by the intention of encouraging the emergence of a good quality of life and such a search cannot be perceived as a solipsistic event, since existence is intrinsically co-existence. If we assume that ethics needs maintain a significant relationship with ontology, and if we agree to talk about the human condition as a plurality (Arendt), singular-plurality (Nancy), original sociality (Lévinas), then ethics can be explained by adopting a necessarily extra-individual discourse. If living is living-with and if our own well-being is a condition intimately connected to feeling-well-with-others, then to worry about others does not signify altruism that reaches the point of self-sacrifice, but is the fundamental way, or in other words the one that best inheres with the ontological quality of the human condition, to interpret the drive towards the good. Virginia Held writes (2006, p. 12) that "persons in caring relations are acting for self-and-other together. Their characteristic stance is neither egoistic nor altruistic; ... but the well-being of a caring relation involves the cooperative well-being of those in the relation and the well-being of the relation itself".

If care is seen simply as unselfishness then theory of caring will run the risk of legitimizing self-sacrifice and of confirming the hypothesis that care, as an altruistic practice, involves a dispersal of being and therefore always implies suffering. At this point, it seems opportune to refer to Aristotle, who puts forward the idea that not only receiving but also giving of good should be thought of as pleasant, "It is pleasant to bestow and to receive benefits; the latter is the attainment of what we desire, the former the possession of more than sufficient means, both of them things that men desire. Since it is pleasant to do good, it must also be pleasant for men to set their neighbors on their feet, and to supply their deficiencies" (Aristotle, *Rhetoric*, 1371b).

The Ethical Core of the Work of Care

The Primary Issue

At the roots of the way of being-there in caring for, there arises an ethical question: what and in what way should we act in order for the other to receive good? The search for an answer to this question requires profound thought on what the provision of good really involves.

Since the moment we define the practice of care in these terms, it acquires an ethical status. If, in fact, we adopt the Aristotelian perspective, the specific purpose of ethics is to show how care for the good, and for promoting well-being, the work of care assumes an ethical status because it is directly intended to provide benefit.[4] Once considered from an ethical perspective, the problems connected with care are made manifest, because what good is and how it should be promoted is one of the

---

[4] In order to analyze the dimension of ethics in care, the interpretative paradigm will be referring constantly to ancient philosophy, in particular to the Platonic and Aristotelian ethical vision. This reference is justified since in ancient thought the concept of a good life and the consideration of the life of thoughts, particularly in philosophy, are fundamental as instruments to facilitate the identification of conditions that allow the individual or the community to realize a good quality of life. The perspective offered by ancient philosophy has to be brought back to the heart of the discussion, not only because it emphasizes the harmony that it has with the thoughts of those who provide care work and compare their experience with this philosophy, but it agrees with the theoretic and practical intention that motivates the commitment to design a philosophy of care meant as a discourse rooted in experience and capable of fulfilling what is essentially necessary for life. Especially in the ethical field, if we keep our thoughts rooted in reality, it result the necessity of going back to the very beginnings of thought.

most difficult questions to answer and, though we are obliged to go on asking it, destined to remain an open question.

Simply because care is so important in our lives, it is related to another fundamental problem of existence: to know what the good really is. As Plato affirms, the idea of good is "the greatest thing to learn" because only by referring to this idea can we understand which things are just, useful and beneficial (*The Republic*, VI, 505a); so great is the ethical and epistemic value of the idea of good that, "if we do not know it, then, even if without the knowledge of this we should know all other things never so well" (*The Republic*, VI, 505a). Every process of knowledge needs a specific enlightenment: for sensitive sight the enlightenment comes from the sun, for the thoughts that search for the truth in experience, the light comes from the idea of good [ἡ τοῦἀγαθοῦἰδέα]. The idea of good constitutes that light that we need to escape from the risk of that gravest injury to being-there: spiritual blindness. Just as thoughts that are not enlightened by solidly grounded knowledge cannot be considered as true wisdom, so our way of being in the world becomes uncertain if it lacks the idea of good (*The Republic*, VI, 506c).

Care is actualized in actions made of words and gestures; the difficult part is to find the right words and gestures at the opportune moment for that specific person; words and gestures that the other can benefit from. So, just as we need sunlight to move among the things of the world, we need the spiritual source of light that is the idea of the good to understand how to act attentively in the relation with the other. In order to make the right decision a source of light is necessary to clarify the question and reach an adequate vision of things. Only if we stay in the radiant light of the idea of good, can we have a fair knowledge, that is also good, of anything.

At this point, however, a statement by Socrates, whose judgment is still considered trustworthy, gives rise to a problem: in his opinion it is not possible for the human mind to form an adequate knowledge of the good (*The Republic*, VI, 505a). The idea of good, that transcends everything for dignity and power, is difficult to discern, "God knows whether it is true" (*The Republic*, VII, 517b). Deriving from the idea of good would be like reaching the highest point of knowledge, which is the highest not simply because we finally attain to it, but because it is the precondition of all other knowledge since it establishes the perfect way in which to act. If the mind could grasp the idea of good, it would understand the first principle, which is not hypothetical but tangible, and from there it could establish what constitutes the right assessment of things in the world without abandoning thought to the mercy of darkness. If the attainment of such an idea were in our reach, we could become experts in everything; every single decision would then be made in the light and every action could go in the right direction.

But this is not the case. There are many unanswerable questions and the one regarding the good is the most difficult of all. Nobody can grasp the essence of the idea of good, or understand its complete significance which would end every question and every investigation, because it would mean exceeding the limits of the human condition, for which the idea of good remains transcendent, it cannot be grasped by our empirical consciousness (Murdoch 1970, p. 93). The concept of the good is destined to be beyond our full comprehension and to continue to represent an area of mystery to the mind.

Once again human life proves to be lacking, because it clearly does not have the crucial knowledge it needs to satisfy its primary aspiration, the aspiration to realize itself in an appropriate form. To achieve this, it would be necessary to have a crystal-clear idea of what exactly to aspire to. On the contrary, this idea is destined to remain obscure to the human mind. Since care is the way of being-there, with oneself and with others, and is directed by the intention to facilitate what is good for life, this practice is destined always to proceed on uncertain ground. Caring actions occur on an uneven terrain, where the parameters for decision are always temporary and uncertain; these are to be object of an accurate reflection.

With Xenophanes, we can say that "the evident reality of good" is not accessible to the human mind, "no man has seen it, nor will there ever be a man who knows about the gods [...] And even if by chance he were to speak the final truth, he himself would nevertheless be unaware of it" (*The Nature of the Divine*, 34). We only arrive at the germ of an idea however hard we try. In more recent times, Iris Murdoch, echoing this way of expressing the disproportion between the power of our thoughts and the idea of good, has stated good is something indefinable (1970, p. 42) and any concept that attempts to define its essence risks triviality. There is a deep-rooted mystery accompanying the idea of good that is destined to remain inconceivable to the human mind because of the limits of our reason. If angels existed, they would be the only creatures capable of defining good, but even if we could communicate with them, we would not understand the definition of the good that they would try to reveal to us (Murdoch 1970, p. 99). The good is appears as an idea that needs to be analyzed *ad infinitum*. A clear and luminous idea of good, that enlightens all aspects of human experience, could only spring from a divine mind. Such an idea would be too glaring for human thought to sustain. For us, merely the gently dawning light of such an idea would be enough to illuminate the mind, a light that from time to time would reveal a chink of sky in the dark forest of life's problems.

When a child shows reluctance to do something that a teacher regards as essential for the proper development of his mind, it is important to know what to do: whether to insist and try persuasion or to leave it for the time being, and risk missing the right moment? When a patient refuses a form of therapy that is essential towards obtaining even a partial solution to his/her problem, what are we supposed to do? Be adamant or respect her/his decision? When we have to decide upon the custody of a teenager and we encounter his/her resistance and desire to remain with his/her family, and the evident suffering caused by leaving this, the most important social structure for existential development, what should we do and how? When a woman who has experienced violence in her family asks for help but does not want to do anything towards solving her problem, what is the best action to take? Respect her will or decide against it and intervene?

There is a constant need of an idea of the good. This undeniable necessity, even allowing for the uncertain forms it might assume, exercises a sort of authority over our thoughts. Therefore, so as to avoid making decisions based on deficient or not properly thought-out ideas, it is of the utmost importance for our existence to reflect constantly about what constitutes the good.

The question of good is the object of ethical theory. However, for some time moral philosophy has totally neglected it. Although the question regarding the good life is at the basis of philosophical reflection in philosophical studies this same elementary question, in the large majority of cases, is scarcely mentioned (Wolf 2001, p. 19). Perhaps the widespread impression of the uselessness of philosophical studies should be traced back to the lack of attention to this fundamental question.

Ursula Wolf attributes the abandoning of this question by philosophy to Kant (2001, p. 19). Starting from the thesis that there is no possibility of answering the question about a good life, Kant (1997) states that the ethical question that is accessible to the human mind should be more limited and, more precisely, should instead be dealing with the problem of right coexistence. By assuming the Kantian theory, the question of the good finds no help in contemporary moral philosophy, since it tends to focus on the topic of justice rather than taking into consideration the idea of a good quality of life (Taylor 1989, p. 3). By adopting this perspective, moral philosophy ended by imparting a limited and narrow vision of moral discussion, thereby causing an impoverishment of the analysis of issues related to the search for the best possible life. If we accept the thesis that states that the most urgent issues in the ethical field deal with respect for life, the integrity and well-being of others and the flourishing of their existence (Taylor 1989, p. 4), then there is no time to be wasted before bringing back to the center of philosophical reflection the ancient Socratic question on understanding "what makes life worth living" and therefore the idea of the good. Since the result of the analysis of caring practices (Mortari 2006; Mortari and Saiani 2013) is that the topic of the good is a crucial one, to design a philosophy of care means to bring back the topic of good to the hub of philosophical debate. Even if we might disagree with the position of those who believe philosophy will not stand up to the criticism of society if it does not make another attempt to face the most difficult question (Wolf 2001, p. 19), it is undeniable that when this question is forgotten, experience struggles to find an authentically ethical breathing space. In contemporary debate, when we oppose the ethics of care to the ethics of justice and define the ethics of care to be of slight importance, unable to guide public life, we are once more slipping into the Kantian perspective of putting aside the question of the good as being too difficult. To avoid dealing with the topic of good, however, is like deciding not to have a map when entering unknown territory.

If we consider philosophy as a science, which must arrive at rigorously grounded assertions according to the model provided by a scientific approach, then there is certainly no room for a discussion of the good. However, the scientific approach is not the only one. There is a way of thinking that springs from sensitive questions that cannot be included within the limits of technical reasoning. Even if the analysis of certain issues does not allow us to find answers in line with the form of scientific theory, this analysis should not simply be abandoned. The one essential factor in deciding on whether to insist on examining certain questions and to dedicate to this examination most of the work of thinking should have as its only evaluation the questions which are of the most value for life.

A philosophy of care is by definition the right one to concentrate our attention on the problem of the good, not just for the pleasure of satisfying a purely speculative curiosity but because, from a phenomenological analysis of the practice of care, it results that the most important and inevitable question with which caregivers are challenged is "what does the good consist of". It is the lived experience of those who act in the world following the ethical tension to care for which makes the question of the good unavoidable. Philosophy makes sense if it is ready to listen to life, and does not fall back on academic disputation where the expression of thought is often simply reduced to linguistic tricks. And just because the philosophy of care starts from past experience and always returns to it, the question of the good arises not only as an essential but also as a plain and simple one. In this sense, the philosophy of care can lend fresh suggestion to moral philosophy, a vital, creative suggestion of new ways of being-there.

Sticking to the Question

The more important a question is for life, the more difficult it becomes; so it appears as a problem that challenges the capacities of reason and shows us our lack of ability to employ exact methods when we act, and finally the more it reveals the densely problematic nature of human experience. Luckily, there are many questions which reason can deal with and find an answer to, but for those that touch the essential part of life we are destined not to find clear definitions. This is why the Italian poet Quasimodo talks about a human condition that is defeated by eternal questions confronting mankind; but it is precisely this indefiniteness of the primary existential questions that make it possible for human beings to have the experience of liberty, which is bitter, sometimes difficult, but which allows freedom of being.

Meditation on what the good is answers the need of giving full meaning to life and also that of finding a practical way of doing so. Even if there is no definite answer to the first question, the vital need for us to know what constitutes the good is so important that investigation of this question is imperative. Even if it is destined to remain as an ineludible discrepancy between the need to know what the good is and the possibility of gaining direct, sure, clear knowledge that is able to enlighten the path of existence, we find ourselves compelled to consider the subject.

The problem lies in finding the way to stick to the question while simultaneously making it make sense. Once we are touching on issues of extreme importance to the problem of being-there, caution and prudence are necessary, in the sense that we have to be careful to reason in the clearest and most rigorous way possible, because when we approach the area concerning crucial issues superficial thoughts need to be avoided. When Glaucon, who was aware of the precipitousness of the pathway of reasoning about the good, attempts to hypothesize that, even though we are aware of our limits, we can still say what we think, Socrates kindly reproves him declaring that opinions divorced from a rigorous "sophia" are ugly things (Plato, *Republic*, 506c). Rather than fabricating unreliable sentiments we should be silent and persevere in our search, accepting the difference between our desire and what we can realistically achieve. When we try to avoid the fatigue of rigorous research, we just see distorted ideas, while only a serious search allows us to "hear illuminating and beautiful things what is luminous and fair" (*Republic*, 506d). To maintain the right balance regarding such difficult questions signifies keeping them open, avoiding racking our brains to find definitive solutions that are not within the possibilities of human reason. As Heraclitus affirms (fragm. 48), "let us not draw conclusions rashly about the greatest things".

The most important question for life, and also for the ethics that deal with the meaning of life, has to be posed while remaining alert to the excess of the question of good and at the same time of the limitation of our reason. As Aristotle states, precision is not to be sought for alike in all discussions, any more than in all the products of the crafts; "we must be content, then, in speaking of such subjects [good] … to indicate the truth roughly and in outline. […] it is the mark of an educated man to look for precision in each class of things just so far as the nature of the subject admits. (Aristotle, *Nicomachean Ethics*, I, 3, 1094b).

It is matter of engaging ourselves in an analysis at the same time broad and profound, to try to reach an idea (I don't use the word *answer* because an answer satisfies the mind, while an idea can be something germinal and open) that though fragile and temporary can constitute the horizon for decisions about the direction and rhythm of our walk of life.

In the world, there are many ideas of the good ready for use, and in many instances without any reflection we adopt a conception of life that does not derive from our independent reflection, but from adhering to a precise cultural context. Human reason espouses forms of laziness that allow it to prefer those types of clarity that are already available instead of making the effort to seek them. In so doing, in crucial moments, when we must choose, the greater part of this decision has already been made for us. The mind tends to economize on vital effort and to utilize ready-made cultural artifacts, but in relation to the good, it is not the result of a personal investment which is the goal. Nothing is clarified, we are kept in the dark, and find no enlightenment.

To take on the problem of the good as a constant subject for thought, from which we can never have respite regarding our responsibility for its careful analysis, means to enter existence, make lifetime something alive. It is like accessing another level of being. As Socrates says, a life without the search for the good is not worth living.

It is a matter of devoting our thought to questions that we know will never find an answer. However, this never finite questioning takes nothing away from the work of thinking on the essence of the good, since every idea we have through pondering deeply on this subject becomes a basis for further thought. It is important to realize this as something temporary, *a temporary anchorage*. This temporariness of knowledge of the good has to be accepted as a necessity, since we are lacking beings, lacking the perfect accomplishment of what is desirable; it is this lacking part that inevitably requires the search for other "fair and good" ways to give shape to our being. Ethics, being a discourse, is developed starting with those questions from which, once examined, we should be able to find clues, however germinal, necessary to understand which way we can give shape to a good quality of life. From this point onwards, the question of the good is unavoidable.

The Platonic theory of *paideia* (*Republic*, VII, 518b-c), according to which teaching, rather than being conceived as a transmission of ideas from the teacher to the students, deals with the cultivation of mind, consisting in questioning essential issues the analysis of which can clarify life's problems. Thus education should teach to keep the mind "looking where it ought to look and redirecting appropriately" (*Republic*, VII, 518d) that is to say focusing on essential questions, those that deal with the search for good, for whatever is just, good and beautiful, so as to give shape to a good life. Only by keeping our mind engaged in this search it is possible to cultivate those "virtues of the soul" (*Republic*, VII, 518d) that are necessary to keep up the search for the things that are of the most value in order to conduct a good life.

If, then, a good practice of care is connected to the search for the good and if the good is the primary issue constantly requiring to be questioned by the mind, then the act of thinking is an essential quality of the practice of care.

When in the *Apology* (29 e-d) Socrates explains the way to carry out educative practice, he uses the term *frontizo* (φροντίζω) signifying either the act of thinking and reflecting or of caring and concerning oneself. Indeed we may say that a good practice of care begins to emerge as being intensely dependent on reflective thinking. The noetic essence of a caring practice is traceable through the etymological analysis of the term that in ancient Greek indicates to having care, *epimeleomai* [ἐπιμελέομαι]: this verb has an evident relation with the verb *meletao* (μελετάω), which has among its meanings not only "I care for, I look after", but also "I exercise, I meditate, I think". In ancient Greek, there exist different words to signify the act of thinking; but while many of them indicate logical, reasoning thought—*logizomai* (λογίζομαι) means I calculate I reflect, I consider, I ponder, and *noeo* (νοέω) means I think, I consider, I project, I excogitate, the verbs *meletao* and *frontizo* indicate a way of thinking that takes care, takes to heart. The thinking that informs the practice of care must necessarily be a thinking from the heart, that feels the presence of another and takes care of him/her.

Where the Issue Is the Good

Drawing together the threads of the argument, it may be affirmed that a good politics of existence assumes care as fundamental, and since the essence of care is moved by the idea of the good, it is even more important to examine this idea. Only if we remain in the radiating light of the search for the idea of the good, may we obtain correct, therefore good, knowledge of things. The problem is that the good is something that cannot be perfectly grasped by the human mind, and because of this it cannot be known or comprehended by any human mind; as a consequence, the phenomenological analysis of care, simply because it lacks the enlightening power deriving from the idea of the good, is inevitably full of gaps. If a discourse capable of being true needs to be enlightened by the idea of the good, then the philosophy of care—just like any other discourse that has human experience as its object—is inevitably weak, because it is forced to measure up to the shadow of the idea of the good and with all the other shadows that mask important aspects of care. Reflecting on the idea of the good, and in general on everything that may be considered as being of the greatest importance for life, in other words all the things of worth described by Plato, might help to gain if not a "brighter life" [φανότερος βίος] (*Republic*, VII, 518a), at least a vision that is less obscured by superficial opinion.[5]

---

[5] When we act we can either help or harm another person. To reflect on what is good is definitely necessary, but not less important in order to reduce the possibility of error, is to understand where evil lies. Evil must be taken into consideration, because we can only understand how to regulate our actions if we know what to look for and also what to avoid. A solely positive polarization of thought produces a conceptual horizon that is not helpful in guiding actions, and blurs the capacity for discretion; in any process of deliberation it is essential to consider negative factors, too, those that could possibly damage the quality of life and how this could happen. But focusing on the negative is as wearisome as thinking positively is pleasant: in the end negative thinking makes us suffer. And if it is true that "human mind cannot bear very much reality" (Preston 1966, p. 14), when reality has a negative appearance, difficulty increases exponentially. Precisely because of our incapability sometimes to bear very much reality, we seek shelter in our imagination, in the conjuring up of a reality that gives consolation. If in some cases this more or less latent tendency of the human mind helps us to find repose during the fatigue of living without interfering with our performance, it could become dangerous when it gets to the point of impeding action. When in the practice of care, we deal with difficult situations that challenge our capability to understand what must be done, we run the risk of allowing our mind to take refuge in reassuring visions that weaken the necessary energy to actively resist the negative and draw our attention towards secondary if or even unrealistic solutions. Faced with someone who is suffering, and whose pain cannot find surcease or when we experience our incapability to find a solution to a practical problem of relationship with another, it is not easy to focus on what it is really happening and silence the tendency to escape and not to resist. We must discipline our attention, and cultivate the capability of keeping the mind focused on reality and on what is actually happening. This is the sort of resistance to what Simone Weil defined as the temptation of the imagination. If the concept were not interpretable through a mystic or esoteric analysis, it would be opportune here to consider the invitation to work constantly on purifying and re-orientating the mind.

However impossible it may be to reach an exact definition of the good, by defining care, that practice informed by the intention to provide what is good for life, we are compelled to include the former problem as well, although we are aware of the inevitable imprecision of every idea we formulate. In order to carry out this duty, we need to return to the Aristotelian argument because, once again, it gives voice to the essence of care practice as it ensues from the phenomenological analysis of experience.

After affirming that every human being is orientated towards the search for the good, Aristotle states that the good in human life is implemented when we live well and when we act well (*Nichomachean Ethics*, I, 4, 1098b 20–21); furthermore, he adds that living well [τὸ εὖ ζῆν] and doing well [τὸ εὖ πράττειν] are the same thing (*Nichomachean Ethics*, book I, 41095a 19–20) and if we assume that acting well means acting virtuously (*Nichomachean Ethics*, I, 8, 1098b 30–31), then we may say that acting according to the passion for the good means acting virtuously. In other words, the ways of being that are in accordance with virtue are essential to continuing the search for the good (*Nichomachean Ethics*, I, 10, 1100b 10).[6]

The practice of care defined as self-care is our own well-being-there; taking care of others is about acting to facilitate the other is her/his search for the good. Understanding what we must do in order to promote the good is difficult but if we accept the Aristotelian thesys that acting for the good is acting virtuously, then to care, since it looks for what is good in life, is in its essence a virtuous action.

Because the good is a difficult thing for the mind to conceive, Murdoch follows Plato and uses the metaphor of the sun (1997, p. 376). Understanding the good is like looking at the sun, but we cannot look at the sun, we are allowed to stay in its light but not to stare at it directly. If we search for the meaning of "to stay in the light" in the perspective of Aristotelian thought we can find that this means acting according to virtue. The fact that virtues have to do with the good, shows them have to be considered of the greatest worth. There are few places where virtue plainly shines; according to Murdoch these places are to be found in "great art" and among

---

[6] In this sense, the good is found in good actions. The good therefore is about doing. We can find this concept in the Gospel of John, when Jesus explains that his food—which what nurtures life—is "to do the will" of he who sent him to Earth and "to finish his work" (4,34). From this viewpoint the good lies not in having, possessing or consuming things, but in doing good works. If we accept the idea that the good is actualized in action, informed by ways of being which consolidate virtue, keeping open the question on what is good, means reflecting on which virtues are informing the way of being-there of taking care in a correct manner. It might help to think that there are two categories of virtues, those that allow us to live well with ourselves, and those that are addressed to others, and the latter, in the opinion of Aristotle, are the most valuable.

"humble people who serve others" (1997, p. 382). I prefer to speak of caring people who take life to their hearts.

Perhaps a small fragment of truth comes to light when theoretical thought results in harmony with feelings that are generated from actual experience; this is the case of the tuning between the philosophy of Murdoch and the results of my empirical research on the practices of care. Starting from the Aristotelian theory Murdoch suggests "to see virtue as the only thing of worth" (1997, p. 381) and from the analysis of the experience of care it is evident that acting in a caring way means acting with virtues: from this tuning we can affirm that virtues are ways of being that improve the good.

But how may we identify and then make these virtues flourish in order to be able to care for life?. In order to answer this question inspiration can be sought in the Socratic reasoning: in the *Symposium* we find Socrates supporting the idea that nothing like love can nurture thoughts that must necessarily remain firm in the soul in order to have the guidance each person needs for his whole life, if s/he desire to live a good life (178c). Replacing the concept of love with that of the good we can say that nothing else like passion for the good is capable of fostering those things of the greatest worth that are the ways of being inspired by virtues.

Talking about ethics, I felt some hesitation in introducing the concept of passion, for the value that our culture attributed to a cool and lucid mind, because an unemotional reasoning is conceived of as the only one that is be capable of truth. However, without passion there would be no transformation in life, life could not find the strength to search for other forms of being: not only other ways to experience things, but also other spaces of thought. Without passion, there is no capacity to resist fatigue or in some cases the pain inherent in cultivating the integrity of our being. When we say that human beings are compelled to transcend, we mean nothing more than the fact that they are always traveling toward forms of being. In order to tread the path of being-there, however, there is a need for energy; sometimes the possibility to decide about an important action of care requires an extra dose of energy compared to normal situations, as in a sort of *meditated passion.* To be passionate about something gives us the necessary energy to initiate processes of transformation; the problem is to give passion a good direction, the one we find when we utilize worthy life goals as indications. The fundamental problem for existence, and therefore for whoever carries out the work of care, is to find this nourishment for the soul.

Only a life enlightened by a passion for the good is worth living. In the ancient tradition, a life that is worth living is when we perform fine or great works (Plato, *Symposium*, 178d). If Greek culture has accustomed us to thinking that great and beautiful actions are those with considerable public resonance, gaining for the protagonist long-lasting fame, a philosophy that examines experience starting from the idea of care invites us to find the right value above all in those simple words and gestures that benefit even only one person, and even simply for a single moment without necessarily having a long-term effect. To be captured by the passion for the good, for oneself and for others, is the necessary condition for the soul to avoid doing anything to bring discomfort to another. If love has the power to fill the soul with divine virtue (*Symposium*, 179a), the passion for the good has the capacity to make us seek for good and right ways to act.

If finding oneself closely involved with someone else's becoming is interpreted in the light of the desire for the good that every person feels, then the politics of existence would undergo a radical change. The fact that the private chasm between our own quality of life and that of someone else's is experientially evident is not automatically translated into a correlated search for the good, on which to base the paths of existence. Feeling deeply alone before the impenetrable mystery of being-there contributes to and encourages our ethical blindness. If, instead, it were possible to cultivate an ontological awareness of the interpersonal quality of the human condition and evince the social value of care, and therefore of the necessity not to live "disregarding others", but "caring for others", then the task of dealing with fragility and vulnerability which all of us eventually find ourselves faced with, as we try as far as possible to avoid evil and find good would gain different nuances and outlines. Of course, unpredictable and uncontrollable events still occur, and human will does not have any control over them, but if each of us could definitely count on a network of relations that are forged according to the principle of care, our quality of life, both private and public, would be different and certainly better. This is the reason that makes care fundamental.

In the *Symposium* (179a), that is the dialogue dedicated to love, it is said that love has such power that, even if there were only a few people capable of real love, they "would conquer all the world". If we venture to replace the word "love" with "the passion for the good", signifying what happens when we care for ourselves and of others, then we can affirm that if more and more people were engaged in caring by nurturing the passion for the good the world would certainly be a better place.

Aside

From now on the concept of the good will recur often. I have attempted while writing to avoid this word as much as possible and I have persevered till now, because the concept of the good is of immense importance for human thinking and because it is something that alarms us because it compels thought towards the risky area of speculation. But then, while always maintaining the development of theoretical reflection embedded in the data of the empirical research I personally carried out in close contact with the work and opinions of those concerned with care, this concept could never be avoided. It is necessary however to specify how it is used here: never deviating from the way in which it is used by those who are considered as witnesses of good care practice. Any dogmatic belief about the reality of the idea of the good should be avoided, and instead a sensitive attention to what everyone perceives as a good life must be cultivated. Therefore, the intention here is not that of promoting a specific theory or vision, but of a necessity of cultivating in the soul a passionate inquiry on the idea of good.

The good has always been the object of moral philosophy. But we are not interested here in the way this idea is treated in systematic thought. Here the Aristotelian principle of *legomena* counts, or in other words the things that are said, in this case the words that describe the sense of the experience of care uttered by those who are in the privileged position of actually practicing care. Here we are relying upon the testimony resulting from direct experience. "Good is non-representable and indefinable" (Murdoch 1997, p. 360), and therefore we are not going to discuss the good, but compliance to reality requires us to use the concept of the good as it is used in daily experience, because this is the necessary condition, even if not a sufficient one, to arrive at a valid descriptive theory of care. There is certainly a lot more to say about this than I am able write here.

Bibliography

Arendt, H. (1958). *The Human Condition*. Chicago (Ill.). The University of Chicago.

Baier, A. (1987). The need for more than justice. *Canadian Journal of Philosophy;* supplementary vol 13, pp. 41-56.

Benner, Patricia and Wrubel, Judith (1989). *The Primacy of Caring*. Menlo Park-CA: Addison-Wesley Publishing Company.

Blum, L. (1994). *Moral perceptions and particularity*. New York: Cambridge University Press.

Bowden, P. (1997). *Caring*. London and New York: Routledge Bow.

Braybrooke, D. (1987). *Meeting needs*. Princeton, NJ: Princeton University Press.

Bubeck, D. (1995). *Care, gender, and justice*. Oxford: Oxford University Press.

Dancy, J. (1992). Caring about justice. *Philosophy*, vol. 67, pp. 447-466.

Fisher, Berenice and Tronto, Joan (1991), *Toward a Feminist Theory of Care*, pp. 35-62. In Emily Abel and Margaret Nelson (eds.) *Circles of Cares: Work and Identity in Women's Lives*. Albany, NW: State University of New York Press.

Hamington, M. (2004). *Embodied Care*, University of Illinois Press, Urbana and Chicago.

Heidegger, M. (1949). *Hölderin and the Essence of Poetry*. In *Existence and Being*, with and introduction by Werner Brock Dr Phil, London: Vision Press Ltd.
Heidegger, Martin (1962). *Being and Time*. Translated by John Macquarrie and Edward Robinson. New York (NY): Harper Collins Publishers.
Heidegger, M. (1992). *History of the concept of Time: prolegomena*, translated by Theodore Uisiel, Bloomington: Indiana University Press.
Heidegger, M. (1998). *Postscript to "What is Metaphysics?"* (1943). In Pathmarks edited by W. McNeill, New York, NY: Cambridge University Press, pp. 231–238.
Held, V. (2006). *The ethics of care*, Oxford: Oxford University Press.
Husserl, E. (1973). *Experience and Judgment. Investigations in a Genealogy of Logic*, revised and edited by L. Landgrebe, translated by J. S. Churchill and K. Ameriks, Evanston, IL: Northwestern University Press.
Husserl, E. (1982). *Idea pertaining to a pure phenomenology and to a phenomenological philosophy*. Transl. F. Kersten, The Haughe: MartinusNijhoff Publishers.
Kant, Immanuel. (1996). *The Metaphysics of Morals*. Translated by Mary J. Gregor. Cambridge: Cambridge University Press.
Kant, I., Mary J., Gregor, and Andrews Reath (1997). *Critique of Practical Reason*. Cambridge: Cambridge University Press.
Kittay, Eva (1999). *Love's labor. Essays on Women, Equality, and Dependency*. New York and London: Routledge.
May, R. (1969). *Love and will*. New York: W.W. Norton & Com.
Mayeroff, Milton (1990). *On Caring*. New York: Harper Collina Publishers.
Mortari, L. (2006). *La pratica dell'aver cura*. Milano: Bruno Mondadori.
Mortari, L. (2013). *Aver cura della vita della mente*. Roma: Carocci.
Mortari, L. and Saiani, L. (Eds) (2013). *Gest and Thoughts of care*. McGrow Hill.
Murdoch, I. (1970). *The sovereignity of good*. London: Routledge.
Murdoch, Iris (1997). *Existentialists and Mystics*. London: Chatto & Windus.
Nancy, J-L. (2004). *All'ascolto*. Tr. It Torino: Einaudi.
Noddings, Nel (1984). *Caring. A Feminine Approach to Ethics and Moral Education*. Berkeley: University of California Press.
Noddings, Nel (2002). *Starting at Home*. Los Angeles: University of California Press.
Nussbaum, M. (1986). *The Fragility of Goodness. Luck and Ethics in Greek Tragedy and Philosophy*. Cambridge: Cambridge University Press.
Nussbaum, M. (1996). *The Therapy of Desire*, Princeton: Princeton University Press.
Preston, R. (1966). 'Four Quartets' Rehearsed: A Commentary on T. S. Eliot's Cycle of Poems. Regno Unito: Sheed & Ward.
Pulcini, E. (2009). *La cura del mondo*. Torino: Bollati Boringhieri.
Rilke, R. M. (1980). *Lettere a un poeta*. Milano: Adelphi.
Rilke, R. M. (1992). *Nuove poesie*. Requiem. Torino: Einaudi.
Rilke, R. M. (1997). *Elegie Duinesi*. Torino: Einaudi.
Rilke, R. M. (2000). *Poesie. 1907–1926*. Torino: Einaudi.
Sevenhuijsen, S. (1998). *Citizenship and the ethics of care: Feminist considerations on justice, morality and politics*. London: Routledge.
Slote, Michael (2001). *Morals from motives*. Oxford: Oxford University Press.
Slote, Michael (2007). *The ethics of care and empathy*. London and New York: Routledge.

Stein, E. (2002). *Finite and Eternal Being: An Attempt at an Ascent to the Meaning of Being*, translated by (Vol. I). Washington: Ics Publications.

Stein, E. (2002). *Finite and Eternal Being: An Attempt at an Ascent to the Meaning of Being* (Vol. II). Washington: Ics Publications.

Taylor, C. (1989). *Sources of self. The making of the modern identity*. Cambridge, MA: Harvard University Press.

Tronto, J. (1993). *Moral Boundaries*. London: Routledge.

Winnicott, Donald W. (1987). *Babies and Their mothers*, The Winnicott Trust.

Wolf, U. (2001). *La filosofia come ricercar della felicità*. (transl. From German by F. Trabattoni) Milano: Cortina.

The Ethical Core of Care

3

In the Heart of Care

The intention that guides caring actions is the search for whatever makes wellbeing possible. Involving oneself in this search means giving an ethical direction to existence. Since the goal of a rigorous philosophy of care is to find the essence, we must now focus our inquiry on the discovery of the ethical core of caring practice.

Having defined care as a practice it has therefore to be investigated as such. Because practice implies action, in order to define it in its complete phenomenological essence it is necessary to find the ways of being-there through which it is actualized. Phenomenology teaches us that in order to understand a given phenomenon we must observe the ways in which it appears and in order to develop a rigorous heuristic work the principle of evidence should be applied. This in turn requires us to consider whatever results from this as valid data; a phenomenological philosophy of care, which searches for evidence based on experience, aims at identifying the ways of being-there that are typical of caring for.

However, because not everything that is real is always immediately manifest, it is also necessary to adopt the principle of transcendence, which compels us to follow the guiding threads of evidence, to grasp what our mind cannot immediately perceive. If we apply the principle of transcendence, we can find the origins of the vital nucleus of care that may not be immediately evident and that manifests itself as *postures of being*. Speaking in phenomenological terms the *ways of being-there* constitute the immediate phenomenological evidence of acting with care, which who-cares-for evinces practically, and that the recipient perceives, when the relationship is at its height; on the other hand, *postures of being-there* are not specific actions that whoever-cares-for manifests concretely in relation to the other, but are

L. Mortari, *The Philosophy of Care*, Phänomenologische Erziehungswissenschaft 11, https://doi.org/10.1007/978-3-658-35175-5_3

more like a intimate dispositions or fertile humus for the action of care. They could indeed be defined as examples of transcendent phenomenological evidence that are enhanced by the ways of being-there.

Regarding the formal essence of care defined in the previous chapter, *ways of being-there* and *postures of being-there* constitute the concretion of the formal structure of care.

Where to begin? Do we first examine *postures* of being-there with care or do we start out by discussing *ways* of being-there? There is no objective precedence in this. The analysis that I followed eventually led to my developing the two planes of the discourse in a circular and dialogic way. If we apply the fundamental principle of phenomenology, the principle of faithfulness to the things that requires us to respect the evidence, we must start by examine the ways of being-there of care. However, having explained in the previous chapter the thesis of an ethical core of the caring practice and that caring postures seem to have an intensely ethical quality, it seems appropriate to start from this part of the argument. We can say that the ethical core of caring actions is actualized in the postures of being-there, and these direct the ways of being with which every person externalizes the orientation of being-there for care.

Care is ethical in its essence because it is shaped by the search for good, or in other words by what makes feasible the determination to create a good life. If Ethics is a product of the mind which is generated by questions about the quality of a good life, care is a practice orientated by the desire of promoting this life. From the perspective of who-cares-for, to act according to what is good means to act in order to promote the well-being of the other. Therefore we can say that bene-vo-lence is the direction of being-there that qualifies care. The phenomenological analysis of the caring experiences highlights the fact that a pragmatic response to this passion for good guides a person to develop specific postures of being-there in which the ethical essence of care is concentrated: feeling responsible, sharing the essential with the other, showing reverential consideration for the other, having courage. Describing these postures of being-there means focusing on the ethical nucleus of caring practice.[1]

---

[1] To enhance the description of the postures of being-there with phenomenological concrete-ness, and also to avoid a too abstract conceptualization, the development of the argument will be punctuated with excerpts and stories of people who are involved in caring practices; these people are considered authoritative because they were appointed as privileged witnesses of the good practice of care. These accounts have been collected during previous research proj-ects aimed to make available experiential data, which I thought necessary for the establish-ment of a foundation of reality to the theory.

Feeling Responsibility for the Other

> I'd say... the story about when we went to adopt Chiara is a lovely one. My husband
> kept telling me for the whole journey ... because the president of the court called us
> and when this happens it means that there is a child with problems... he kept on tell-
> ing me for the whole journey: "For goodness sake, don't do what you always do.
> Don't say yes immediately, but hold on for a while before answering". He kept repeat-
> ing this for the entire trip. And before we entered the room, he said to me once again:
> "Keep the answer to yourself, because it is true that we can say yes, but we also have
> other two children and we cannot force them to accept a choice that might require
> some sacrifice on their part...so let's give it some thought". When we introduced
> ourselves to the judge who proposed... Chiara, who had psychological and psycho-
> motor difficulties, and also had trouble walking... I kept the answer to myself. But
> when the judge asked: "What do you want to do?" my husband said: "We are taking
> her. Immediately". And he was the one who answered! (from an interview with a
> foster-in-care mother)

Caring actions for others are moved by the sense of responsibility for the other.
Feeling the responsibility not only for our own quality of life, but also for someone
else's is a necessary condition to care for another.

Responsibility comes from the Latin *respondere*, whose original meaning was
answering to a call. To feel responsible means answering actively to someone
else's need, with consideration and promptness. Taking on the responsibility for
another person means being open to doing as much as is necessary for the well-
being of the other, wherever possible. This openness not only has to be active but
declared, in order to let the other know that he/she can count on us.

When I pay attention to someone else I cannot feel disconnected from the quality of his/her being-there. If this is true in general, it is even more so in caring
contexts: in the educational context of early childhood where the teacher is faced
with a child who needs everything, in a healthcare context, where the sick person's
face reveals all the vulnerability and fragility of his/her condition. If I pay truly
sensitive attention to another, his/her past cannot be indifferent to me, and by involving me and challenging me, an active response on my part is obligatory. It is an
unconditional command, that turns into awareness and acceptance of the impossibility of separation from the other. The person who is capable of care is the one
who is guided by the imperative from the Old Testament: "(and that) Thou not hide
thyself from thine own flesh!" (Is 58, 7 b).

The responsibility of who-cares-for shows itself with variations of intensity according to the degree of neediness of the other. There are situations where the level of independence of the other is so scarce that it requires direct responsibility from who-cares-for, the newborn who needs everything, for instance, or the sick person temporarily incapable of looking after himself, or again the disabled person who is totally dependent on someone else. There is also a care that is expressed through an indirect responsibility, where who-cares-for interprets his own actions as putting the other in the condition to take responsibility for her/himself. Educational care cannot be conceived of as taking over the direct responsibility of someone else's well-being oneself because this would mean depriving the other of her/his own ontological responsibility. Replacing the other in this case would mean betraying the purpose of education, that is supposed to enable the development of someone else's being and to guide her/him towards her/his own responsibility.

Answering the call to responsibility means acting in the mode of "being for others". Acting for others is the way in which ethical action is realized/actualized. Lévinas hypothesizes a grey and "anonymous there is", that he calls "il y a", (Lévinas 1987, p. 35), a dense web of becoming subject to forces that are not contingent on our existence and in whose trammels we find ourselves enmeshed. However, this entrapment within the anonymous flowing of things does not stop other different and creative ways of being-there, because the human being may establish relationships of care with others and it is this type of relation that interrupts the bleak confusion of the anonymous hum of becoming. The assumption of responsibility for a caring relationship manifests itself as an answer to the call of being-with-others in a meaningful dimension.

Lévinas talks about the individual's "infinite" responsibility towards others (Lévinas 2006, p. 34). As we will see in the following paragraph, the concept of infinity carries out an important function in qualifying the noetic space of the practice of care. But relying on this idea to qualify the posture of being responsible can present problems, because the infinite does not belong to the essence of the human condition, which is always finite. The ancient Greeks, who recognized the risk of excess, considered the infinite to be negative because non-finite; everything that is non-finite is excessive and as such could lead to an unmeasured and unbalanced interpretation of being-there. In a fragment of Heraclitus, we find that the sun, or in other words that entity life on earth depends on, "cannot overcome its own proper measure" (Colli 1993, 14[A 81]). Precisely because the human condition is finite, the vital energy of each of us is limited, so we cannot ask any finite being, fragile and vulnerable as it inevitably is, for endless responsibility. What is required of us is endurable responsibility: this indeed is enough for us and is also within human reach. For that matter, without hypothesizing ways of being that are beyond the limits of human capability, it would be enough for each of us to respond to the call for responsibility according to our own capacity and the quality of life would have a completely different, better, aspect.

Good care is appropriate care if it answers the other's requirements to the necessary degree. The primary virtue for Aristotle is that of trying the right measure: a form of harmony between opposite poles. To expect too much from ourselves is risky, because excessive fatigue can harden one's heart and the resulting inflexibility is not a characteristic that makes for a good relationship with the other. Helen, in her prayer to the goddess Cyprid, explains that if she had a sense of proportion she would be "the sweetest" goddess for mankind (Euripides, *Helen*, vv. 1105–1106).

The moment at which we apprehend the sense of responsibility starting from the idea of infinity is one of a total disruption in the conventional order of things: "there is, literally, no time to look back, no time to escape responsibility, no inner hiding place to retire into self, it is marching straight ahead without concern for self" (Lévinas 1972, p. 34). But for the human being, anything immeasurable is risky. An endless demand for responsibility may exist as a hypothesis, but it is not tolerable from a practical point of view. When we take on the responsibility of caring for another, it is part of the order of things to feel the need to stop and think, to keep a private corner in which to collect our thoughts and regain the vital force of being-there, to the point that we can deny our own presence when we realize that we have come to the end of our reserves of energy. We have to look after ourselves, because care for another cannot take place if we fail to care for ourselves. Putting ourselves at the disposal of others must be squared with avoiding any form of excessive presence, that is a sign of the desire to exercise power over reality instead of aiding in its transformation. Explicit in the principle "love your neighbor as yourself" of the gospel is the reminder to be in the world with equilibrium.

From another philosophical perspective, even Iris Murdoch interprets in a rather excessive way the ethical manner of being-there she defines as an "active moral agent", when she states that morality occurs when "we cease to be in order to attend to the existence of something else, a natural object, a person in need" (1997, p. 348). "Ceasing to be" is not feasible. The caring relationship requires our presence and even if this is puts us at risk, it cannot be avoided. What has to be learned, though, is to sustain the awareness of our egoism in order to keep it under control; this is the necessary passage for an ethical presence. It is undeniable, in as much as we are dealing with experiential evidence, that excessive attention towards the self prevents the forming of an ethical stance, but invalidating self-reference that precludes the attention for the other does not mean erasing ourselves, since without the subject the ethical action cannot take place. Consequently, there is a way of being present where the subject acts with entirety of thought and feeling, with the necessary attention for self, but at the same time focused on caring for another.

Resorting to concepts, such as the one of infinity, which the human mind has always placed in relation with the other world of the divine, is a fascinating pursuit because it sanctions the destruction of certain worn-out paradigms that limit the ways of thinking and opening our minds to others' thoughts. This, in turn, enables us to discover other ways of thinking. However, we must not forget that such concepts should be used with caution and that the drawing of a different noetic space[2] should be a question of trial and error. Having said that, the idea of infinity, has to be assumed as an unattainable idea and not as principle that can be concretely operational; it may be considered valid if we change its operational level from action, or in other words from being-there with another, to thought, assuming this as a heuristic ethical principle. If a clear and perfect idea of acting well cannot be found in the human mind, the duty of thinking what it means to implement good and appropriate care and to be responsible while maintaining a sense of proportion seems an endless task. Since every concept that directs our presence in the world is remarkably imperfect, the never-ending task of continually thinking our thoughts is up to us. This imperfection is as inevitable as the unexpected obligation to focus our attention on another so as to understand what is really happening and what we should do. In this case, a deep knowledge of the other and of his/her uniqueness can be considered as a form of love, if we translate love with the ancient Greek term *"agape"*, that is a spiritual loving, intense but delicate.

---

[2] The concept of responsibility of Lévinas helps to identify the ethical quality of acting with care. However, this concept has to be used carefully, since there is the risk to legitimize a sacrificial conception of care. Lévinas talks, indeed, of a "sacrifice without reserve", the sacrifice of who acts in the position of a hostage designated who has not chosen himself to be hostage, but possibly elected by the Good, in an involuntary election not assumed by the elected one (1998, p. 15). Interpreting responsibility as the position of an hostage ends up to put the ethics inside a discourse that if it has the merit to show that this comes before any ontology, at the same time it subtracts its positioning towards the other in a conscientious dimension, the only one where ethical actions finds the fertile humus that it needs. Without counting the warlike borders of this discourse, because talking about hostage and sacrifice without reserves makes us think about an hero at war.

According to Murdoch, reality is revealed to the patient eye of love (1970, p. 40). But I prefer to say that reality is revealed to eyes imbued with knowledge of the value of care. If being ethical means obeying reality, the ethical agency needs a glance which is capable of paying profound attention to reality in order to grasp its essential qualities. A phenomenological analysis of a different good practice of care reveals that "carefully observing reality" constitutes an essential practicality of care.

At the Origin of the Sense of Responsibility

Understanding the Quality of Being-There of Another

Phenomenological analysis of experience suggests that the generative root of ethical practice, which is manifested by being responsible for others, must be found in cultivating awareness of the fragility and vulnerability of the other, and in understanding how to detect his/her ontological weakness.

Considering a child as a being lacking certain skills or imagining him/her, on the contrary, as a complete person whose forms of being are already present in a germinal form, and that it needs to be nurtured, has implications which are relevant to the way of perceiving educational care. In the field of healthcare, to think of the patient as a sick body which in order to be treated merely requires a certain therapy, or to think of him/her as a person whose suffering is also present in her/his mind and, therefore, as a living, breathing soul are two very different things.

Being is being-with, so it is not enough on its own, it does not suffice for its own needs: we need others and they need us. The fact that everybody needs care highlights the fact that everyone needs to care for someone else. It is the constant exchange of care that makes life possible. The evident ontological data of existence as co-existence makes care for the other something necessary. In this sense, caring for others is not just an existential ideal, but a necessity of being-there. This necessity of caring for the other besides caring for ourselves is particularly evident at the moment we become aware that the need to care for is typical of the human being. This in turn constitutes the idea of the other as someone who needs care, from which in its turn springs a sense of responsibility. The awareness of someone else's vulnerability and fragility binds me to her/him, and it is something that I feel first of all inside myself. Elena Pulcini talks about the "power of weakness", since in someone else's weakness there is an undeniable appeal to responsibility.

The sense of responsibility needs a specific ontological view, the knowledge that we all share this weakness, the perception of our individual weakness and the understanding that the other is in our same situation, because only by knowing that we are all fragile and vulnerable can we feel the urge to take action for the other and do for the other what we would like to be done for us. In this sense, the Christian commandment: "Love your neighbour as yourself" expresses the first truth of ethics. Feeling someone else's ontological weakness has the power to make us feel how binding our responsibility for him/her is.

Even if empathy for another's weakness greatly contributes to our feeling united in our shared awareness of the quality of being, our perception of the ontological quality of existence, however, is not enough by itself to generate concrete responsiveness towards the other. The urge towards responsibility is generated when we realize the needy condition of the other: when we recognize the other as someone who is weaker than us, someone who is in a condition that we can help or for whom we can do something.

Let us imagine that we are standing still at a point in a city from which we can observe people going about their business, people who may very well be as fragile and vulnerable as we are but even if this is so it is not enough to activate that sense of responsibility that spurs us on to perform caring actions. For us to decide to place ourselves at someone else's disposal we to feel that s/he has an overwhelming need of help that only another person can give. The caring relationship, as we already said, is asymmetrical and responsibility comes from feeling this asymmetry of power in relation to the other's being-there. Not fortuitously, when Lévinas is discussing responsibility he quotes Isaiah, who demonstrates his own sensitivity to the concept of the asymmetry of power when he says "Share your bread with the hungry, bring the homeless poor into the house" (Is 58; Lévinas 1998, p. 74).

When we assume that the needy condition of the other is a fact of reality that requires our responsibility, we must also make sure that we are not thinking of responsibility only in terms of a response to another's difficult situation. From previously developed arguments (Chap. 1) it results that care is not merely a case of curing injuries, but also of allowing possibilities of being to flourish. Even the child who does not present any particular problems at school requires my responsibility, even the friend who is trying to change his/her existence, but without being at risk, makes me feel responsible for his well-being; even the citizen who intends to initiate an important political action, that would be impossible by her/himself, makes me feel involved. In these cases, the other is perceived not only in terms of his weakness, but also of his potential; his needy condition means having to receive from others the necessary support to make his own possibilities successful. To exist means to be open to the possible and care is what is needed from being-there in order to move forward.

In general, the literature on the topic of care only refers to this phenomenon in terms of the healing of injuries brought about by being-there, or as intervention in the more difficult circumstances of existence, and it omits to think of care as a duty to help the other to actualize her/his potential, which represents the main importance of the work of care. When we examine practical examples in the field of the work of care, which respond to someone else's need to find ways of fully cultivating their possibilities of being-there, it becomes clear that the readiness to take over the responsibilities of being present for the other is generated by a specific mindset: the passion for the good. A passion that encourages the inclination to dispose ourselves towards being available for others and allows them to actualize their own essence. The decision to take on the responsibility of care finds its motivation in the desire for the good.

Feeling Touched by the Other

Understanding the quality of someone else's feelings is not enough, however, to deciding (on our behalf) us to become responsible for him/her; if this were true, it would be impossible to explain the reason why we do not always decide to help someone else even if we see the necessity. It is feeling touched by the other that is the crucial factor. A kind of thought that is ontologically aware is not enough, it has also to be existentially sensitized. Knowledge by itself is not sufficient to trigger the movement of being-there. There is a need of sensitive knowledge, that feels the quality of someone else's existence. "Sensibility is exposedness to the other" (Lévinas 1978, p. 75) and only this stance puts us in touch with his/her feeling. Being sensitive means getting in touch, feeling the quality of the other, understanding the direction of his/her thoughts, tensions and desires.

Feeling the quality of someone else's feelings can assume the form of *empathy* or of *compassion*. When the neediness of the other is positive, in the sense that the other needs to be accompanied and supported in the work of constructing her/his own being, feeling becomes *empathy*. On the other hand, when someone else's need reveals a situation of difficulty such as subjection to some form of injustice our reaction may be termed *compassion*.

When the teacher of a child learning to read realizes that his/her desire to acquire knowledge is mingled with the uncertainty of any success the specific sense of responsibility on the part of who-cares-for comes into play and engages him/her in finding all the possible conditions to help the child and his/her development.

This is the case when Socrates becomes involved with the education of Alcibiades and shoulders the responsibility of helping the adolescent to cares for himself. Socrates feels Alcibiades' need of self-realization in public life (Plato, *First Alcibiades*) and his desire to find ways of giving consistency to his own unique and individual possibilities empathetically; as at the same time the sage experiences the tremor of the soul when it is facing a decision intrinsic to its own becoming and which activates the responsibility of guaranteeing the other his own presence either in responsiveness or receptiveness. When, instead, the other is in an abnormal condition of need, as is the case today of, for instance, an immigrant without house or job or of a child who is neglected by his/her family and who needs to find a guardian, then, since we perceive profound injustice in both these cases, the consequent affective posture we feel is compassion.[3]

When we talk about feeling, we find ourselves in the affective dimension of human experience. Pulcini, who is among those who theorize the priority of feeling in care practice, writes that the other's vulnerability stimulates feeling, and by mobilizing our emotional side, it provides an affective foundation and a motivation for responsible action. Wherever issues with high ethical value are involved, it is evident that feelings play an important role in the life of the conscience. Moral reason is not neutral or aseptic, but sensitive.

In contemporary ethical reflection particular attention is dedicated to the role played by feelings; in Jonas (1984), this attention increases to include love itself as an important moral feeling. Love should be fundamental not only for family but also for political ethics, because both familial care and care for the world share a love for a similar object, the love for relatives in the family context and the love for the community in the public context, where politics are implemented in order to better the quality of life. On the basis of Jonas' thesis, Pulcini considers love as a constitutive element of the practice of care, a motivational push towards the ethical imperative of responsibility. On a similar basis, we find Murdoch (1970), who holds that moral philosophy, compressed between an

---

[3] From this premise, it becomes clear that the contrast that one school of thought has established between the ethics of justice and the ethics of care is incorrect. In point of fact care is inexistent if there is no sense of justice. Care is moved by the passion for the good, and reasoning on the good implies understanding what it is right and virtuous to do. This is not the place to initiate a critical discussion on contemporary moral philosophy, but it is necessary to mention the evident givenness of the ethics of care as a discourse whose logos is not only not in opposition to the concept of justice, but intrinsic to it. Attributing a broad significance to the ethics of care does not exclude that the ethics of justice may assume its own exclusive identity, its specific formalization that is necessary to lend order to the field of public life.

existential and an empirical vision, can only come into being if it puts the concept of love at its center.

Nobody can doubt the value of love in our existence and since care deals with what is essential in life, it seems imperative to grant love a mandatory place in the philosophy of care. However, it should be emphasized that in our culture the word love conveys a meaning which is different as regards the feeling that has an essential relationship with care. While care should utterly permeate all relationships with its presence, the concept of love is used to indicate privileged affinities. If we translate the word "love" with the Ancient Greek term "*eros*", then the word indicates passion more than sentiment and it signifies only a certain, very particular kind of bond marked out by specific intimacy. If we adopt the Greek "agape" then the use of this term in the philosophy of care would be more appropriate since the verb "*agapein*" conveys the sense of a love intended as protection, care, rather than passion, equivalent to the Latin verb "diligo". However, even if love as "agape" gives the intimate idea of care as looking after someone, owing to the semantic weight with which the word love is overburdened today, it is better to keep it separate from discussions whose aim is that of defining the general essence of care. Jonas affirms, indeed, that even though it is important, love is still an optional element, that can strengthen and ennoble the duty towards another, but is not its source. The true source of the sense of responsibility is, in point of fact, the evidence of the other's ontological weakness "necessary, therefore, is an ontic paradigm in which the plain factual "is" evidently coincides with an "ought"" (Jonas 1984). The essential role of thought is brought back to the center of attention, together with the ideas forming the lens through which we see the world. But the importance of the noetic dimension should not distract us from the affective aspect: the problem lies in finding the right relationship between thought and feeling.

Moral sentiment is important, that sentiment that awakens my sense of responsibility towards the other, but we must know what we mean when trying to define the essential quality that is typical of this sentiment: it is not an irrational feeling from the heart as different from a rational one from the mind, but is generated by a sensitive, emotional reason or in other words by reasoning deeply with the heart upon the quality of reality and therefore upon the other's situation. For as the Stoic philosophy states, sentiment is not something that is added to thought, but a structural part of it. Thought is always emotional. In this sense, the human mind is always pervaded by a specific emotional atmosphere.

If we could develop a phenomenology of the life of the mind, we should see that each part of our affective past is intimately connected to an act of thinking: to a more or less meditated certainty, but always to a product of the cognitive activity. From the parable of the "Good Samaritan" (Lk, 33) we learn the power of the feeling of compassion: first one person and then a second one sees someone who is injured on the other side of the road and neither of them stops; but a third person does stop and not only sees the victim but feels compassion. Compassion emerges if there is the idea of justice at its basis; it is this idea that allows me to perceive reality in a certain way and to decide if it is just or unjust, and then, if I realize it is unjust, I feel compassion. Attention to reality is a way of being that is ethically dense when it is nourished by a certain way of interpreting this reality. Feeling compassion is possible if my perspective on the other is one that is permeated by the idea that the other is just as weak as me, s/he is fragile and vulnerable like me, and therefore s/he needs care like me and s/he feels pain when others pass by with indifference. It is this ontological orientation of the mind that makes the principle of the Gospel understandable: "Do to others as you would have them do to you" (Mt, 12). It is evident that at the root of the sense of responsibility there is not "only" a feeling just as there is not only thought without feeling, but *thoughts from the heart*.

In the past, the affective sphere was decidedly underestimated. According to some modern conceptions, that have deeply influenced general opinion, emotions are the expression of the irrational aspect of a person and because of that they seem unmistakably separated from the rational sphere. In this way, emotions appear separate from any cognitive activity that aims to understand them and eventually modify them. On the contrary, the idea that the ancients, in particular the Greek philosophers, had about the emotions was very different. Indeed, they understood emotions to be strictly related to beliefs, and because of that as being provided with a cognitive structure. This concept is developed by contemporary philosophy, specifically by the school of Modern Stoicism (Nussbaum 2001) that, in synergy with cognitive cultural psychology (Oatley 1992) conceives of emotions as being connected to a cognitive nucleus and because of this as being capable of transformation in relation to changes in the cognitive area. Therefore, starting from the convergence between philosophy and psychology, we can hypothesize that if emotions have a cognitive structure, work in this area can also modify the sphere of feeling.[4] And this is an important fact in the ethical field,

---

[4]Within this theory different interpretations are developed which range from the thesis holding that at the basis of every emotion there is a belief, to the position of stoicism stating that between belief and emotion there is a *relationship of identity*. From the perspective that establishes a strict relation between emotions and thoughts Nussbaum (1996) separates rational from irrational emotions according to the thoughts on which they are based. On the basis of this theory, it would be interesting to understand if we can identify the precise thoughts at the root of the emotion of compassion that moves the caring action and, in general, if we can identify the specific ideas that generate the predisposition for care.

which enables us to reaffirm the necessity of replacing the out-of-date dualisms that produced a reductive vision of experience. The mind's life cannot be fragmented: wherever the mind is emotion is too, wherever emotions are, there are also cognitive issues. Just as spiritual life is intimately connected to the body, so thinking life is one thing with the flow of affective life.

The analysis of empirical data confirms this hypothesis, as we can see from the report of a nurse who finds herself faced with the problem of a patient who is suffering unnecessarily because of an organizational deficiency:

> I could perceive her anguish [of the patient] at the thought of two days of pain until Monday when the technician would come on duty and fix the infusing pump. Her husband was beside her and I could see his visible concern, demoralization and frustration, I had the feeling that he felt abandoned by all of us. He was only too justified in his opinion. I too felt frustrated, if silent, anger because you cannot let someone suffer uselessly in this way with a clear conscience. I stayed with them for a while trying to understand what had happened that morning and above all how the patient was feeling: despite the administration of sedatives she continued to be very agitated. So, I told her and her husband that I was going to see what I could do to find a solution.

Indignation is not an irrational emotion, but it is a consequence of the evaluation of the unfair situation of the other and it implies profound concern for her wellbeing. The account reveals that for this nurse it is not acceptable that a person should suffer pain that could easily be avoided and she made certain that whoever was responsible should realize this and intervene. It is evident that in her opinion the patient needs to be protected because she is vulnerable.

If we accept the ModernStoicism and cognitive vision of the emotions, in order to promote a culture of responsibility of care, it is not simply a matter of boosting the level of affective sensibility, but more one of cultivating a way of thinking, a specific ontological vision: one that comprehends the value of the other and at the same time her fragility and vulnerability. It is of the utmost importance to perceive not only the ontological weakness of the other, the fragility that makes her needy and the vulnerability that requires the maximum respect for her being-there, but first of all to know how to recognize the worth that makes her sacred and inviolable.

The idea that caring actions require a particular way of feeling the other and that this feeling, rather than being considered cheap sentimentality should be thought of as a source of energy that is capable of shifting being-there, is intimately connected to a particular way of thinking the other, does not mean that we should fall into a sort of rationality, or in other words into the abstract concept that erases individual differences and thus the very possibility of feeling the other. The type of thought that is at the basis of responsible actions is not a rationalistic thought, that derives from reality only what fits the structure of the concept, but is like a horizon, a lens that makes it possible to see in a specific way: it enables consideration of the other not only without losing sight of his/her singularity, but in such a way as to activate the facility to feel-with his/her situation and experience. If thinking and feeling are one thing, then to feel the other we must gain a specific ability to think the other.

This integrated vision of different levels of being-there contributes towards the formation of a philosophy of care if it is reinforced by a different way of conceiving reason. Reference can no longer be made to the cold, analythical Cartesian reason, but to a sensitive, fertile and maternal reason. A reason that maintains contact with reality, with the slightest detail of reality and, moreover, which it then obeys. A reason that is immersed in the materiality of life without finding consolation in abstract systems and in the imagination that distracts one from how things really are; a reason that, in order to stay close to reality while it is actually happening, also knows how to be present itself as a narrative reason not only an argumentative one, because narration keeps thought close to reality in its temporal occurrence. A reason that is not afraid to feel, because it knows it cannot think correctly without feeling/with the heart the quality of things.

Obeying Reality

Being Obligated

When discussing responsibility we must inevitably turn to Lévinas, who makes us reconsider our ethical stance towards this concept which possibly errs on the side of too great a rationalization.

According Lévinas, responsibility should skip all the passages of rational mediation, because the other when entering my vital space, obliges me, by his/her presence, to be responsible. And this obligation is not the consequence of rational deliberation, but of an imperative that precedes thought. I am called to responsibility simply because the other is there. The other commands me. My responsibility for others is something that happens before any discursively constructed decision. We find ourselves obligated to responsibility starting from the glance of the other that guides me (Lévinas 1998, p. 13).

To feel oneself immediately responsible when faced with the other is a consequent on the idea that we are obliged to assume responsibility "without this obligation having begun in me" (Lévinas 1998, p. 13). Assuming responsibility for the other precedes any freedom and lies beyond any deliberate action; this particular posture of being-there implies "a passivity more passive than all passivity" (Lévinas 1998, p. 14). It is simply the fact that we perceive the vibration of being in the other that compels us to be responsible; the other "orders me before being recognized" (Lévinas 1998, p. 87), in the sense that the command is actualized before any other reasoning on my part that leads me to decide if and how I want to be part of the relationship. The other is introduced by his presence, and his presence is a call to responsibility. The other's face summons me to an undeniable responsibility, regarding which care is perceived as a necessary and inevitable reaction.

The conceptualization introduced by Lévinas overturns the way we understand responsibility as a posture of being that has its beginning in premeditation and then becomes the result of a deliberate act. On the contrary, responsibility for others is perceived as a "debt contracted before any freedom and before any consciousness" (1998, p. 12), like a task that everyone is compelled to accomplish without being able to decide whether or not to, like a sudden command furtively inserted in our conscience by ordering me toward the other (Lévinas 1998, p. 11). The extremism of Levinas' perspective consists in putting responsibility outside the action zone of conscious deliberation. Since we assume that anything that is not the result of conscious premeditation as extraneous to and incongruous with the very idea of consciousness, thinking that the subject acts in obedience to an obligation beyond its will would attest that we are no longer in the region of consciousness. […] It is as though the act of responsibility "could not consist in a waiting nor even welcoming the order…, but consists in obeying this order before it is formulated" (1998, p. 13).

Noddings (2002, p. 52) also speaks of obligation towards responsibility, meaning by this word an inner "I must", that is not an answer to a universal imperative, but to the need of concrete care that we feel in another person. Faced with someone else's call we have no choice; it is someone else's reality that is imposed on our will. This obligation to answer the call to responsibility should not be intended as a reduction of freedom, since in point of fact the call to answer the other refers to an authentic way of being-there, which is the relationship with the other, a relationship ethically imbued with the lifelong search for the good.

A Simple and Essential Thought

It is difficult to accept that something so important for life as the sense of responsibility for another that moves our being-there towards caring-for could be considered as extraneous to the self-awareness of conscience. It is difficult, especially for someone who grew up in a culture that has invested so much of itself in the power of reason, to accept that our being-there is moved by something that comes before consciousness and that, as far as the ethical posture of responsibility is concerned, action is set off by a command that comes before reflection. I struggle to accept this idea, perhaps because by depriving consciousness of the power to play an important part in ethical behaviour, we make the perception of our lack of sovereignty over existence more radical. This resistance towards Levinas's vision, that may disguise a desire to look for consoling visions to counteract our fear of the fragility of reason, requires further thought.

Realism forces us to focus our attention on actual facts. With the application of the phenomenological method which calls for access to experience as it is perceived in order to understand the horizon of meaning within which we move, an obligatory epistemic passage to build up a valid and grounded theory is that of access to the experiential data derived from meeting witnesses of good care.[5] One of the most important features of their reports is the emergence of an out of the ordinary way of thinking which in order to be understood in its essential quality suggests the necessity of redefining the concept of responsibility within a hermeneutical space revealed by the philosophy of María Zambrano.

The Spanish philosopher invites us to consider that reality is not only what reason manages to capture and analyze, but that there is something more to it and the usual way of envisaging consciousness is not sufficient to apprehend this ulterior aspect. However, as soon as its outlines may be discerned, consciousness emerges "like an island of light in the darkness (Zambrano 2020, p. 227). Reason is usually interpreted by moral philosophy according to a scientific model and rationalism has accustomed us to believe that, when we have determined a correct method, it

---

[5] Investigating in the concrete life the practice of care through an analysis of the lived experience of those persons who are identified by people as good caregivers is fundamental towards constructing a well-grounded theory of care. In this sense, therefore, theoretical research and empirical investigation cannot be separated. On the basis of this epistemological thesis of the philosophy of care that I am defining here, constant reference is made to empirical research carried out during recent years. The results of this research are evinced in the narrative excerpts which accompany the study. The "*legomena*", or in other words the things that we say, are the first data upon which we can elaborate a descriptive theory of experience.

can penetrate any chink in reality, with the consequence that ethical actions, the expression of a free individual, are always made up of rational acts and come about by premeditated and well-defined deliberation. On the horizon that is bounded by rationalism we build up a vision of the human condition that is rationally enlightened, governed by a consciousness that is capable of lighting up every event and to penetrating the innermost areas of reality. Locked within this rationalist approach, it is difficult to accept the thought that in reality there is something invisible that we cannot see and cannot be seen (1973, p. 175) and which affects our being-there in a vital and intimate manner. What we perceive and what we are aware of does not reveal all that happens, it does not exhaust the whole of reality; there is more, and this more follows non-rational ways of moving our being.

A certain moral philosophy has accustomed us to the idea of the person as an empty will that is guided by general imperatives; every moral action has its own reasons and moral behaviour is implemented when the subject acts following a specific idea. Indeed, if we follow the vision developed by Lévinas who speaks of an obligation towards the other coming before any rational deliberation or that of Zambrano who suggests that our thinking is moved in certain cases by the logos that permeates the original ground of life, it results not necessary to search for a clear and rigorously reasoning. But we are used to the idea that the person coincides with the presence of a perfectly conscious and all-powerful will, it is difficult to think that not all our actions spring from the work of reason so as we conceive it.

Perhaps it is true that we are not just reasoning subjects surrounded by a world that can be reduced to the horizon of analytical thought. Perhaps it is true that the life of the mind which makes itself visible to the reflective gaze does not explain everything and that there may be more, that does not lend itself to any attempt at rationality. This does not mean, however, that when it seems that logic reasoning can find no space, there is not the work of thinking; there may indeed exist a form of thinking that is different from what moral philosophy hypothesizes as the founding element of ethical deliberation. I think here about the answer that, in the context of a research on the practices of different caring professions, was given to me when I was asking care-givers the reasons for certain brave and intense kinds of care for another: "I do it because I have to. It is very simple", they told me, and I would catch them looking at me curiously, as if they could not understand the reason for my question. This kind of answer I found out later was also recorded by Patricia Benner and Judith Wrubel in the field of nursing care. When these two researchers, faced with nurses who implemented caring actions that implied complex evaluations of the situation and required difficult decisions, asked them to explain the reason of their actions, they generally got answers such as: "I did what I had to do" (Benner and Wrubel 1989, p. 4).

If we carry on the argument by accepting Lévinas' s point of view, it seems as if a particular form of responsibility for the other is acting in these people and that this comes before any systematically constructed reasoning has had time to develop. It occurs when we find ourselves obligated towards the other before any deliberation and beyond any other decision that comes from the depths of our being, as if the first motion of responsibility is an act of obedience towards reality, emerging before any other thought, a passivity that is more passive than any passivity.

Nevertheless, a further interpretation is also possible. Zambrano herself, who moves the idea a long way beyond the myth of clear and coherent reason, recognizes that, even if we often find ourselves in the condition of passive subjects when facing a reality that exceeds all rationalizing efforts, this does not mean the absence of a subject, a thinking subject who is still able to make decisions based on deliberate calculation (2020, p. 235). The very fact of passivity implies that there is a subject who decided to assume this experiential position. It is true that when people who are capable of important caring gestures, who know how to take on forms and levels of responsibility that are perceived as extraordinary and because of this are almost frightening, are invited to explain their actions they provide such simple answers that they lead us to suppose that everything happens in answer to a mysterious command. Nevertheless, if these brief, simple answers are interpreted using the parameters of systematic thought, they do not mean that reflection is absent, that between the obligation that the other demands from me and my answer to him/her there is nothing but an extreme passivity towards the imposition of someone else's will. Thought is indeed present, but it is very simple, radically simple.

It is simple in the sense that it is essential and it is essential because it knows where the essence of things lies. What is fundamentally essential for life is radically simple. These people are able to see the other's need, see and think the other's weakness, just as well as they can feel a more usual concern for the other's well-being. They are also fully aware of this: of the other's condition, of their own position and of a possible way of being-there; if then they have to explain their reason for taking action they say "we do it in this way because we simply have to" and this elementary explanation must not be understood as an indication that action does not include the consciousness. In point of fact, it demonstrates a different way of voicing the thoughts that accompany the action. In the same way, in the parable of the "Good Samaritan" we do not find much talking: he saw the other in a critical condition, felt compassion and took care of him.

An ethically oriented decision is not in need of sophisticated rhetoric, or of reliance on rules or systems of scientific knowledge of the world; its need is rather that of a superior perception of reality, "a patient and just discernment and exploration of what confronts one" (Murdoch 1997, p. 330). This perception of the quality of reality is not the result of simple observation, but of a sustained attention already ethically oriented towards the search for those things worth their possibility of being-there.

An elderly woman I met during my research on the practices of care, whose only means of transport was her bicycle, every evening, after helping with the family chores, went to spend the night with a neighbour who was ill and lived alone. When asked why she was doing this, despite her age and her few resources, she answered: "She is all alone and she deserves a bit of comfort as much as anyone else. It doesn't take a lot just to give her a little time". A concise statement reduced to the basics, but which is reinforced by a clear idea of what is important and by a way of reasoning that, even if not expressed in philosophical terminology, is readily understandable in its ethical meaning. This is reasoning without the architectural rigor of systematic discourse, but it has another type of rigor, which comes from measuring oneself the quality of reality. It is a thought that abides where the sense of being-there is at stake; it is not directed by pretentious philosophical systems, but by profound concern for the other's good. In the simplicity of these thoughts there is an ethical strength that does not precede consciousness, but is certainly the voice of a consciousness that understands when there is no other option and orientates being-there from this perspective.

In care we are dealing with an *essential thinking*, that is a *simple thinking which holds fast to the essence of things*. For this reason, it needs no rhetoric. It seems as though we are going to the core of the authentic idea of care, the essence of that evangelical formula so difficult to interpret: *poverty of spirit and purity of heart*. Poverty is the quality of a thinking that adheres to the essential and does not expect anything more from speech than for it to express the basic sense of things; purity of sentiment belongs to whoever is engaged wholly in the search for what makes us feel good, or in other words the primary and original goal of life.

Only when we are capable of this essentiality and purity can we focus correctly on reality. Looking at reality in the right way puts us in the condition of understanding what must be done and this comprehension excludes any other choice besides that indicated by the quality of reality. To act with justice and care is an ideal to which the ethical person aspires, and that ideal requires the pearson to search with the just attention to see what is necessary and to obey reality when it requests a bit of good.[6]

---

[6] Murdoch was engaged in deconstructing the myth of free will, when she identified good quality of action as the obedience to reality. Starting from the point that the basis of a good

A craftsman who decided to give an apartment that he owned to an immigrant without asking anything in return or for any references, when invited to explain what brought him to do such a thing, said: "Well, it was the only thing I could do". To be moved by the principle of caring for another, to search for what is good, makes us experience situations where there is no other option. This means the choice has already been made, guided by passion for the good. The only option is obedience to reality from the ethical point of view. This is yet another way of conceiving the ethical stance.

We find a confirmation of the possibility of interpreting the ethics of care according to a paradigm of essential simplicity of thought in Murdoch's observations. She suggests that there is not even one moral thought that works as the complex reasonings indicated by moral philosophy; indeed, if we consider a concrete situation of moral deliberation we find that the agent, as compelled by obedience to the reality, "will not be saying: 'This is right'" and then "'I choose to do this', but he will be saying: 'This is A B C D ... (normative-descriptive words) and the action will follow naturally" (Murdoch 1997, p. 333).

The thoughts that nurture care are different from those that a philosopher uses and the philosopher cannot understand this if s/he simply stops at those that have already been thought, and if s/he fails to keep her/his attention fixed on reality, bound to the network of meanings with which people implement actions. This is the lesson of phenomenology: to keep ourselves and our thinking in a close relationship with things and their occurrence. Only by observing what others do and listening to what they say can we understand that besides our own often limited approaches, there are other ways of conceiving the life of the mind and our possible way of being-in-the-world. Without seeing the quality and the movement of reality we cannot understand, and without understanding reality and its intimate happening

and just action, one which complies with reality, must be particularly significant, she states that there is nothing more significant than "purity of attention" (1997, p. 356). Since purity is something that evokes a different reality from what is considered the norm, the immediate temptation is to avoid this term, but then, if we accept the challenge of Murdoch to assess thought while using unusual terminology, we are inclined to remember Platonic theory, that identifies the mind able to see the truth as "pure and tender" (Plato, *Phaedrus*, 245a). For Plato, the pure soul is one that mounts up on high to contemplate valuable things, and above all these the most valuable is the idea of the good. If we consider the meditations matured on the basis of a phenomenological analysis of caring experiences on the basis of the Platonic vision we can hypothesize that the mind is potentially pure when it is in search of the good, since the good is the most essential thing. To keep the mind anchored to this search, to sustain the effort of coping with a disproportionate demand without looking for misleading shortcuts is not easy; but the search for the good must necessarily remain our major concern.

we end up by inventing false explanations, that only work in a world of ideas detached from reality.

The other's face calls me to an undeniable responsibility when a certain way of seeing and understanding his/her real situation is activated within me. This understanding of the quality of the other's existence does not need elaborate philosophical ramblings, but simply a thought able to capture the quality of reality and that has no need of being formalized using far-fetched argumentative systems, since the effective statements are essential and straightforward.

Nevertheless, thinking is not enough. Feeling responsible becomes a dynamic principle of being when we feel passion for the good. It is not someone else's face imposing itself on our mind, but rather the need for the good that we perceive in his eyes. This is the quality of sensitive and vital reasoning.

Feeling Reality

Sensitive reasoning, generating responsible caring actions, is a way of thinking that allows reality to be seen and felt. If I feel the need for care in the other and I think of care as something essential, I shall have no other choice but to answer. Feeling and comprehending the essential constrains me to answer the call to be-there for the other. The ethics of care prove radically different from current ethics, according to which any effort should be moved by the intent to increase the sphere of freedom, by keeping open the maximum number of possibilities of action. In care, ethical action answers a need and in its best acceptance the term *acting* does not convey the meaning of unqualified movement, but something similar to obedience: *an obedience to reality in its essential necessity*. I am constrained by necessity not because I relinquish my freedom, but because I accept the fact that I must submit to necessity and I do this because I recognize its value.

Caring requires obedience to necessity of reality. It is not the deprivation of freedom, but the expression of a different order of liberty, one that requires *awareness of necessity bearing in mind that the essential dynamics of the good are at stake*. This is a position that does not imply a choice, not because this choice does not exist, as Lévinas hypothesizes, but rather for the reason that the decision to stay on the side of the good and the right, the valuable things make life worth living, has already been made. Iris Murdoch would say that, when we pay the "just attention", there is no other choice but to act upon what reality obliges us to do (1997, p. 330). If attention is paid to reality and this attention is orientated by a passion for the good, the only right action is to obey the reality that is revealed by this ethical attention. And all this is not a mystery, a strange way of being-there which defies reason. When we obey the call to do good things, we give our assent and assent is an action of the mind. Assent implies a mentally conscious action. We are always thinking. It is inevitable. The attention to reality, that for Murdoch is a condition of that ethical action that consists in obeying reality, is thoughtful and it is activated in a space opened by a horizon of thoughts.

The phenomenological analysis of experiences makes clear that the search for the quality of an ethical posture of responsibility must not be squashed between the idea of an almighty will and that of a mind that is overwhelmed by dark forces, between the idea of a universal reason that acts on the basis of impersonal norms and one completely stable which reacts to reality in its singularity. For this reason, it is possible to conceive of a mind that, though irremediably imperfect, assumes the endless task of thinking about the quality of reality so as to discover a horizon of thoughts which in turn help to develop that ethical sensitiveness that allows a sensibly rational reaction to reality and thus be able to obey it conscientiously.

For Murdoch the essence of ethics is that of focusing "a patient and just discernment" on reality (1997, p. 330). When she states that moral action is closely linked to knowledge—not however with the general knowledge of empty abstract principles, but with that of an exactitude founded on a highly developed perception of what happens to the other which is possible only after a careful exploration of his vital space—she affirms the moral role of attention to reality (1997, p. 331). The essence of virtue is to perceive the quality of the human condition and to stay faithful to this vision.

This realism, that is not merely epistemological (to be able to perceive the quality of the human condition), but ethical (to be able to accept the reality for what it is without looking for consolation), does not exhaust ethics, but actually establishes it, because ethics is actualized by taking action with others in the world. We were not born to contemplate, but to act. If ethical action is an action that deals with reality, with its necessity, then we can hypothesize that at the root of ethics there is a passive virtue that is actualized as realistic attention as it embraces the qualities of reality, nonetheless responsibility is the primary virtue, the one which answers the call of reality. Starting from this assumption, ethics requires the receptive and passive action of seeing and embracing whatever reality tells me about itself, but then it is actualized in actively answering reality with concrete gestures. There is not only the scientific truth, but also the truth of existence. In the gospel according to John, which can be defined as the text where the essence of loving care (*agape*) for the other is enunciated, truth is not something that we say but something that we do (3, 21). Thinking is essential, but reality needs actions by which to be transformed, words and gestures where thought is embodied: caring words and gestures, that implement the Aristotelian principle of "acting well".

There still remains an issue raised by Murdoch which is impossible to ignore. After putting forward the idea that we are similar "to an obscure system of energies from which choices and visible actions emerge in ways that often are not clear", she affirms that one moral question can be the following: Is it possible to identify techniques of purification and reorientation of an energy that is naturally selfish, techniques that are able to make us act in the right way when we are facing moments of choices? (1997, p. 344).

First of all, more than an "obscure system of energies" which would influence the guiding principle of our way of being by inhibiting any act of free choice, a hermeneutics of experience leads us to hypothesize that in some cases cognitive actions are governed by a system of ideas acquired by direct participation in the cultural environment where we live and that they unobtrusively influence our consciousness. If the *ordo amoris* theorized by Max Scheler indicates a scale of criteria that is arrived at with full awareness, we can hypothesize that there are ideas that bring consistency to the cognitive flow, acquired unconsciously, which structure an *ordo tacitus*, or in other words a system that functions silently. The network of relevant ethical concepts that constitute the background of deliberative processes, is not build up only through intentionally developed reasoning, but structured also in an intuitive way during our daily conversations. However, the silent performative presence of an implicit background does not exclude the elaboration of a meditated horizon by the mind, on which other free and aware acts depend. With this premise, the problem enunciated by Murdoch takes on a complex profile: how do we reduce the power exercised by the implicit background, and find an order of thought that makes us perform good actions that is those that are in harmony with the drive towards the good?

If we continue to apply the phenomenological method, a possible answer may be found through an analysis of lived experience as described by those who can be defined as "witnesses of a good care practice". When these people tell of the way they matured the vision of life that guides their daily actions, they generally attribute a particular importance to direct experience of the actions of people engaged in care practice. What is even more relevant here is that these people not only act but also mention the underlying reason for what they do, and the way they report their perspective on care is in no way either aggressive or authoritarian, but rather descriptive and self-questioning.

Analysis of experience shows, therefore, that action acquires its meaning when it is accompanied by a discourse that describes this meaning; that discourse has the power to transform reality by activating the consciousness of the listener when it adopts a non-assertive, modality that evinces the speaker's awareness that s/he is not in possession of any hard and fast truth and that owing to this s/he is bound to constantly interrogate her/himself. What defines the ethics of care is therefore a way of being in reality which is not only actively engaged but also intensely meditative, since the action is accompanied by constant mental effort that fosters and animates the search for those ways of being-there that we use to respond appropriately to the necessity of care that reality asks of us. A good practice of care is strongly impregnated by ideas, and by a philosophy engaged in understanding the phenomenology of relational life, in finding the most opportune action and in the critical evaluation of the impact of practice on experience.

If care is a practice and this practice is shaped by thought, then the source of thought regarding care is in a different region from the one we usually imagine. The sensitive area that guides being-there with care may possibly be alimented by a type of thought which is quite out of the ordinary. The idea of a "winged soul" that Plato promulgates in the *Phaedrus* can help in understanding the quality of this way of thinking (249c-d), where it is said that the search for true ideas requires the mind "to take flight" and the philosopher is able to use his mind in this way when distancing himself from the ordinary way of relating to things and addressing his attention to another order of reality. If, on the other hand, one recalls the example of the Thracian slave-girl, who ridicules Thales for failing to keep his mind on the ground beneath his feet (Plato, *Theaetetus*, 174a), thought that takes flight can be interpreted as that of a person who knows how to keep her/his attention within the flow of life with a regard that is sensitive and free from preconceived ideas, that fill the mind with prejudices and prevent it from seeing the essential qualities of reality. The winged thought that we need does not aspire to go elsewhere, rather it is a embodied and down-to-earth thought that maintains contact with the things that are actually happening, but at the same time it does not give up the wings that allow it freedom of movement and that spread themselves when thought is moved by passion for the good. Indeed, the winged thought finds its right direction simply in the attempt to remain within the order of the good.

Modern culture has taught us to follow an intellectual reasoning, which denies the value of personal growth, denies that ethical action is knowledge and gives importance to systematic moral reasonings based on general criteria. Nevertheless, the reason which remains in touch with life is the one that seems to shape caring practices. We may recall maternal reason, that before all others takes care of the quality of being and because of this can enrich being-there. This is indeed a reason which is essentially ethical and poetic. Without underestimating the search for evidence and the precision of scientific research, it derives its strength both from the emotions and also from even the slightest details of materiality. The life of the mind that shapes caring practice is characterized by the fact that thinking and feeling are united, and it is motivated by its need for a living knowledge because it responds to the necessity of discovering a horizon of meaning for to give life to a good shape. Life does not need a reason that is subject to sophisticated rhetorical systems of thought, which keep it imprisoned within the scaffolding of logic, but one that is concerned above all else with "serving the need" (Zambrano 1998, p. 22), that is to say with answering the questions that are raised by experience and that help to find a solution to the urgent necessity of tracing those threads of meaning that can make life worth living.

Acting with Generosity

The Act of Giving

> That night I was in the ward and an accident had just happened. The police called me to be an interpreter, since they know me. In this accident, a young family with a five-month-old baby were involved. Luckily, the child was uninjured. Knowing that mine is a foster family, at some point a policeman asked me what could be done with the baby, so as not leave him in the hospital. I was about to tell him what to do, but at that point I met the baby's eyes. He seemed lost and as if he were looking for someone, so I said: "I'll take him home". And so he stayed there for the entire convalescence of his parents. I couldn't do anything else. (From an interview with a nurse)

The above experience shows the exact truth of Simone Weil's thought when she says that "generosity and compassion are inseparable" (Weil 1973, p. 146). I act for the other when I can feel the quality of his lived experience and it is then that the face of the other sounds the depth of my being. Caring-for is giving time and since time is life, giving time is generosity in its pure essence. We are capable of generosity when we feel the other's necessity and we fully understand that her/his appeal to receive care cannot be denied.

There are people for whom caring work constitutes the mainstay of the meaning of experience; it is that particular way of being-with-others that brings meaning to our own presence in the world. From their words in telling of the practice of care, it emerges that in dedicating time and energy to caring for others enriches them in being, because they know that what they are doing brings relief to another person. For this reason, caring work is essential not only for who-receives-care, but also for who-cares-for (West 2002, p. 89).

Doing caring work also means realizing where the greatest need for it lies. The knowledge that we are doing what must be done, and that this is obligatory because the other has a vital need of it, offers a reward of meaningfulness that lies far beyond any idea of exchange. For this reason, we can say that in caring work there is an intrinsic element of gratuitousness. The care that takes another to heart goes beyond the perimeter of calculating, measuring or negotiating. We care for another because we feel this action is a necessity. In this lies the giving quality of care.

Generosity, and thus gratuitousness, results a constitutive element of care, because caring for the other manifests itself in the form of benefit, which in turn is about giving something to someone else without expecting anything in return. Giving without asking for anything in return does not imply losing something, because when a good action of care is actualized both the cared and the caregiver experience the good. From a just action, that is a necessary one in order that in reality something good happens, the outcome should not be harm, but benefit to both parties. The only thing is that for the person who-gives-care the advantage does not derive from who receives-care, but from the action of care itself, that is, from the consciousness of having done what is necessary for the benefit of the other.

While repudiating any easy sentimentality about the subject of care, it should be emphasized that it is not actually true that the gift of taking the other to heart does not require anything at all in exchange: it requires the other to respond positively to caring actions. Maternal care requires the baby to go on surviving; the care of the teacher needs the other to care for him/herself in order to give a shape to his/her own existential possibilities; the care of the therapist requires the patient to start a new path in redesigning his posture in the world. Every caring action that we receive reminds our consciousness about our needy condition and about the ethical responsibility to give a shape to our being-there. And it is at the very moment when the sense of being takes shape, that generosity is decisive.

The argument for putting a high value on gratuitousness might be taken as naïve, by those do not understand how the world works. On the contrary, when reality requires it, the space for generous action pertains to the person who lives life according to other standards, those at the basis of deeply spiritual ethics, that do not rely on rules but on the passion for a good life for the greatest number of people.

In the Christian culture the gift, an act of giving in order to increase the other's quality of life, is a fundamental action. We may recall the works of mercy: feed the hungry, give water to the thirsty, clothe the naked, welcome the homeless. The action of caring for whoever is in the condition of not being able to do anything by him/herself is related in the parable of the Good Samaritan and in this story the essence of the ethics of care is condensed. While the fable that Heidegger reported (1962, p. 242) tells about the ontological quality of care, the parable of the Samaritan (Lk 10,25–37) condenses its ethical sense.

A traveler on the road sees an injured man and feels compassion: he stops and he cares for him giving his time without expecting anything in return; then he gives another person some money and asks him to care for the man since he cannot stay any longer, telling him that he will return to complete his action of care. The action of the Samaritan is a giving which has the quality of generosity: he offers his time and takes it upon himself personally to relieve another's suffering without expecting anything for himself, then he uses his own means to make others responsible in the action of care.

In the generous action of care nothing is lost, but on the contrary something is gained, something essential; the gratuitous action is not a simple leaking away of our own energies, because there is a gain in meaning: this is caused by the thought that we have done what was necessary. Life is a journey in time and we need to take extremely good care of time; but time is replete with meaning only when we act in the light of a search for the good. This is why the Samaritan does not hesitate to interrupt his journey and devote his time and energy to someone in need.

This interruption of our own time so that we may give time to someone else is an example of an action with the right proportion: to stop and help another implies only a pause in the journey without jeopardizing our personal projects; in fact the Samaritan, after caring for the other, goes on traveling. The giving action occupies a some times in our existence, but it is never all-consuming; were we to expect the opposite, the matter would be unsustainable. The caring action is such if it happens in the right measure we need to discover the right degree of time and energy to provide. So as to contribute the right proportion of helping actions, the Samaritan involves another person. It becomes a political action of sharing the responsibility of care; he calls on someone else to share in the action where it is necessary. In this way any form of attention-seeking-behavior and of omnipotence is stringently avoided because often in order to care for we need to realize our limitations and, in our turn, to rely on others. Recognizing our own limits and from there seeking the right measure of being-there leads us to call upon the help of another and the involvement of this third person gives rise to the existence of the community.

In the Samaritan's way of acting lies the answer to the question that Alcibiades asks Socrates: "What does perfect caring mean? [θῶς ἐπιμελεῖσθαι]" (Plato, *First Alcibiades*, 128b). Socrates uses the term "orthos" that in ancient Greek indicates the point of perfect balance, when one line meets another and creates a right-angle. We can attempt an answer to the Socratic question by affirming that perfect care is a care put in place in due measure. We are right when we find the right proportion, the balancing point between opposite poles within which we always operate: to care for ourselves and to care for the other, to do things on our own and to delegate things to others; and then specifically, to recognize up to what point we should act for another or, on the contrary, whether it is the case to interpret care as a request to the other to act independently. Our job is to learn to distinguish between how far we must be actively responsive and how far we should remain passively present.

A thing is good if it is right and a thing is right if it keeps itself in the right proportion. In this sense, the good always requires "the right measure", the right way of being-there. There is no opposition then between the ethics of care and the ethics of justice, since both acting with justice and acting with care require "the right measure of being-there.[7]

Among the many experiences of care that I collected during my research, some of them underline the need felt by who-cares-for to find the right degree of availability, because they feel that an excess of care is not right: if in one of the two poles of the relationship there is excess, on the other there is a lack, and this imbalance does not serve the order of the sought-after good.

> Some time ago, Anna,[8] together with her family, gave her consent to fostering in situations of emergency. She decided to welcome Maia, a migrant woman with a new born daughter, to her home. This hospitality was prolonged beyond the established time and during this period Maia began to feel comfortable and at her ease. At some point, however, Maia's behaviour was perceived as too demanding, and her requests affected not only her relationship with Anna, but with the entire family, because her manner became unbearable. At that point, after a difficult decision, Anna made up her mind to suspend the custody in her home and to find a solution that would allow her family to regain their wellbeing but without abandoning Maia, who had the right to keep on counting on the foster family. It was a very difficult decision that meant a good deal of deliberation in the family, but the driving logic behind this process was not simply that of the subtraction of a problematic element, but actually the search for another way of maintaining the caring relationship, which implied the right degree of availability and avoided the useless and negative leaking away of being.

How is it that one person decides to share with others what is essential for themselves, such as family life, knowing that welcoming a person "with problems" will

---

[7] Aristotle places one virtue above all the others, the one he defines as the primary virtue (*Nichomachean Ethics*, II, 6, 1106b 16–28): this is the one that consists in finding the right point of balance, the golden mean between opposites. If it is true that care practice finds its cornerstone in the Aristotelian primary virtue, then two consequences may be argued: (a) there is no difference between the ethics of care and the ethics of justice because the search for the good is inseparable from the search for the perfect action; (b) care may be interpreted as an ethics of virtue from the moment that the primary virtue according to Aristotle is the pivotal part of acting with care.

[8] Names are invented in order to protect anonymity.

need a great deal of time and energy? Certainly, as we said, that way of attention that sees and feels the other's situation is essential. Nevertheless, it is not enough to feel the quality of the other's situation. The passion for the good inspires the giving posture, together with the refusal of evil and the feeling of the injustice of suffering as something that cannot be tolerated and that calls us to respond. Pulcini talks about "passion for the other"; in the most intense experiences of care this may be termed *passion for the other's good*.

Murdoch (1997) would like moral philosophy to regain the idea of the good as its primary object of focus. If we pay attention to experience while it is happening, who-acts-with-care seems to possess a certain familiarity with the process of reasoning on the good; s/he takes for granted its priority in the hierarchy of things of value and acts *obeying the call for the good that springs from reality.*

Without Expectations

If we were to follow the discussion that Jacques Derrida (1991) develops on giving, we could not talk about an ethics of giving in care practice because he states that a gift exists only when an action of giving does not appear as such either to the receiver or to the giver. In point of fact, when care practitioners describe their solicitous actions towards the other, they themselves do not usually consider these actions as gifts, but rather as things they do that need to be done. Nonetheless, they maintain that any such action, even if it is free because it does not expect anything in return, eventually and almost inevitably does receive some kind of recompense. We can define this action as a giving act precisely because it is outside any idea of exchange, any calculation that governs financial exchanges. The true and unique exchange that is actualized in the good practice of care is an exchange of being, that follows a logic that is totally unpredictable and that is not calculated by who-cares-for at the start of the action. If the person who-receives-care defines the caring action as a gift and consequently shows gratitude, it does not wipe out the generous sense of the action, because if I recognize something as a gift I do not necessarily feel obliged to reciprocate, I simply receive. To accept is certainly not to ignore the gift but to confirm the meaning of someone else's action, a meaning that finds its reason in the fact that the act of offering is, *in nuce*, a compass-reading directing us towards the whole sense of existence.

The phenomenological analysis of experience evinces that giving with gratuity does not represent a marginal phenomenon. In contrast to what Caillé affirms, a gift is not something continues circulating in a cycle of goods and services such as that of a social network (Caillé 2007), because it could no longer be defined as a gift, it would not belong in the ethical dimension of generosity. Gratuitousness breaks away from all circular logic of exchange and it manifests itself unilaterally. The gift seeks nothing; therefore, it is not looking for the consolidation of the social bond either. It is certainly unrelated to the value of use and of exchange and it is equally evident that it has no place within the logic of social ties: in fact, the Samaritan does not look for an exchange, he simply takes care of the other. The gift is something that somebody gives after feeling called to respond to an essentially onto-logical necessity of which he is aware in the other. The value of the gift lies in the complete displacement of attention on to the other which has nothing to do with calculation.

Without generous acts, life would not find ways to flourishing in its possibili-ties. In order to function correctly, a community needs rules that include the pos-sibility of building up and maintaining social ties; if rules were missing, selfish interests would prevail. But although they are necessary, norms and rules are not enough to create a community able to generate a good quality of life. The good requires the ability to act beyond the rules that precondition the way of being; what is needed is the ethical break caused by the gesture of giving. Only in the gift, ac-cording to Lévinas, lies the possibility that an authentic community may come into being; in order for a community to be created it is necessary to recognize the other and "to recognize the other is to give" (Lévinas 1969, p. 75).

The thinkers who endorse theory of the gift as the third paradigm, reason within a vision of social life that does not see the importance of care. The exponents of the anthropology of the gift think and speak about it while remaining within an intel-lectualistic vision, constrained by the logic of self-referential knowledge. If we think on the logic of gift, starting from a phenomenology of caring experiences, or in other words from a thought connected to concrete facts, the theorization of the gift manifests a different essence. Caillé, while commenting the Maussian para-digm of the gift, is concerned with establishing hierarchies of importance between sociologists and ethnologists (Caillé 2007), whereas the task of mapping out a philosophy of care has as its only intention the understanding of the quality of ex-perience and the attempt, if possible, to underline those acts that are of the highest existential value.

The radical distance between the two perspectives is rendered particularly con-spicuous by the fact that central to the formulation of the theory of the gift is the idea that society has to be conceived of as a reality with a symbolic order, a totality linked by symbols. According to the Maussian theory of gift society is kept to-gether by ideas and beliefs, while the theory of care puts actions at its center. True, every action is inseparable from the thoughts and feelings that accompany it, but it is above all a concrete gesture directly affecting experience. If for Mauss symbols and gifts are identical (Caillé 2007), and therefore the gift may remain in the circular logic of giving-receiving-reciprocating, from the analysis of care practices the fact emerges that the gift is a concrete gesture that is tangibly complete and finds the whole of its reason in *doing* something.

The supporters of Maussian thought, though commending the value of giving, maintain this gesture within the paradigm of exchange: we give, we receive, we give again and this exchange generates other alliances. But the gift of care in its authenticity, must be considered as being independent of all mercantile paradigms, even the third Maussian paradigm, because it breaks with the logic of exchange, and its value consists in generating meaning. The care-giver does not expect anything in return, only wishing the gift will be the cause of some good, even if only a very little, for the other. A metaphor of the meaning of giving is to be found in the story of the Three Wise Men (Mt 2,11) who travel afar bearing gifts for a baby in a stable without expecting anything in exchange but the awareness of having done what was right. In care, the gift is not part of the phenomenology of symbolism, but a concrete phenomenon; a gift is a gesture that responds to a vital necessity.

An Extraordinary Ordinary Life

A primary school teacher's story:

> In school, all pupils have different rhythms of learning. When someone does not understand something important, I try to find alternative ways of explaining it. At times, however, I cannot always make myself understood. I then try to set up a time in the afternoon, during which I can pay more attention to those who are having problems. In some cases, just paying attention is enough to encourage and stimulate a different approach towards study. It might seem as if I were wasting time, but in reality, the next morning coping with the job is much easier and quicker and my pupils feel better.

The practice of care is revealed in different ways: organizing educational experiences that take account of everybody's needs and possibilities; paying special attention to the other with the intent of showing one's readiness to listen; searching for a therapy appropriate to the other's situation without relying on readymade guidelines. All these actions need time. Dedicating time means giving what is essential in life: namely, time, because it is the stuff of life.

The ethics of giving concerns the essential, and the essential element of existence is time: we care for when we offer the time of our thoughts, the time of our sensitive words and gestures, and the time of our acts to forge our meaningful relationships with others. The act of giving, understood as devoting our thoughts and emotions, gestures and actions to the other, is the ethical essence of care. People who practice care in the sense that they care deeply about the other's well-being know where the essential lies. In other words, they know how to search for what does good, and the importance of searching for the good shows them what must be done. First of all, it insists that we should give our time in order that something good may happen. So great is the value of donating our own time that not even the most intense gratitude can restore to us the time spent in thoughts and actions dedicated to others.

The imperative, be it expressed or tacit, that pervades our culture, commands us to be efficient, and efficiency is judged above all by the fact of not wasting time. At school, we need to learn as much as possible without wasting time in seemingly sterile activity, such as moments of detached reflection, or pausing to talk about things that catch the student's attention; in healthcare structures the amount of time spent at the patient's bedside is established on the basis of stringent organizational timekeeping, that leaves no room for a proper chance to get to know the other. It must be said that just when time is overly organized something essential is lost for ever. In the literature on nursing mention is made of "*lost care*", or in other words of a way of going about things that loses sight of the practice of care. Keeping time for ourselves gains nothing for us, but constitutes a self-depleting outlay that has no profitable or meaningful result.

While donating time to what gives meaning to life, we are not risking any loss of being, neither is there any self-sacrificial ideology that makes us lose the right way of acting. There is a lack of meaning when we no longer gain pleasure from our actions.

Aristotle affirms that we choose certain actions for their own sake, and not for any calculation of the advantages that may accrue to us (*Nicomachean Ethics*, X, 3, 1174a, 6–8). There are actually two typologies of the good: one which is instrumental and one chosen simply for its own sake, the first being functional to something else, the latter chosen for itself (*Nicomachean Ethics*, I, 6, 1096b, 13–16). Something that is chosen for itself is something that is valuable in itself, therefore an action that is chosen for its own sake is an action whose goodness is produced while we derive pleasure from it. The giving action of care finds its meaning in an *ethical pleasure*, that is to say *the pleasure that derives from knowing we are doing what must be done*. We gain experience in the sense of being-there wherever we feel pleasure in what we are doing, an intrinsic pleasure, that comes from the thought of doing something necessary to the good.

There are actions that make us realize their necessity, even without having to refer to sophisticated theoretical analysis, and it is this realization—supported by experiential evidence—of the rightness of the thing to do that is the reason for our decision to do it, independently of any thought of financial profit deriving from it. We do not choose to take care for an extrinsic, adventitious gain; the pleasure and the profit lie in the feeling of doing something that is right, that is to say good and just. There is therefore a form of pleasure in doing something in a generous way to respond to someone else's vital necessity, the pleasure that comes simply from thinking of doing something necessary in order to make something good happen: it is an ethical, rather than a hedonistic pleasure. Ethical emotion is an event felt in the consciousness which it seems we must experience so that we manage to uncover the vital force to do what is essentially necessary.

In care as consideration for and attentiveness towards the other, the gift becomes apparent as a free and benevolent act, unrelated to that circuit of mutual obligation that is hypothesized by the Maussian vision. As complete generosity is not sustainable for the human being, the person who is acting within the logic of giving may be seeking for something as well, but this something is not a request to the other, since it is inherent to the very action of caring for. If we turn to Aristotelian theory, every human being aims at *eudaimonia*, a term that we tend to translate as happiness, but that literally means a good condition of the spirit, therefore spiritual well-being, and this well-being of the soul can be found when we live well (εὖ ζῆν) and we act well (εὖ πράττειν). Reasoning on the basis of the Aristotelian assumption, when a person is engaged in a caring action because s/he feels the whole value of this, s/he acts well and by acting well s/he can experience a form of spiritual well-being. In this sense, valuable actions performed for their own sake are excellent actions. We may affirm, then, that whoever acts with care is moved by the idea that her/his own well-being coincides with her/his own well-acting and that acting well consists in being capable of offering experiential situations where the other can find her/his well-being. Knowing that we are acting in response to the other's need of something essential is sufficient to our spiritual well-being, because when we can see that the other is feeling well it makes us feel well ourselves. The profit that derives from giving-without-asking consists in knowing we act obeying the necessity of good. Therefore, the action of giving causes pleasure in itself and lies beyond any logic of exchange. Aristotle (*Eudemian Ethics*, I, 1214a, 5–10) affirms that *eudaimonia*, or in other words, the spiritual experience of the good, which derives from doing good, is the best of all things and because of this it is the most pleasant. The gift is born from feeling the necessity to share with others, because we know that this form of action generates meaning.

When it is understood thus, the ethics of the gift that is activated in some actions of care, even if they need an expenditure of time and energy, does not imply a loss of being. At the root of good care, the logic of self-sacrifice has no place; instead it is the knowledge of the essential, of understanding how this is a matter concerning the whole meaning of being, that drives us to experience the pleasure that comes from doing what we need to do.

From stories collected from other people who had witnessed caring practice in the demanding form of taking the other to heart, we realize that giving with gratuity is a key element in developing the action of care and it happens quite normally, simply as something that has to be done, without calculation or evaluation. If something is essential to a successful response to the need of well-being-there of the other, then we do it. The well-being of the other is a value, and this value becomes fundamental, it comes before anything else, especially when the other is in a position of extreme fragility and vulnerability. For who-cares-for, the essential thing is to desire what is good; if the good is donating what is essential for life and if the essence of being-there is time, abiding within essentiality is giving time to the search of what makes us feel good.

Giving time, engaging our own energy in a generous action, when we have no expectation of return, knowing that we are acting according to the necessity of reality, is not something easy to understand if we let ourselves be driven by a selfish vision that equates goodness with self-affirmation. From the acquisitive perspective, which only understands action profitable to ourselves as appropriate and reasonable, the giving action appears a nonsensical waste of time, a risk that puts us outside the usual boundaries of everyday life. The meaning of a certain way of acting that can be caught in the following stories of *extraordinary normality*, as I like to call them, is in fact quite different.

When, during interviews with people who were said to be reliable witnesses of good caring practice, I mentioned to them their exceptional way of acting and thinking, I was frequently asked not to speak in these terms and to consider their way of being in the world as behavior within the confines of normality.

> A nurse who is married and has two adopted children with her husband offered her availability for emergency fostering. The request from social services to take under her responsibility two little brothers for an emergency custody of forty days was made to her when she herself was ill in hospital. She accepted anyway. Then, once she was feeling better, she decided to host two children with epilepsy during the week-end, as soon as they were discharged by the hospital. She told me during an interview: "Something that bothers me a lot is when people say to me: 'Yes, but you are such a special family'. It really gets on my nerves".

At first I did not understand why she did not want their caring actions to be defined extraordinary and I tended to pre-judge it as a useless effort to hide the quality of their actions, then I realized that I was being asked to make their way of life seem "normal" because this was the necessary condition to make it become part of ordinary life, to avoid confining it to spaces that if defined as extraordinary become inaccessible. Whoever acts with generosity and gratuity thinks according to an ethical grammar that overturns the ordinary way of thinking, simply because s/he doesn't feel as if s/he were doing something exceptional in giving with gratuity, but simply what is necessary. It is here that lies the being-different that is the real value of being-there.

Things that are valuable for existence shy away from the calculating logic of the market and are governed only by desire for the good. Whoever lets her/his own actions be generated by the desire to facilitate the occurrence of what makes the other feel good does so because s/he thinks and feels that this is what really matters. It is not the feeling of obedience to rules that dictate the disposition to let oneself driven by the desire of good, but feeling and accepting the necessity to respond to an unavoidable request that comes from the other.

We understand from the words garnered from those who are working in care, that their implementation of the demanding actions required is contingent on their knowledge that care, on which the whole of life depends, is of inestimable and crucial value. Knowing that they are devoting time to something necessary to ensure a good quality of life suffices for them to find the energy needed to take action. Rhetorical strategies, sophisticated philosophical and political theories that bring pleasure to some intellectuals when they write, but that more or less remain in the realm of theory, all these go by the board. What is necessary for the good to happen is often an enigma, but what is certain is that people who know how to take care think in an essentially simple way and with a feeling that goes to the heart of things. When we know we are facing something that is essential for existence, then choices that are not made in the ordinary way of things, which theoretically we label as phenomenological concretion of the ethics of giving, are not felt to be an impoverishment of ourselves, but as a benefit in terms of the real sense of being-there.

We have said that care in its intensive form is devotion; being devoted means, among other things, also "being ready" to respond to someone else's call. The person faced with an abandoned child who does not hesitate to welcome her/him into his family, even if the child's presence will absorb the little free time s/he has; the friend with a friend affected by depression who does not hesitate to dedicate time and a sympathetic ear to her/him as s/he needs to feel that s/he can count on someone, even if this availability requires a great deal of cognitive and emotional energy; the teacher dealing with a student with difficulties who strives to invent learning activities that are personalized in order to facilitate the development of self-confidence, working overtime to prepare a specific didactic exercise, knowing full well, however, that this work will never be formally recognized: all these manage to find the energy to act in a generous way because they know that the good of the other is at stake, or in other words it is matter of what is obligatory for existence.

When Kant, in the *Critique of Pratical Reason* (1997), talks about imperatives in the field of ethics, he means when using the term the essence of thoughts that generate ethical actions. But the imperative of care ethics is different from the sense of the imperative for Kantian intellectualist ethics. For those who-care-for the imperative does not derive from a statement to which the reason attributes a general regulatory value, but from another person we meet, from the need that we feel in her/his eyes and in her/his words of the good that is of vital importance for everybody's life. In this ethical obedience to the individual reality of the other it is not a mere question of the situational context, because ideas that are collapsing towards simple contingency, with no reference to a cognitive context within which to understand how and how far to act, would not be ethical either. The thinking of care is situational because it is attentive to the other and to her/his singularity, but at the same time it is general because it is based on the idea of the essence of good upon which the mind is always focused. It is a realistic thinking, that is conditioned by the singular and concrete life of a person, but at the same time it is idealistic, because it never abandons the idea that guides the action.

The Vital Necessity of Giving

There are moments and situations in life where the generous and free action of care is absolutely necessary. At the beginning of life everybody needs to be cared for. When the newborn is in the situation of total dependence, s/he constantly needs caring actions that can only be considered as gifts, be they time, attention, or cognitive and emotional energy. Being born is the same thing as finding ourselves burdened with the duty to preserve life and realize our being in the best way possible. The task of being born over and over again and in this way bringing into life new forms of being-there needs to be sustained by the life force, the one thing that permits the soul to make unusual efforts of being-there. This force originates from experiencing, at the beginning of our existence, a relationship where we have received prolonged periods of gratuitous care. Care as a gift of attention, of gestures and of words that bring value to someone else's being is a necessary condition for the other to find the necessary energy to cultivate the passion for caring for him/herself. Receiving the gift of caring actions makes us feel valued and it is when we realize our own value that we find the strength to be-there meaningfully.

The care that welcomes being-there as it comes into the world and leads it to its first encounter with others and with things, with the world of ideas and affection, plays an essential role in life. When our entry into the world, after we have been dried off, exposed to the air and deprived of the contact with the original nurturing material of life, consists of a welcoming embrace that communicates to us the loving pleasure in making us feeling good, this caring reception leaves reserves of vital energy in the soul that in the course of time will help our being to open up and, so to speak, 'breathe in' experience, thus making it possible to feel all the pleasure that this should signify. To experience good care at the beginning of our life is vital.

When, instead, this gift of attention is missing, the sense of privation of something essential is suffered in the deepest part of the soul. And the need of something essential that was missed lasts through time, constantly urging the soul to search for that original care that was never received. But the emptiness of original care cannot be replenished, because the lack of something so essential—and it is essential because it concerns the very core of being-there—cannot be replaced by anything else.

In order that this lack may not turn into something harmful, other kinds of care must occur during life. Among these, it is essential that educational care help the other to transform the pain of lack into a compulsion towards self-care, care for others and for the world, so that this becomes the most important daily action. If it is true that while we act with care we obey our own ontological need, obeying reality and practicing that part of care that we are capable of makes us dwell where the soul feels it will be able to receive vital energy.

But not less important is the action of whoever really has at heart the other's being, helps him/her to reconcile him/herself to this lack. We cannot do anything for many of the wants that we suffered at the beginning of our life: we can only learn to accept them, and from this point onwards, where everything seems difficult, begin to be-there.

We cannot always manage to learn to recognize the empty spaces of the soul and, as soon as possible, to accept them. Living may then become a continual strain, as if the loss of that first embrace places our inner equilibrium at risk so that we are always afraid of tumbling into the abyss. Nevertheless, the good can arrive at any moment, quite unexpectedly. And this good does not need to be much, it is usually to be found in very small things. At the precise moment we feel that we are near to breakdown, an unexpected hug, that arrives as a gift of being, calms and relaxes our soul and we learn that there is something else, that we can still experience the good.

Approaching the Other with Respect

A Kindergarten Teacher's Account:

> When the children arrive in class every morning, I greet every single one of them, I wait for them at the door and, bending down to their level, I shake hands with them. This is to let them know that I know that each one of them is there. They are happy, they smile. Every child has its worth, but not all of them know it. It's up to us adults … and we can make them understand this if we are capable of reverence, that is something more than simple respect …

Who-cares-for another person is in a position of power regarding to those who are not independent. Precisely because whoever is dependent is also extremely vulnerable, the asymmetry of power is typical of the relationship of care. From the moment we assume the responsibility of caring for the other and we feel capable of acting in a giving sense without needing anything in return, things can change the power-to-do, if we are not careful, into a kind of violence against the other. Responsibility and generosity, even if they may be qualified as essential dimensions of the ethics of care practice, are not enough to guarantee good care. Responsibility and generosity structure good care if they are intimately connected with the capability of being respectful towards the other; the respect which is reverence.[9]

Having respect means allowing the other to be-there starting with her/himself and according to her/his own way of being. In other words, it signifies considering the other as transcendent in relation to myself, and keeping the other completely separate from my way of being and thinking. When Lévinas affirms that "the col-

---

[9] According to Kant respect is a feeling (1797, p. 75n). A feeling that is not received as the effect of an action that comes from outside, but "stands before its own tribunal, too, and must give account of itself" (ibidem, p.75). Therefore, respect is differentiated from all other feelings. It is a feeling that takes shape the moment I recognize the significance of moral law. Respect is indeed the effect of law upon the subject and this effect consists of the immediate determination of the will. "The most important object of respect is the law, and specifically that law which we impose on ourselves and yet recognize as necessary in itself. (…) Respect for a person is in point of fact simply respect for the law" (ibidem). In the practice of care the respect is different. Since acting with care is a consequence of feeling the call for the good that comes from the other, respect does not mean respect of a law but respect of the other person in real life: this is the major difference between Kantian ethics and the ethics of care, or in other words between an ethics whose predilection is the law and an ethics that concentrates on the person in his/her singular essence.

lectivity in which I say "you" or "we" is not a plural of the "I" (1969, p. 39), he is demonstrating the necessity of maintaining difference and distance, to know how to envision the other in her/his particularity and then to accommodate her/his uniqueness. Respect for the other and her/his own being requires us to understand how to cultivate a rapport where who-cares-for engages with the other while maintaining a distance between their individual realities, while at the same time ensuring that this distance does not widen into a break in the relationship and furthermore that the relationship itself does not impede the establishment of the right degree of distance.

A primary school teacher says:

> Usually children react negatively to negative evaluations, but in Matteo's case his face fell and he became silent and withdrawn even though he had gained a very good grade in his composition. He sat down and didn't want to talk to anybody, not even to me. So I sat next to him and I asked him what was wrong. For a while he wouldn't say anything, then after I went on asking him why he was so sad, he pointed to my corrections in his exercise book, where I commented that in that particular case it was out of place to talk about his friend. I didn't understand. Then Matteo told me: "I need to say this because he is my friend and I don't want to lose his friendship. I would rather you gave me a lower grade". Eventually I understood: for him, his feelings were more important than my idea of the correctness of a composition. We rubbed out the corrections together and looking much happier he told me that he liked this way better and that I could lower the grade.

We must be respectful if we wish to avoid the considerable risk of unkindness that can occur every time we deny the other the possibility of being-there according to his/her own desire of good. If, on the other hand, we allow ourselves be called into question by the other to let her/him be-there starting from her/his own conception of her/his need is the precondition of an ethical relationship.

The Essence of Respect

In Word and in Deed

Respect is expressed in gestures and words: a teacher shows respect when any necessary criticism of the result of a learning process is put into words that express the truth of the situation without hurting the student's feelings; there is respect in a therapeutic manual treatment of the patient's body if it is done gently; there is respect in listening to a friend who is having difficulties when we know how listen attentively without prejudice, which would prevent us from understanding the quality of the other's experience; there is respect on the part of a social worker who, when helping a maladjusted teenager, tries to change her/his attitude to avoid imposing readymade solutions which fail to take account of the young person's past and horizon of meanings.

Respect is shown while approaching (going towards) the other gently, aware of being ready to accept his/her subjectivity (welcome). Respect is hospitality; it is about letting the other's being speak to me without fear of being judged. There exists, in point of fact, a particularly concrete violence: that which deprives the other of living space or which harms his/her body; but there is also an intangible violence, which is no less painful, that of words or thoughts, when with my language I prevent the other's being from prevailing over my own ideas and expect to confine it within my own theories and interpretative schemes. Respect leaves the other all the necessary room to situate her/himself beyond ideas dictated by my own mental devices and makes itself apparent in the search for an adequate language for the ontological substance of the other.

However, even when we have due consideration for the other's ideas, when we try to empathize with her/his past experience and do not pass judgement before making allowance for his individual being, we should never make concessions when faced by what we consider as unreasonable or even unjust. Any initiative should be considered as conceding space for the other, as an important and undeniable act of respect. Before any other action, the other needs to be listened to and understood starting from her/his way of placing her/himself within reality.

From an interview with a nurse:

> I remember a young woman with a tumour who was suffering from a very severe dermatitis caused by radiotherapy and also had had inserted a nasal-gastric tube that could only be put in by undergoing gastroscopy. She was in terrible pain, when we were on the wards we could hear her screaming as soon as we came into her corridor. She had been ordered a totally inappropriate type of sticking plaster by the doctor, and after two hours everything underneath it was suppurating.)
>
> One afternoon, after having noticed that the sticking plaster was incorrectly positioned, I told her: "I am sorry, but I need to re-do your medication". She started: "No, don't touch me, please! It hurts too much". She was screaming in terror. It was hard to say: "I am sorry but I really have to do it, you must resist… for your own good". I knew only too well that I was hurting her and she knew it too but it was the only solution, I couldn't leave her like that, she would have felt worse and worse. The lesion covered by the plaster was a very big one… I really tried to come up with some way of pulling it off without hurting her too much. Eventually I thought that maybe cod liver oil could work, so I found it and I tried to detach the plaster, not a centimeter, not half a centimeter but a millimeter at a time… I was in her room for more than an hour

and a half doing this for her. When I finished applying the gauze, which was medicated with protective ointment this time, and put on the bandage, she was in tears, but looking in my eyes she whispered: "Now I am fine, I feel better".

The time I dedicated to her was useful. The medicated gauze worked and it went on improving matters during the next few days too. She even kept up the same type of treatment at home. It had been a difficult job but it was worth it.

The suffering that the other is undergoing is shared by someone else, the nurse is subjectively involved in her patient's pain, and since she comprehends the physically painful quality of the patient's lived experience she feels that something has to be done, she feels the necessity to take action by dedicating her own time and her own energies to reduce the patient's suffering. Not only does she try to find a specific solution for her patient, but her physical intervention communicates respect and attention.

When we talk about respect we are often envisaging the relationship with the other in its spiritual dimension, forgetting that the other is also a body, and that some areas of care, for example maternal and therapeutic procedures, involve an intense physical relationship with the other. To show respect for the other's body means to exercise care with a sympathetic yet at the same time detached affinity. The way of being of the meeting of bodies with responsive consideration is expressed by a caress. The caress is the attestation of a concentrated closeness, that knows exactly how to pay sensitive attention to the other without seeking anything in return.

The person who needs care entrusts her/himself to who-cares-for, because s/he lacks everything that derives from being in this specific relationship; but since s/he is relying on someone else because s/he is lacking and in need of something s/he is does not have which others can provide, dependence intensifies her/his condition of vulnerability. It is the escalation of this condition that requires the carer to be extremely respectful, which is what must happen when we have grasped the concept of reverence for the other. The difficulty for the person who-cares-for lies in maintaining the right measure in the relationship between actively responding to the necessity of the other and acting without diminishing his/her position as subject and not object, the area in which s/he can act with autonomy and thus the possibility of doing things on his/her own. Even in good caring practice, it may occur that the right degree of presence of who-cares-for is jeopardized; at this point the only option open to the cared-for is resistance to any action, word or gesture that transform receptiveness into possessiveness. Anyone capable of practising good care can realize when respect for the other's space is at risk, because s/he knows how to read the signs of resistance that the other shows every time an action lacks reverence. We can admit generative relationality when who-cares-for is capable of an openness towards the other that has no trace of an appropriation of her/his experiential space or of those forms of intrusiveness that deprives the other of the ethical responsibility that belongs specifically to her/him.

A respectful relationship, however, needs something more: it needs the skill of who-cares-for to avoid the possible tendency to obliterate his own identity through excessive availability, which can never be right. A good caring action, able to nurture the other's being-there, needs from the very first a total respect for ourselves. Caring for the other needs time, cognitive, emotional and physical energy, but it also needs availability, as does any other way of being-there. In order to practice a good care, it is necessary to find the exact balance between an action that could risk the expropriation of the other from his position of subject and one so distant that it could slip into the category of neglect. The balance is obtained by knowing how to establish the right distance and the appropriate nearness. In other words when approaching the other we should always restrain the expression of our own selfhood and our own personality with all its expectations and opinions. In a good caring relationship, the other must be conceded his/her own space where s/he may resist any potential reduction of her/his diversity and who-cares-for should demonstrate their ability to cultivate a relational space where the resistance activated by the other is not strong enough to interrupt the dialogue.

First of all, respect is an operation of the mind, an action that consists in not assimilating the singularity of the other according to into stereotyped concepts that make his/her uniqueness invisible.

Every human being is unique. We are singular and at same time plural beings, or in other words we share the essential qualities of the human condition, and at the same time each of us interprets in an original way his/her presence in the world. To be respectful means to welcome everybody in his/her uniqueness. The first and undeniable form of respect is actualized, therefore, in that way of perceiving the other and his/her uniqueness. The encounter with the other cannot be anticipated by concepts that, whilst attempting to define his/her nature beforehand, actually eliminate the possibility of appreciating him/her and his/her originality.

If we don't try to meet the other in his singularity, in his unique and distinct being-there, we cannot authentically care, because the other's diversity is missing. A caring relationship is a relationship with each other; Lévinas interprets ethics as the work of justice in the relation of the face to face (1969, p. 78) relationship when he describes the meeting of two people whose respective uniqueness is safeguarded.

There is always the risk of assimilating the other according to our own visions and desires. One of the greatest difficulties in human bonding is that of maintaining a relationship with another while safeguarding his/her difference. It is already problematic in informal relationships of care such as mothering or friendship, because even when they are nurtured by profound respect, there is always the risk for the caregiver to filter the other's being through his/her own interpretative strategies. However, it is even more difficult in the caring professions, where we act within specific cultural boundaries, following predefined theories and often obeying rules that get in the way of a relationship with the other in his/her singularity. The person who in doing the caring job is dealing with a number of people all at once (the caregiver at the baby-care center, the teacher in the classroom, the nurse at the hospital) risks losing the possibility of having an idea of the other which is faithful to his/her original profile. In order to act competently it is necessary to have theories (which are didactic, related to welfare, medical, etc.); but any competence worthy of the name has to have the broadest significance possible and the general vision masks the evidence of the particular.

Knowledge may be defined as such when it has (or is considered to have) a general significance, permitting an efficient approach to the control of experience. Nonetheless, the efficiency that is based on general knowledge implies a loss in relation to the singularity of individuals. The teacher who comes into the classroom with a precise theory on the way students learn, risks overlooking the ways and means of acquisition that differentiate each student. Reducing the individual learning potential of the other within interpretative boundaries of specific theories signifies trapping him/her within conceptual limits where his/her singularity has no value, because according to systematic competencies knowledge means seeing the individual in front of me as the pre-defined element of a theory and not as a being unique in his/her individuality. Assimilating singularity inside generality—which happens when the diversity of the other is absorbed by the hermeneutic limits of a general concept—is an exercise of power that borders on violence. Any form of thought that interrupts the resistance of the other in his diversity goes in a totally opposite direction to the relational essence of the human condition since, as it prevents the other from being perceived as an individual, it actually makes any relationship impossible. For a relationship to take place it is necessary for two people to meet. Should the other's diversity disappear and the relationship fail, then it is impossible to take care.

Concern for the protection of the other's singularity is, on the other hand, at the core of the philosophy of care. Here the indicator of the essence of caring for is the capability of paying sensitive attention to the other in as detached a manner as possible from any preconception and free from expectations. For, if I envisage the other in advance in the way in which I should like him/her to be, I should render his/her difference invisible. The caring relation summons us to go towards the other "as towards an absolute, unanticipatable alterity" (Lévinas 1969, p. 34). Who-cares-for needs to keep her/his action for the other free from boundaries of pre-defined theories that prevent to comprehend the singular original situation of those she/he cares for. The ethics of respect underlies an epistemology that confirms the validity of situational and personal knowledge.

General knowledge contributes in a great way towards efficiency, and for that it is necessary and unavoidable. However, if it is not supported by knowledge of the particular that facilitates the understanding of the other's uniqueness, it ends by making his singularity invisible. The more we tend to rely on general knowledge, without dedicating time and energy to try to comprehend the individual essence of the other and on the strength of this personalized knowledge to regulate own actions, the more we risk a sort of subtractive violence, or in other words we cheat the other of what is his/hers.

The first kind of respect is realized therefore in that thinking that allows the caring relationship to be a meeting between two subjects. Thinking singularly is alimented by the exercise of sensitive attention, that entails from who-takes-care the cognitive discipline of keeping the mind free from ties with anticipatory conceptual systems so that it may remain to the highest degree receptive towards the other's quality.

In order to interpret the development of respect as acceptance of the other and of her/his singularity we should envisage the other starting from the idea of infinity, because if infinity is something that resists any form of encapsulation then imagining the other from this perspective means to set conditions to protect it from the power of our discourses, a power that becomes violent when it makes the other's alterity disappear inside anticipatory forms of thinking. Thinking of the other as infinite means to conceive her/him and keep her/him as transcendent, while protecting her/him from being trapped inside her/his own epistemological strategies.

When the relationship with the other is formulated in this way, it seems as if there is no room for care. On the contrary, however, the request to keep the other as transcendent, extraneous, is not an imperative for a non-relationship, but for a relationship that is brimful of respect for the other. Indeed, it requires all the power-systems of our language to be deactivated in order to find a meeting-point with the other that is free from anticipatory meanings, so that we manage to fully embrace the sense of her/his experience. Considering the other in the light of the idea of infinity, means to keep the movement of the mind alive so that it never surrenders to pre-established hermeneutic forms and always continues the search for an understanding that is as faithful as possible to the singular quality of the other's being. Other people cannot and should not become objects that may be reduced to categorization using worn-out concepts.

The other's alterity is always beyond any pre-conceived thought. As hard as we try to get to know the other in order to adjust the caring action to his uniqueness there is always something that remains other. For this reason, the search for comprehension of the other should be intended as in-finite, or never complete. Envisaging the other starting from the idea of infinity means acknowledging both the limit of all knowledge and the obligation always to always rest go on searching for an adequate comprehension of the other, avoiding the imprisonment of the process of understanding the other in the homogenizing tangle of pre-given theories. For the very reason that it prevents the objectifying of the other, the idea of infinity gives life to a different way of thinking from the ordinary way. It is this way of thinking that generates ethical relationality with the other. An authentic caring relationship keeps the other in a position of infinity, because it knows that no cognitive tools, nor well formulated theory can contain the other's otherness.

The Roots of Respect

If we adopt as a premise the fact that at the basis of all our ways of being with others in the world there is the specific idea that the essential qualities of the entity towards which we direct our intentionality are to be respected, then it is essential to identify which conceptualizations of the other are essential to the generation of the way of being of respect.

Certainly, the origin of being capable of respect is the idea of the other as an intrinsically valuable entity and, because of that, sacrosanct. To know the other's value is one with hearing the imperative of the other's inviolability that demands the utmost respect. The necessity for who-cares-for to conceive of the other as a being of an intrinsic worth, which cannot be lessened by any situation or event, derives from making the readiness to act according an ethical principle dependent on the perception of this being's value. When we realize the value of the other, the reverence for his being becomes an evident and unavoidable necessity long before we succumb to any logical argument in its favour.

We feel the ethical necessity to have respect if we perceive the other as valuable. As affirmed by Aristotle, "For he who disdains, slights, since men disdain those things which they consider valueless and slight what is of no account" (Rhetoric da mettere in corsivo), a value that is intended as something intrinsic, innate in being, something that we cannot calculate because it comes before any other thought. Something that is given as a primary fact, or in other words that type of fact that constitutes an unarguable "*archê*".

The respect of the other's value situates the relationship in a "sacred" dimension. The other is sacred, both in his/her material and spiritual life. Over time we have lost the meaning of the sacredness of life. The sacred dimension does not only belong to a transcendent reality, outside time and space, but is embedded in life itself: in the newborn that I must keep in my arms to protect him/her while I feel all his/her vulnerability, in the child who asks me to listen to him/her while s/he tells me something that concerns her/him, in the teenager who is in the custody of another family and expresses his anger and pain to me, in the fragile patient who no longer feels independent and looks at imploring her/him for understanding. *Care is a participation in the sacredness that is in the other person.*

The other, inasmuch as s/he is a living and feeling entity, is sacred in her/his being, in every nook and cranny of her/his existence, and must be treated as such. Sacredness is not only a typical quality of another order of reality, divine and immaterial. The materiality of bodies and lives that we meet in living relationships are sacred: just as is the body of a baby, the fear of a patient who does not know what to expect, the mind and heart of a child who explores the worlds of knowledge, the concerns of an adolescent who discovers a new life. Where holiness is, there is always mystery too, and the other always bears this mystery within her/him. Considering the other as a unique and sacred being requires us to control our tendency to use knowledge as power.

Light is a metaphor that has always been used to describe a cognitive act, which looks at a knowledge that is faithful to the things. Knowledge means throwing light on a problem, illuminating an issue. However, there are different ways of using light. There is a way to cast light over the other that annihilates her/him, to the point that s/he prefers to retreat. We know through experience that too much light is harmful: when light hurts the eyes, they close and our being would like to withdraw. There is, however, a gentler way to illuminate matters, which delicately touches the outlines of things, allowing them to appear as they are. The muted light softly irradiates entities as if to invite them to manifest themselves. Respectful attention defers to the other, reverences her/his reality, her/his "transcendence" since the reality of the other "exceeds the idea of the other in me (Lévinas 1969, p. 50).

That feeling of taking something to heart that gives life to good care needs a thoroughly ethical way of thinking, capable of considering the other without pre-confining her/him within conceptual boundaries that are already defined. Furthermore, the ability to stay outside the limits of its own conceptual frames is absolutely compulsory. It is a type of thinking that is independent of the usual hegemonic order, and becomes a way of thinking that is able to receive the other and to surrender itself to her/his being. A good and right care needs a mind that thinks outside the ordinary, a mind that flies over (Plato, *Phaedrus*, 249a) because it distances itself from ordinary cognitive movements. Thinking outside the usual order, almost ungrammatical. But this approach towards usual norms is not to be conceived as a distortion of the mind, but as a different way of thinking, that breaks with normal habits to access something else. The thoughts that put us in touch with the other are beyond the ordinary because close to the mode of contemplation which avoids any desire of possession, and because of this knowledge is interpreted not as capturing the other but as acquiring the facts that the other wants convey about her/himself. This indeed is the way of thinking that puts us in touch with the intangibility of the other without which his being may be compromised.

In tracing the ethical essence of care, it is clearly revealed that the postures of being that characterize it reach back to those that are defined as virtues. Aristotle distinguished between ethical virtues and dianoetic virtues (*Nicomachean Ethics*, I, 13, 1103 5). It is evident that the philosophy that epitomizes the work of care requires the exercise of rational virtues: respect for the quality of the other to whom the thoughts are dedicated, the attempt to find the words which fit the shape of his being, avoidance of forms of reasoning that transmute into possession of if not violence to the other. Ethically informed thinking is free from possessive fixations; it is moved only by the desire that the other remain inflexible in the face of any ideas, or any expectations; it is capable of maintaining the other at a distance from the subject who is adopting it, and this distance prevents the creation of inclusive relationships and of power. Not only the concepts with which we think the reality, but also the cognitive practicalities with which we elaborate knowledge have strong ethical implications and given the fact that care is ethical in its essence, it requires an ethically informed way of thinking.

Being Brave

It is hard to talk about care, because to the great majority it appears ethically weak, out of place in a world that follows other types of logic. Care would seem an atypical practice for our times because of the individualism that so strongly characterizes it. The dominant tendency is essentially that of worrying about our own life, and of considering that what really matters is the condition of freedom seen as having no ties at all (Benner and Wrubel 1989, p. 2). There is little desire for responsibility for others or for solidarity because the prevailing orientation in our society is fundamentally narcissistic. In place of the moral feeling represented by attention to the other, self-love prevails, which in Kant's opinion is the absolute opposite of ethics.

1679 Elena Pulcini describes the postmodern subject as subject to an unlimited impulse towards self-realization and entropically closed inside the self-referential circuit of his own desires, to the exclusion of all alterity; he is indifferent to the public sphere and the common good and incapable of projecting himself towards the future. According to Charles Taylor (1991, p. 4), individualism—considered by many the most important conquest of modernity—leads to an existential projecting towards the future so completely concentrated on itself that in comparison the others are just simple background actors. The individualistic vision leads us to imagine our own self as independent from others and therefore not to consider it as part of an extensive network of social and biological relationships. Individualism is a way of interpreting life "centering on the self, which both flattens and narrows our lives, makes them poorer in meaning, and less concerned with others or society" (Taylor 1991, p. 4). Among the losses that the individual experiences Taylor sees the failure of great ideals and of passions; but, above all, the impulse towards centering on the self, causes an undervaluation of all those ways of being that focus on the relationship with the other, because they seem to impoverish the project of self-realization (Taylor 1991, p. 4).

Individualism, that permeates the vision of modernity, makes us believe we can be autonomous; it conceives our existence as a complete space in itself and considers the contact with the other from a supposed individual completeness. The idea of a subject who is considered as capable both of pursuing his own interests and of serving a social vision that is inspired by the principle of realization of the common interest, is no more than an ideological residue with no roots in the cultural context; often a subjectivity without depth and without thought prevails, one that is dependent on provisional economic and cultural movements, that acts on the basis of ephemeral projects that are strongly conditioned by a spreading conformism and by a consumerist relationship with a world reduced to a large market. The evidence of strong disparity in buying power seems to leave everybody indifferent and without the slightest feeling of political indignation; a vocation towards the unlimited expansion of selfish desires and expectations seems to prevail which combines with insensitivity to the needs of others. A glance at the relational phenomenology of our time reveals a widespread incapability to feel an affective bond with the other and consequently to cultivate the ethics of relationship that is the precondition for building up shared, participated worlds. A hedonistic and narcissistic spirit is dominant, one that actualizes an existential self-referential attitude inside which the subject perceives himself to be free from ties.

It is becoming increasingly obvious that the prevailing political climate favors the practice of pragmatic not to say careless utilitarianism: events that prove indifference for the other, if not isolation and violence are commonplace. In daily life— at work, on the street, in public affairs, in welfare—we often come across examples of an excessive self-love together with indifference towards other people that shows our loss of attention for them.

But in contrast to those issues that tend to emphasize the dreariness of our time, we should acknowledge two things. First of all, exasperated individualism and narcissism are not a characteristic only of present society, as if ours is a period whose degeneration has no precedent; this would obviously constitute a false view of reality. Plutarch (I century A.D.) wrote that during his times the main cause of "the culture of bad living" was "self-love which is chiefly to blame for making men eager to be first, to be victorious in everything and to desire to gain everything without ever feeling they have enough. For not only do men demand to be at the same time rich, learned, strong and convivial spirits good company, and friends of kings and magistrates of cities, but unless they may also have champion dogs, horses, quails and cocks they are inconsolable" (*On Tranquility of Mind*, 12b). Furthermore, we need to consider that the negative that was there in past times and that is still here today, is mixed with the positive, as it has always been. It is always dangerous to see reality from only one perspective. If this blinkered way of seeing things were suitable to reveal the spirit of the times in general, then the culture of care would find no ground upon which to seed itself, talking about care would be like throwing grains of corn on concrete.

Global information focusses on negativity, on precarious forms of relationship with others and with the world in general; it leads consciousness to disregard the good in reality. It is necessary to see if there is anything else, and of course there is, as without care every civilization would end. To avoid being influenced by monological visions of reality, it is necessary to go and look for the proof of what we can define as "good care", because it is from there, from its positive aspects, that we can build up a culture of care. One of the chief duties of a politics of existence is that of searching for green areas even in the cemented and asphalted city. And it is a fact that vegetation can be found almost everywhere, even if only in the form of hidden lichens clinging tenaciously to stones or flowers that have managed to seed themselves along the city walls. The positive aspect of care may here find its metaphor.

In order to find witnesses of good care we should look at that area of life that is particularly, and in general, correctly, subjected to harsh criticism because of the little attention that it pays to the other's being: the healthcare system. Here the complaints of negligence, carelessness or offense to the other are frequent. But something else is present: there are many acts of care that soothe pain, and return his sense of worth as a person to the patient. In some cases, the act of care takes on a political meaning, because it expresses itself as a denunciation of situations of carelessness that cause useless suffering to the person concerned. These are the gestures of care that require *bravery*.

A head nurse tells this story:

> I remember the case of Marco, he was not even forty, and he was suffering from terminal melanoma. One night a group of nurses before me had already tried to do everything possible to reduce Marco's pain. Since nurses have no power of decision the doctor had been called several times because the pain was so bad that nothing worked; every prescribed painkiller had been administered, but it was like giving him a drink of water, not even morphine was able to make his suffering at least bearable [...] it was a particularly bad night. The next morning, when I received the report and I heard what had happened, I was overwhelmed by anxiety. I understood that I had to do something that I couldn't passively accept that someone could suffer so much. So, I made my report personally to the doctor, asking for a meeting with the team to modify the therapy. But as I feared, the doctor underestimated the situation. At this point, I couldn't bear any more, I decided to take my courage in both hands and I flew into a rage: I expressed my frustration very strongly regarding the situation and how it was being handled, I made our position as nurses extremely clear, and in my fury I told him/her of the many terrible moments experienced by me and my co-workers by the bedside of that patient. It was an awful row, I knew that from that moment my relationship with the doctor would no longer be easy, but I had to do what I did.
>
> The important thing is that in the end the doctors decided to do what we nurses asked: they called a consultation and as a result a more suitable pain therapy was introduced [...] and with that type of treatment at least for three or four hours Marco could sleep. From that moment I noticed that even his family were much more relaxed [...]. And the doctors should never say: "We can't do anything more than this" or "We are afraid"... Because if you doctors are afraid, what should the patients say? Or what should we nurses who are side by side with suffering all day long say? [...] When you are there with him and he cries and he holds your hand and asks for help, and this goes on and on because the pain never lets up... it is not easy [...]. In one way or another we had to solve the problem. I needed to take the responsibility to heart, to take it upon myself, and for this reason I felt that I must do it even if I knew I had to fight a really hard battle.
>
> We are in the year 2000, and with all the drugs available it seemed inhuman to me to let a patient in that condition suffer without trying everything possible. There are possibilities sometimes, often what is missing is the humility to look for the best one.

The story tells us about a difficult experience, one of a patient who is having to bear unbearable pain; a pain that makes him wish to die so that suffering will cease. But confronting this pain the nurse knows how to perform an act of good care. This nurse knows how to do this since she is guided by compassion, and how properly to treat the other, what Zambrano defines as "pity" (Zambrano 2020, p. 241). The nurse not only cares for the patient as requested, administering prescribed therapies, but she shows attentiveness and receptiveness. The phenomenology of the act of care reveals that, because she empathies with the patient's pain, she decides to take the responsibility of a *brave* gesture: to challenge the person who has the authority to decide the therapy and question his/her choices.

We are dealing with a real case of what in ancient Greek is called "parrhesia", that is, to speak frankly even if we are in a position of disadvantage of power respecting our interlocutor. It implies not only freedom of speech but also the capacity take the risk of denouncing what is not right and the obligation to speak the truth for the common good even though there exists a personal risk for the speaker. There is also the intention of returning the interlocutor's perspective to a right relationship with the truth of things and the danger lies in the fact that this position is one of greater power than the speaker's. In this case the gesture of "parrhesia" is a caring one because it is born from the attention to the other's (the patient's) situation and it is moved by the intention to start a process of change for the good.

We are capable of "parrhesia" when our being-there opted for a responsible and brave stance towards a person who has the power to decide the quality of life. This does not mean that who-cares-for decides to be brave as an answer to a must-be that is expressed in the form of being subjected to categorical imperatives that are formally codified, but s/he is "simply" there because s/he is in a responsible relationship with reality. As it is explained by Patricia Benner and Judith Wrubel (1989, p. 4), we act bravely because we feel that there is no other option that is compatible with the other's need of care.

At the root of this way of being there is the ability of feeling the other's condition so closely that we let ourselves be touched by his/her suffering, and instead of avoiding the experience of the other's pain because it is too great, we use this feeling to push ourselves to take action. I act for the other when I know how to feel him/her, when I do not simply look at his/her face, but I feel the quality of his/her life. We are capable of care when we feel the other's appeal to take care of him/her.

A nurse responsible for an intensive care unit says:

> When I went back home at night I couldn't stop thinking about my patient. I felt the injustice that he was experiencing and it was unbearable for me. But what could I do more than I was already doing? I felt I didn't have any more energy. Do we always have to struggle? And is anybody thinking about me? The next morning though, the moment I saw the patient again, the questions in my mind returned worse than ever. I started to work, and I was sad and angry inside for the entire day. Then, I didn't stay on after work as usual—to tidy up the files, to talk to my colleagues—I left the ward as soon as possible. My daughter was waiting at home to do something with me as I had promised. But after stamping my card I managed to take only few steps, then without thinking too much about it I went back to my ward I entered the consultant's

room and, without asking permission, I forced him to listen to me for few minutes. I told him all the negative aspects that in my opinion were typical of the management of the unit, where the person in charge, who has the power of decision, prefers to hide himself behind rules and norms, behind political logic and selfish ideas. "But who cares about the patients?", I told him, "We are here for them, not to get into trouble". Then I told him that the respect I had had for him as a professional had gone for ever.

I knew I had gone beyond the customary limits of my position. But could I do anything else? I couldn't refuse to listen to what was inside me. If I had how could I face myself in the evening? The next morning when I arrived in the department, the patient wasn't there any longer. He had been transferred to another department. I went to the consultant and thanked him for having done what had to be done. I was happy. And I must say that then for once he thanked me.

The story of this nurse emphasizes her sensitive attention to the patient, to whom she dedicates rational and emotional energy, to find an adequate solution for his real necessity of care. This type of engagement implies not only a dedication of time, but also an investment in terms of the politics of relationships in the workplace that requires not a little courage. Indeed, the women jeopardizes her position as a figure responsible for the department, as a point of reference for the medical staff. Care practice often requires bravery: the bravery to oppose prevailing ideas, to declare our disagreement out loud to whoever is in a position of power. This is the strength of the parrhesiastic gesture, or in other words of telling the truth even when we put our position in danger.

Responsibility, generosity, respect, bravery, all are mentioned in our culture as virtues. The description of the ethical core of care here developed is intended as a verification of those theories of care that discuss an aretic preparation in the ethics of care. Whoever practices care never uses the word virtue, but from the phenomenological analysis of practices what emerges is that the terms that in moral philosophy are adopted to name virtues are able to enunciate and to conceptualize the directions of sense that guide the narration of experiences of care.

Aristotle, thanks to whom we have the first and most important ethical theory of virtue, distinguishes, on the one hand, between virtues that everybody expresses towards him/herself, for instance when we practice self-care, and on the other, virtues implemented for the other. We need both of them to conduct a truly human life, but the those carried out for others are the most important among the virtues (*Nicomachean Ethics*, V, 1, 1130a 7–8) because if acting with virtue is motivated by the search for the good and if well-being-there is something that happens in relationships with others, then the relational virtues are those of greatest value. In this sense virtues that are implemented in the relational space are those complete in themselves (*Nicomachean Ethics*, V, 1, 1130a 9), even if their implementation is extremely difficult because the relational space is unpredictable and uncontrollable.

If we then consider the Aristotelian concept of dianoetic virtues and using this we analyze the quality of cognitive processes that support a good care practice, we can see how the ethics of care is aretic not only in the postures of being but also in the practicalities of the life of the mind that inform caring actions. Obeying reality, keeping faithfully to our point of view even when faced with difficult moments in the experience of care, keeping our mind free from preformed theories so as best to embrace the other and his/her original experience, and, not least, resisting the temptation to be content with conventional ideas of the good but rather remaining constantly in search of the very best way of being-well with and for others in the world, these constitute the ethical orientations of the life of the mind of who cares for.

Bibliography

Benner, Patricia and Wrubel, Judith (1989). *The Primacy of Caring*. Menlo Park-CA: Addison-Wesley Publishing Company.

Caillé, A. (2007). *Anthropologie du don: le tiers paradigme*. Paris: La Decouverte.

Colli, G (1993). *La sapienza greca*. III Eraclito. Milano: Adelphi.

Derrida, J., Kamuf, P. (1994). Given time: I. counterfeit money. The University of Chicago Press.

Heidegger, Martin (1962). *Being and Time*. Translated by John Macquarrie and Edward Robinson. New York (NY): Harper Collins Publishers.

Jonas, H., (1984). *The imperative of Responsibility. In Search for an ethics for the technological age*. Chicago and London: The University of Chicago Press. Originally published as DasPrinzip Verantwortung: Versuch einer Ethik für die technologische Zivilisation, Insel Verlag Frankfurt am Main, 1979; and Macht oder Ohnmacht der Subjektibität? Das Leib-Seele-Problem im Vorfeld des Prinzips Verantwortung, Insel Verlag Frankfurt am main, 1981.

Kant, I., Mary J., Gregor, and Andrews Reath (1997). *Critique of Practical Reason*. Cambridge: Cambridge University Press.

Lévinas, E., (1969). Totality and infinity. Translated by Alphonso Lingis, Pittsburgh, Pa: Duquesne University Press.

Lévinas, E., (1998). *Otherwise than being., or, Beyond essence*. Pittsburgh, Pa: Duquesne University Press. Originally published as Autrement qu' être. Dordrecht.

Lévinas, E. (2006). *Humanism of the Other*, translated from theFrenc by N. Poller, Urbana and Chicago, IL: University of Illinois Press.

Murdoch, I. (1970). *The sovereignity of good*. London: Routledge.

Murdoch, Iris (1997). *Existentialists and Mystics*. London: Chatto & Windus.

Noddings, Nel (2002), *Starting at Home*. Los Angeles: University of California Press.

Nussbaum, M. (1996). *The Therapy of Desire*, Princeton: Princeton University Press.

Nussbaum, M. (2001). *Upheavals of thought*. Intelligence of emotions. Cambridge, MA: Cambridge University Press.

Oatley, K. (1992). *Best Laid Schemes. The Psychology of Emotions*. Cambridge: Cambridge University Press.

Pulcini, E. (2009). *La cura del mondo*. Torino: Bollati Boringhieri.

Taylor, C. (1991). *The ethics of authenticity*. Cambridge, MA: Harvard University Press.

Weil, S., Waiting for God (1973). Introduction by Leslie E. Fiedler. New York, NY: Putnam's Sons -Harper Colophon.

West, Robin (2002), *The Right to Care*, pp. 88-114. In Kittay, Eva and Feder, Ellen (Eds.), *The Subject of Care*, Rowman & Littlefield Publishers, Boston.

Zambrano, Maria (1998). *Los sueños y el tiempo*. Madrid: Siruela.

Zambrano M., *El hombre y lo divino*, Madrid: Alianza Editorial, 2020.

The Concrete Aspects of the Essence of Care

4

Care is a practice motivated by the ethical intention to facilitate the other in having a good quality of lived experience; the principle of benevolence distinguishes the generative matrix of care. To be oriented to the search for good is embodied in some postures of being-there: the assumption of responsibility towards the other's being, that is moved by *thoughtfulness* for the other, the sense of reverence for the other, the authentic disposition to *share the essential* and the *courage* to take the initiative.

Since the being-there of each of us always reveals itself in our ways of being-there (Heidegger 1992), the practice of care can be understood in its essence if we identify the ways of being that reveal it. It is the task of a phenomenological investigation to understand which are the ways of being or "behavioral indicators of caring" (Noddings 1984, p. 12) that attest responsibility, respect, generous sharing with others and courage. We will consider as indicators of care those ways of being that evince the intention of who-takes-care to benefit the other.

Some of these indicators require a posture that is more passive-receptive and others one that is more active-responsive, for this reason we can affirm that "receptiveness" and "responsiveness" are two categories that organize the ways of being of care. For receptiveness, I mean making room in our own mind for the being of the other and for responsiveness the action of putting into practice concrete gestures on behalf of the other. Receptiveness and responsiveness are essential conditions of the conscience of the caretaker.[1]

---

[1] This thesis constitutes the basis of Nel Noddings' theory of care, where receptiveness is defined as *"engrossment"* and responsiveness as *"motivational displacement"* (1992, p. 16). To be capable of *engrossment* means being able to feel and embrace what the other shows of

L. Mortari, *The Philosophy of Care*, Phänomenologische Erziehungswissenschaft 11, https://doi.org/10.1007/978-3-658-35175-5_4

Paying Attention

Keeping One's Eyes on Reality

Receptiveness is expressed essentially through attention (Noddings 2002, p. 14). "Attention is nothing but receptiveness that is taken to the extreme (my translation)" (Zambrano 2008, p. 51), in the sense that it is the adoption of an attitude of mind bent towards the reception of as much feedback as possible from reality. For this reason, it is actualized as deliberate and intense concentration on the intended phenomenon, and the resolve to examine the signs of reality as carefully as possible.

To practice a good action in the care relationship, we must appreciate what is actually happening, and to pay attention, understood as a sort of concentration on the outward aspect of events, will allow us to comprehend their reality. In this sense, attention is a primary cognitive act of caring. We recognize the quality of reality by paying attention. Attention is taking the right time to observe and listen others. When attention is passionate and continuous concentration on the other, it will not let itself be distracted, but keeps the mind fixed on the other's reality.

Paying attention means having consideration for the other. And for the very reason that this disposition is directed towards the other, this kind of attention may be defined as an ethical gesture: focusing on the other is the first form of care. If, when we are in the presence of others, we have the feeling that we are not the object of their attention, it seems as if we do not exist. Because of this, the lack of attention constitutes a threat for our personal identity.

Our involvement in activities that are often hectic and exhausting, makes it difficult to find the time for prolonged attention for others, such as lingering contemplation or slow and repeated regard, so as to gain a reliable impression of the other. It is more frequently the case that our attention is frequently interrupted, and we give the other a series of brief and summary glances, just enough to let her/him understand that we are aware of her/his presence. But even these fragments of attention are important, because if they are not accidental, but rather the result of a habitual attention for the other, taken comprehensively, they can have unpredicted results.

Attention as a caring gesture is not a simple glance, but an intense concentration upon the other person. A concentration that is not caused by the desire to capture something from the other, to penetrate his life experience, but that actualizes itself

---

her/himself. Making room for the other is the prerequisite for *motivational displacement*, or in other words for a sympathetic reaction to the other, thus implementing the necessary energy to act in her/his favor. The essential quality of both these attitudes of being is the readiness to "let ourselves be absorbed by the needs of the other" (Noddings 1992, p. 16).

as the simple readiness to receive what the other shows of him/herself. It is not the attention typical of a sort of scientific research that intends to penetrate reality, but rather an attention that is collecting facts deriving from evidence.

I pay attention to the other because his/her face speaks to me (Lévinas 2006, pp. 31–32), it tells his/her desires and his/her pain, his/her hopes and fears. But to capture the quality of his/her past, my attention needs to be sensitive and receptive, because even if the face speaks, what it has to communicate is not immediately understandable. Sensitive attention is not intellectual, but participant; it is attention that comes from the mind and the heart. Iris Murdoch (1997, p. 327) defines attention as "a just and loving gaze directed upon an individual reality", and this type of attention is the characteristic of a moral agent. In order to act morally, clarity of vision is needed; only a constant, intense and sensitive attention make a clear vision of things possible. Paying attention is therefore itself a moral posture of the mind and the heart.

If attention to the other's individuality is important because it provides my thought with facts about his/her reality, first of all it is an ethical act because it recognizes the other's face, his/her being and therefore his/her call to be-there responsibly. Ethics is not a discipline to be referred to only for important decisions, but is a way of thinking and feeling that is always relevant, because in every moment in the relationship with the other we have problems to face and decisions will have to be made that can be decisive for the other's life. To care is to be ethical and Ethics implies attention. For this reason, we must always be attentive in order to make right decisions. From this point of view, sensitive attention for the other is an undeniable ethical gesture, and because of that it is the "daily bread" (Murdoch 1997, p. 335) of the practice of care.

Attention accompanies every moment of care: the initial phase of the relationship when, making the receptive disposition concrete, we make room for the other's being, and then the responsive phase of acting on the other's behalf, because while I am taking action I need to understand what effects my action has over the other's condition and how s/he reacts. Monitoring the effects of our actions is an essential part of the practice of care and, in order to monitor what is happening, so as to collect facts to reinforce the process of understanding, an intense attention is necessary.

The practice of attention is fundamental for any activity and therefore for any cognitive action. If we can say that "no attention means no life" (Zambrano 2008, p. 53), from the perspective of the practice of care, lacking attention means precluding that intensive presence for the other that is an essential and decisive condition for the exercise of good care. If simply looking is a spontaneous action, attention is rather a posture of the mind, and the acquisition of this frame of mind requires specific training.

Attention is realized in the willingness to grasp reality in all its detail, because we may best understand its complexity from an analytical perspective. This interpretation of the meaning of an act of attention must not be understood as an expression of that reductionism that conceives of the whole as the sum of its parts, but as proof that the grasp of the complexity of situations is not simply a matter of an overall, approximate perception but one which is founded on the dynamic vision of details.

To care for the other it is necessary to know how to see the other and realism, intended as the ability to perceive reality (Murdoch 1997, p. 353) requires the exercise of attention, an attention meant as detachment from the self and concentration on reality.[2] Noddings (1984, p. 25) talks about "displacement" to indicate how being-there with care requires us to switch attention from the self to the other.

Sensitive attention to the other that is typical of care is a way of being-there activated not through simple obedience to a behavioral rule, but as a consequence of the respectful consideration that we have for the other; when we are capable of consideration and respect it is impossible to be inattentive and deaf to the entreaty in the other's eyes. To pay attention with one's sight and hearing is a response to the ethical call that we feel coming from the other.

The way of being of the attention is moved by the interest that the person feels for that specific phenomenological field and its function consists in bringing that phenomenon into the full presence of consciousness. Therefore, attention, because it is an intentional act, is determined by the degree of worth that we attribute to the other, and the value of an entity is something that we learn in the cultural community where we live. *The attention that cares has its generative matrix not only in the recognition of the other's worth, but also in knowing and accepting that the prime necessity is the necessity of the good.* In this sense, attention is an ethical posture.

---

[2] The experience of an accurate vision of reality requires complete awareness of what is happening and this form of focus on the external world reduces the possibility of using fantasy. Indeed, Murdoch defines fantasy as the tendency to be self-centred, that is, concentrated on our own desires and our own images. Focusing too much on ourselves prevents us from paying attention to the other. From this premise, Murdoch also questions the practice of self-inquiry, that is to say a meticulous exploration of our own way of functioning (1997, p. 355). It is true that self-inquiry may simply mean nothing but a retreat into oneself and as such it represents an obstacle for being-there in the world as is signified by the term taking care, but self-inquiry, when it is stimulated by the ethical impulse to get to know ourselves in order to act as well as we possibly can, is instead a discipline essential towards developing an ethically connotated presence, since if it is performed with rigorous consistency it allows us to acquire the knowledge of our own way of functioning in a relationship and therefore to supply data about the possible starting-points of processes of transformation.

Loyalty

However, paying attention is a tiring thing. Attention is "a tension, an effort" (Zambrano 2008, p. 51), because if it is to actuated as complete concentration on the other, it requires the ego to be set aside. Furthermore, in order grasp the essence of a phenomenon at the height of its manifestation, the required action for the mind is "a sort of inhibition, paradoxically, a withdrawal of the subject itself so that actual reality can be manifested", the attention that knows how to receive the quality of being of the other "it has to carry out a sort of cleansing of the mind and of the soul" (Zambrano 2008, p. 52). We can welcome the other's being, make room for his lived experience to the extent that the mind becomes lighter, or in other words it is relieved from the weight of all those theories that anticipate the other and enclose him within a process of interpretation that was decided before the encounter. A mind that is capable of attention is a mind that is welcoming to the other, and to be hospitable it has to make room, a space that is generated carrying "the concentration of the subject to the limit of ignorance, not to mention innocence" (Zambrano 2008, p. 52). If when we focus our attention on the other, we project our theories, expectations, fantasies and desires on her/him, then a thick mist seems to form between us and the other, which impedes our vision of reality and its actual limits.

When we are asked how can we "purify attention and make it more realistic?" (Murdoch 1997, p. 356), we may hypothesize that the ability of paying attention can be learned through practice of putting our self aside, of not considering ourselves as the center of everything. Attention is a discipline inspired by the principle of clarifying the mind to the point that when it is, so to speak, a well-polished lens, it is no longer visible, having become merely a means through which light may pass. Thus attention cannot exist as a way of being-there with care if there is no discipline and critical reflection on the part of the self.

Paying attention is also difficult because, "if it is true that human beings cannot bear much reality" (Murdoch 1997, p. 352), when reality has a problematic connotation, just as, for instance, when we find ourselves confronting pain, the difficulty of paying attention increases notably. Because of our very incapacity to bear too much reality, in some moments we find a refuge in our fantasy by picturing a reality that brings consolation. If this more or less latent tendency of the human mind sometimes helps us to rest from the work of being without the possibility of acting, it may become dangerous when it assumes characteristics that alter our actions. When, in the practice of care, we face difficult situations that challenge our capacity to do what we feel it is necessary, there is the risk that the mind, instead of enduring, seeks refuge in consoling visions that inhibit its necessary energy to bear the quality of reality and, instead, focus attention on unimportant or even completely unreal possibilities.

Confronted by a situation where the other suffers seemingly unbearable pain, or when we feel completely unable to find a solution for a practical problem regarding the other, it is not easy to keep on paying attention to what is happening and to avoid the tendency to withdraw and give up the struggle. The effort of attention makes itself felt, above all, when the reality are faced with is a situation involving suffering; it is hard to focus on this, whether the suffering is our own or someone else's, without somehow altering the scene to make it bearable. To keep one's gaze on pain requires endurance in the heart and loyalty to reality in the mind. Since we are not used to observing reality carefully and, above all, to keeping our eyes on negativity, we must cultivate a discipline of attention that knows how to stay anchored to the epistemological principle of searching for the truth, a condition that requires the self-control of keeping our thoughts focused on reality and what is actually occuring.

However, to give attention its proper direction it is not enough to keep the mind faithfully absorbed in reality, because, in order to find a happy medium between observing and getting lost in the complexity of reality, the mind needs to look forward, it needs to keep its gaze focused towards what constitutes the principle of the order of being, or in other words on the idea of the good. It is a matter of making the idea of the good a primary object of attention. It is only in a constant dialogue between the level of immanence [to obscure what happens in the reality] and the level of transcendence [to pay attention to what could happen in the horizon of the good order of the things] that attention finds its right orientation. Attention is fully realized if it is able to dwell both in the world of things that happen concretely (the world of the senses) and in the world of ideas (the world of the reason).

Both levels of reality may disrupt attention: as Plato said, the world of the ideas should not be contemplated for too long (*Republic*, VII, 517), but neither should the world of the senses, that constantly requires us to understand before we can make the right decision. Plato talks about the turn of the soul that occurs when we avert our eyes from the senses and we direct it towards the reality that he considers most worthy of value, the world of things that are the object of the glance of soul. We are obliged to live in the complicated and complex world of the senses, where people need to be protected and nurtured, fostered in their being and helped in moments of difficulty. The change we must make is not that of averting our eyes from one world and focusing them on the other, but keeping our eyes open in a sort of dialogue with both levels of reality. There is not only one right direction of our gaze which the soul should privilege (Plato, *Republic*, VII, 517); the change consists in resolving to make the dual effort of paying attention both to the material world as it is and to the ideal world, starting from our inmost impulse towards goodness. We should not forget that Plato considers the turn of one's gaze towards transcendence as a single instant in the complex dialectic of life, in facts he asks those who keep their eyes on distant things of value to return their attention to the world of the senses and learn how to do both things: because only by keeping one's attention on the reality of life and testing one's gaze against the luminous reality of lengthily contemplated ideas may we take on the proper posture of the human being, that is one of a tree firmly rooted in the earth that raises its branches to the sky. The exercise of a way of thinking that knows how to keep itself within reality and its occurrence, that at the same time weighs up what is desirable, that expresses the drive towards the good, constitutes the condition necessary "ἐπιμελεῖσθαί τε καὶ φυλάττειν" (Plato, Republic, VII, 520).

Listening

Paying attention is manifested not only through sight, but also through speech, that is through words, either spoken or silent. Silence, what is more, leaves room for someone else's speech. Since the structure of being of the entity that we are has a relational quality, listening to others is one of the essential ways of being. Without listening, indeed, there is no understanding. It is a phenomenologically evident fact that our being, since it is relational, is originally posited on the way of listening to each other (Heidegger 1992); it is because of this evidence that knowing how to listen is a structuring action of the caring relationship.

Listening requires the other to start talking, and the action of listening becomes a caring action when we know how to give the other consideration for what s/he is saying to us. In ancient Greek the act of listening to is expressed by the term "ἀκούω" that means not only "I hear" and "I perceive", but also "I learn" and "I obey". When we listen to the other we learn, we learn from his experience; therefore, the time dedicated to listening is actually a time full of meaning for ourselves, too, because listening to the other creates the posture of reflexive presence concerning our own lives. Furthermore, the act of obeying as interpreted within the relationship of care, can be understood as consideration of what the other has to say, without simply accepting the meaning but welcoming what this meaning indicates, in other words caring for the meaning of the other.

If we subscribe to the ontological idea that the human being can be defined as an entity which possesses language, then speaking becomes a humanly relevant action and since acting with care is in its essence an act of consideration for the other, listening to the other's words means communicating our consideration for him/her. It is because "we are language" and because it is with words that we reveal our being and while doing so we render ourselves accessible to the other, listening is an essential way of being for the implementation of a relationship of care.

When Heidegger affirms that "language itself has Dasein's kind of being" (1992, p. 270) he expresses in dry philosophical language what each of us feels when we are actually talking: when we pronounce words to say something essential, we feel we are revealing ourselves to the world and this disclosure makes us feel the need for the other's thoughtful attention to our speech that is also a declaration of ourselves. Talking is always talking about something: it may be about what is happening in the ordinary, utilitarian world, when we are engaged in care seen as providing things for the work of life, it may be something about ourselves, to share the horizons of meaning within which we build up our vital relationships with the world. When people talk about themselves, they reveal themselves, they lay bare their own being; in that case if they find someone who is willing to listen means to experience another's consideration for their being-there, while feeling that nobody is interested enough to listen may indeed be interpreted as a temporary abstraction but also as a denial of their worth. The child who is talking about her/his game is telling me something that for her/him is important and the significance s/he attributes to her/his words requires respect on my side for her/his act of communication, respect that is shown by listening. The sick person who talks about her/his fear and her/his anxiety is looking for help: not listening means to deny the value of her/his lived experience and therefore to worsen her/his condition with another type of suffering, which comes from not feeling sufficiently considered.

A caring way of listening should, be likened the readiness to understand the sense that the other communicates to me. Putting ourselves in the position of listening to someone else means to be on the very border of meaning, a meaning that is present beyond the sound of the words that express it. Listening with an authentic receptive intention is not a simple demonstration of being able to receive the other's words, but means to lean out towards the comprehension and espousal of the possible sense of these words; for this reason, listening is the action of making the other's words resonate inside ourselves: an open and reflexive presence at the same time. It is only when the posture of mind is open and reflexive, that listening becomes an ever-opening space that will accommodate meeting.

Listening requires passivity, it needs the ability to turn into an empty container that makes room for what the other wants to say about her/himself. The action of passive listening is fundamentally that of being quiet, a quietude that has not only and not always to do with sound, but rather is intellectual, since it is really the capacity to suspend the motion of our own thoughts and attune ourselves to someone else's words. When we are quiet and we really want to understand the other as fully as possible, we can "summon and call Dasein back to its ownmost being" (Heidegger 1992, p. 267).

Therefore, in the action of listening there are both receptive passivity and responsive orientation towards the other. Passivity is necessary to make room for the other in our mind and responsivity to access the sense of the other that in order to be grasped completely always requires the effort of understanding, which strengthens when sense seems not to be immediately accessible.

Being-There with Words

Nonetheless, after listening in silence, the gesture of the word is important because who-cares-for must demonstrate that s/he has received the other's words and intervenes with words of communion with the other. With these words, the essence of experience is manifested.

We are a dialogue, as Hölderlin says in one of his poems. To say that we are a dialogue is different from simply saying that the human being possesses language or that s/he feels at home in a world of words. Dialogue is not a simple uttering of words, but a lively exchange of words between two people, words that nurture life because they are nurtured themselves by the fact that the act of dialoging is driven by the desire of meeting the other and together. We are the words we use with ourselves and with other In a caring relationship, looking at our interlocutor and listening to them lead to dialogue, to uttering words so that we understand one another, to building up a space full of shared meaning. The "sensed sense" that Nancy discusses (2004, p. 2) does not exist in the intraindividual area of thought in our mind, but it springs from the dialogic encounter with the other, who while s/he is receiving our words and returning to us the sense that s/he construed from them, s/he helps us to access another level of meaning.

The inseparability of our being plural and possessing speech to talk to one another is an ontological quality already clearly explained by Aristotle, who defines in the Nicomachean Ethics the human being as a political animal with language. Before this, Plato talks about the "gift of speech" (Timaeus, 20c). The word that is a real gift is the word that cares, a word that needs no analysis since it enters the very breath of the other's mind with hardly any effort. As it is of incalculable worth, language can have the same effect as medicine, but it can also reveal itself to be a poison. Language makes manifest what is most concealed expression to what is most concealed, as well as what is confused and common (Heidegger 1949, p. 298). To guard one's tongue is therefore an ethical imperative of the practice of care.

So exactly what is meant by a caring word? A simple word, with no rhetorical emphasis; a word that keeps to the truth and is inspired by the search for good. The word that the child needs so s/he may grow up in accordance with her/his own potentialities is a word that reveals good possible way of living life, that reveals possibilities, that conveys trust in our own possibility of being, but at the same time it is a realistic word, that states things as they are. The students who is facing a difficult moment needs to hear a word that helps him to find self-confidence, but without hiding the real picture. The word that cares is a word that opens spaces of being-there and at the same time is realistic and sincere.

The simplest words are also the most essential: care, thanks, good, truth. There is an intimate relation between goodness and truth. Who-cares-for, simply because s/he is looking for the other's good, is in search of the word that expresses the truth, the word that states how things are, without hiding anything and without idle chatter. Good care expects the sincerity and directness. But in point of fact the word that places itself firmly in reality, even when it is painful, has positive consequences because it starts a process of critical self-understanding.

It is, nonetheless, of great importance that frankness, when it expresses something that is not easy to admit, is accompanied by the Ciceronian principle of "*suavitas*" (Cicero, *Laelius. On Friendship*, XIX, 66 e XXIV, 89), or in other words is voiced in a manner that makes the truth acceptable for the other. Speaking with delicacy does not necessarily mean diminishing the strength of meaning of a message, but taking care that the import of what we are saying may be acceptable to the person listening so that it permits her/him to initiate a change in her/his behaviour.

Whoever-cares-for must from the very start of any communication make sure that it is made in the spirit of extreme reverence and respect. A word that communicates respect for the other is permeable and open: it does not expect to say everything about the topic of the dialogue, but it is discreet and careful to leave plenty of room for dialog. When a speaker expects to be able to say everything, to exhaust all topics at once, her/his discourse runs the risk of becoming violent. A caregiver who lets her/himself be guided by the ethical gesture of respect for the other while s/he talks, understands that s/he must implement her/his awareness that language is always inadequate, especially when we are asked to put what we think we understand about the other into words. Too many words, uttered, perhaps, too quickly and forcefully, could complicate matters instead of clarifying them. The word of communion that builds relationships comes from measuring what we say, lightening, simplifying. In this sense, the expression of Lévinas: "unsaying the said" (1969, p. 30) becomes an ethical principle of discourse.

The caring word is the word that gives consistency to a hospitable discourse, one that frees itself from concepts that would keep it bound to an assertive logic, incapable of distinguishing the uniqueness of the other, of letting the other express her/himself in her/his own words or of accepting the risk that alterity might cause confusion in our thoughts, demolish certitudes, or show up our hermeneutic limits. Hospitality is letting the other enter our space without giving up her/himself, permitting her/him to bring her/his subjectivity and, in doing so, disrupt our habits and challenge our silent inflexibility.

But we do not always need words to convey consideration. In some cases, "being-there" is enough. To stay there, with our presence, without action, but to be there. To be there with vital attention in silence does not mean dumb proximity, but an abstention from action to concede the initiative to the other for his appeal to us. Even simple being-there communicates our availability to the other, it lets her/him know that we will be there at the right moment. It is pure availability. Feeing in the other a readiness to be there at the opportune moment is the prerequisite for us to decide to risk the leap into the space beyond. As Hölderlin says, in the poem "Homecoming", the feeling of the possibility of counting on the availability of someone makes us find the necessary strength to "travel forth into the distance, a place of promises".

Understanding

As stated by Heidegger (1962, p. 159), the act of understanding is an essential quality of being-there, since existing is essentially understanding, and considering that the essence of the human condition is being-with, the understanding of the being of being-there does not depend on an isolated-I-point, but on an entity that is always being-there-with-in-the-world (Heidegger 1962, p. 156). Understanding is a fundamental existential phenomenon, in the sense that the human being feels the necessity to understand what is going on, not only in her/his own existence but also, since s/he is a relational being, also in the other's existence. It is the act of addressing the other with the intention of understanding her/him that makes relationship possible, because it allows us to build an ontological bridge between ourselves and the other. Consequently it is evident that an essential quality of acting with care is the intention to understand the other.

If someone's being-there is her/his own personal possibility of being-there, understanding the other means understanding the series of possibilities through which being-there becomes an existent. The comprehension of caring for is determined by the intention to grasp what the other needs in order to actualize the possibilities of her/his very own existence; understanding what the other needs more than anything else means getting in touch with the center of his existential reality.

The understanding that contributes to a good action of care can be developed on two different levels: it can be seen as a theoretical act that interprets the other's situation in order to help her/him to understand her/himself, to find her/himself and her/his own essence, but—on a higher level of practical involvement—it may also be that of helping the other project her/himself into her/his own individual possibilities. This second mode of actualization of the understanding, which friendly and educational relationships of care define in a particular way, closely interprets the Heideggerian vision of the understanding, according to which understanding is not a simple cognitive action that is manifested through an abstract awareness of the other's situation (Heidegger 1988, p. 277), but it is realized according to the degree of facilitation of the process of manifestation of the being of being-there.

Understanding requires knowledge, the knowledge of the other's condition. There are actions that, even if they are motivated by the intention to care, not only do not reveal themselves as such, but cause problems for the other since, as they lack adequate knowledge of the other's life, they fail to take into consideration her/his real situation and her/his true needs. Many social and political initiatives miscarry because they are not supported by crucial knowledge of real needs to satisfy (Noddings 2002, p. 58). Since the possibility of doing something good and just is allied to knowledge and since human beings are almost inevitably misunderstood by one another, trying to find something that brings well-being to the other, requires knowledge of her/him. Annette Baier sustains that a clear sign that we are doing an authentic work of care is shown when there is no toleration of any form of ignorance about the other's real situation (1985, p. 94). Hence the need of constant communication in order to acquire information about her/his situation, because gathering information allows us to implement that necessary knowledge to comprehend if the other really needs care and if so, what type of care s/he needs.

It is not easy to acquire information understanding about the other, about her/his condition and her/his way of interpreting experience, not only because the human heart is an enigma (Hölderlin, *To Hiller*), but also because the other does not always want to tell things about her/himself to another person; perhaps because s/he is reticent or is trying to dissimulate. It is therefore inevitable that special procedures must be adopted to obtain knowledge about the other. Reliable knowledge of the other's situation presumes "a refined and honest perception of what is really the case, a patient and just discernment and exploration of what confronts one" (Murdoch 1997, p. 330), and this accurate vision of the other's state is not the result of merely observing, but of the sensitive attention that has previously been defined as a moral discipline.

Dependable knowledge is based on an honest vision of things, that entails a form of "obedience to reality" (Murdoch 1997, p. 332): the mind is capable of obedience to reality when it approaches the phenomena without prejudice, with receptive attention for the form through which the reality is revealed. Obedience to reality, with the care to recognize in detail the shape of the other's being, bids us to learn how to exercise the cognitive way of *epoché* (Husserl, 1982): to approach the other without the screen of ideology, without pre-constructed theories on what is and on what could be.

In order to know the other adequately, we must exploit cognitive acts that can help us discern the shape of the other's being and accept the givenness that his being reveals without deforming it through our pre-formed interpretative schemes. Because of the intrinsic limitations of the quality of the life of the mind the risk of an assimilation of reality to these scheme is always there. Therefore, it is also possible to deform the alterity of the other within our cognitive devices. The subjugation of her/him to the interpretative possibilities of the means at our disposal subsequently entails an imposition that deforms the way of her/his being, thus leading to the elaboration of inaccurate knowledge of her/his identity. A knowledge that can never result in a faithful picture of the other's original personality jeopardizes the possibility of an adequate comprehension. When who-cares-for is engaged in the phenomenological discipline of *epoché*, s/he has to keep her/his mind free from pre-comprehensions, from preformulated theories and, on the contrary, look for paths that lead to the true way of being-there of the other. In order to access the other's knowledge, cognitive practices must be as unauthoritative as possible, so that the other reaches the evidence of her/his being in her/his own way; this calls for a method of gaining knowledge that is as receptive as possible.

When Plato, in the *Phaedrus*, works out his epistemology of ascent, according to which true knowledge entails raising oneself above the world of ordinary things, he affirms that the soul must be pure in order to go in touch of the truth, and to gain this most important quality it has to let go of its bonds with the body and withdraw completely into itself. The pursuit of a condition of purity is an ultimate idea, because it indicates an unattainable state; the mind, indeed, is always full of something, or in other words of the same ideas that it is made of, so without the ideas the mind itself would not exist. However, the regulative principle of finding a condition of purity and lightness, even if it is impossible to achieve, can discharge a positive function, since it forces the mind to follow a metacognitive discipline of analysis of its own functioning with the aim of verifying if and how we are improving our understanding of the other in the closest way possible to her/his being-there.

When our mind is obstructed with too many preconceptions and with theories that suppose a general hermeneutic evaluation, it is difficult to make room for true knowledge of the other, a type of knowledge that respects her/him and gives her/his alterity consideration. Restriction of cognitive acts by anticipated interpretative systems permits little if any consideration of the alterity of the other. Instead, keeping the other in transcendence requires a pure mind, which does not, however, mean a mind empty in its aridity, but one that activates all its receptive skills towards the manifestations of reality, and that at the same time makes sure that it keeps itself free from already formalized hermeneutic devices. Renouncing the tendency to rely on pre-judgements, reducing predefined ideas to the essential, practicing the discipline of noological moderation is the expected task for a mind that lets itself be guided by the principle of pursuing authentic knowledge, authentic because realistically subjected to the qualities of the other's being. Pursuit of the principle of purity of heart and poverty of spirit does not signify risking aridity of thought, but means finding the essential: without aspiring to excess that can obstruct the mind, but abiding in that less that allows us to find spaces of thought where the other's being has room to reaffirm itself.

However, even when we are convinced, perhaps after numerous and difficult attempts, that we have understood the other, we should immediately doubt this conviction which would lead us toward an illusory comfort zone, because the process of understanding others as well as ourselves must never be considered as accomplished. Human beings are and remain obscure to each other (Murdoch 1997, p. 326). To understand how the other is destined to remain an enigma for us it is helpful to accept Lévinas's invitation to consider the other's face as a sign of the Infinite; in contrast to the phenomenon that tends to reveal itself in answer to a request for attention, the sign of the Infinite is an enigmatic glow (1998, p. 12). Conceptualizing the other's face as a sign of the Infinite forces us to think that the finitude of understanding is called to measure itself against a never-ending task. It helps to eliminate the tendency to rely too much on our own theories and also to cultivate some degree of humility, and get into the habit of not taking the results of our thoughts too seriously.

Feeling-with-the-Other

Understanding cannot arise if there is no ability to *feel the feeling of the other*. There is no understanding in an emotionally neutral attitude. The action of understanding is always emotionally guided (Heidegger 1962). An efficient responsiveness to the other involves the ability of "emotional tuning", that goes beyond the simple rational acknowledgement of the situation in which the other finds her/himself.

Feeling is experiencing sensitivity for the other. According to Lévinas (1998, p. 75) sensitivity is exposing oneself to the other; being open indicates a condition of passivity, even of vulnerability. Sensitivity is letting ourselves be questioned by the other's difference. If we accept the idea that the experience of being sensitive is always an embodied one, then becoming sensitive to the other's lived experience means feeling his state of being in the flesh, and it is this embodied feeling that makes true comprehension possible. If we never let ourselves be touched by the other then our apparent solicitude is not heartfelt, and this is embodied feeling what it must be to actualize the condition in which the most intense forms of care are carried out.[3]

The fact that many of those who deal with care pay particular attention to the sphere of feeling is not of secondary importance. Some, indeed, actually identify care with feeling. Feelings are indicators of qualities that we attribute to things, they are interior forces that nurture action, they keep the heart warm and stable. In the gospels, every time that a significant action is described, the heart is mentioned and when the action is negative the expression "hardness of heart" is used. Referring to a prophecy of Isaiah, Matthew (13,14–15) says that a hard heart cannot understand simply because it is hard.

In order to understand the quality of feeling that is specific to good and right care, the Platonic concept of the soul, that "tender and pure" soul described in the

---

[3] When commenting on Heidegger's thought, Lévinas affirms that "every understanding comes about in an effective disposition" (1996, p. 29), and that the emotional tone of care is anguish. There is some truth in this affirmation, but at the same time it restricts the hermeneutics of the experience of care. It may be true that when we deal with care in some problematic situation we experience a sort of anguish, but we cannot assume that anguish is the most important feeling in the work of care. Every kind of understanding occurs/happens within an emotional situation. Since the quality of being-there is problematic, because it is fragile and vulnerable, the understanding of being-there may be accomplished with anguish. Reflecting about the ontological weakness of the human condition can expose the mind to a sense of anguish, but It is indeed this ontological sentiment that allows being-there to comprehend its condition in an authentic way (ibidem, p. 30). In this sense anguish is the same as understanding. Since caring means taking responsibility for existence, consequent on understanding the neediness of being—neediness of things that are in the world and of others without whom our deeper possibility of being would not be fulfilled -, care may be burdened by anguish; for this reason, Levinas talks about "anguished care" (ibidem). However, it should be noted that the philosophy of care here theorized is based on the complex agency of care. If experiences of anguish may be associated with care when it is understood as the effort of keeping oneself within being, care as cultivation of the other's being and of the encouragement of her/his most characteristic possibilities, comes into contact with other lives, that often reconcile us to the quality of existence. The educator in day-care who helps a child to develop his first forms of autonomy experiences the other's joy; the teacher who, after adopting a different teaching/learning methodology, sees the student who was previously struggling regain his confidence, experiences the pleasure of doing good that relaxes the mind. The implications of theorizing care starting from a dissimilar semantic field are easily understood to be different, because the potential variability in experience that care opens to being-there are made evident.

Phaedrus, seems to have the necessary hermeneutic power. The feeling that is promulgated by the search of what is good for life belongs to a pure mind, but if for Plato the pure mind is one which is relieved from the polluting relationship with the reality of the senses, instead a vision that is in contact with reality considers the pure mind as one that does not in fact renounce its relationship with reality. When this sort of mind engages with the other it keeps itself as free as possible from the residue of negative feeling that might contaminate or interrupt relational exchanges while, at the same time, it focuses on positive feeling which alone can further the generation of good things. If the first sort of mind is like an empty vase, like pure crystal, oriented towards another order of reality, the mind of whoever-cares-for does not take the divine as a compass-bearing, but the bodily life of the other who is asking for care. Therefore, a pure mind is one that knows how to dwell at the heart of reality with an attention that is immersed in the often difficult becoming of things, without losing the impulse that supports the search for the good.

In the *Rhetoric*, Aristotle distinguishes between two different levels of emotions: those that bring pain and those that bring pleasure (II, 1, 1378a). This basic distinction, that relies on experiential evidence, tells us that the first principle of order of emotional phenomena is represented by the distinction between positive emotions (those that bring pleasure) and negative emotions (those that bring pain). Only the heart of a god or of an angel is ignorant of the negative feeling which causes suffering; but we are of this world and our heart has contrasting feelings. Thus a pure heart conceived of as one that feels and fosters only positive feelings is unrealistic, but one which is guided by the intent to put its feeling to the service of the process of comprehension of reality is pure: meeting the other with the maximum degree of feelings that give pleasure and limiting those that cause suffering, and, when the circumstances call for the knowledge to interpret negative feelings such as anger or scorn, giving life positive guidance.

Feeling Empathy

In order to act with care, it is indispensable to be able to feel the other, and feeling the other's feeling is empathy, or in other words the ability to grasp someone else's lived experience (Stein 1989, p. 6).

In the Gospel of John, there is a powerful description of empathy: "When Jesus saw her crying, and the Jews who had come with her crying, He was angry in his spirit and deeply trembled" (11,33) and it is this precise trembling within him that urges him to engage in that act of care that caused the resurrection of Lazarus. An extreme form of understanding requires the capacity to feel empathy.[4]

I would define empathy as letting our own being vibrate with the feeling of the quality of the other's lived experience, the evangelical "tremble in His spirit". To be empathetically present involves entering a state of emotional resonance with the other, an emotional alignment that allows the other 'feeling felt' (Carse 2006, p. 43). A person capable of emotional resonance manages to access the other's lived experience in all its fine distinction and this allows the understanding of the significance that the other attributes to his situation. According to Carse (2006, p. 42) the way of being that defines "compassionate engagement" makes establishing contact with the other possible even when he/she is in a difficult emotional situation. To be capable of an empathic presence means being able to approach the other even when he/she is in the most difficult situations and in some cases the ability of emotional resonance of the other's lived experience can lead to breaking the gacial immobility of the solitude of suffering.

Empathy is never intrusive, but is a way of connecting with the other with receptive attunement, that involves bracketing one's own frames of reference and welcoming the other. Empathy involves the capacity of keeping the other in transcendence, or in other words of building a relationship where the other remains distant from me, without letting this distance cancel the possibility of a relationship and "yet without this distance destroying this relation and without this relation destroying this distance, as would happen with relations within the same; this relation does not become an implantation in the other and a confusion with him, does not affect the very identity of the same" (Lévinas 1969, p. 41).

In phenomenology, empathy is defined as an act of presentification, that is bringing the other's lived experience into the present and it is this capacity that puts us in relation with the situation the other is experiencing. The other's experience that is the object of empathy has not been experienced by me but it is still there, manifesting itself in my non-original experience. If the act of empathy indicates the

---

[4] Michael Slote's thought resonates powerfully in some theories of care (Held 2006; Noddings 2002), but nonetheless —as I had the chance to tell him—I don't think it is possible to take his ideas as a source for the thesis of the importance of the empathetic attitude in the care relation, since Slote uses terms that suggest a reductive vision: indeed he speaks of empathy as a "primary mechanism" of caring (2007, p. 4). Considering the need to break away from the limitations of traditional discussion, that has neglected care for far too long, and to find words that are able to express all the cultural potential of care practice, it must be noted that Slote not only confines the discourse back within the limits of the philosophy of Hume but he also uses terms that could provoke an interpretative distortion of the phenomenon we are talking about.

capability of the human being to enter in a syntonic relationship with the other's being, it is still necessary to specify that experience brought into the present always belongs to a foreign consciousness, and this separation between me and the other makes it impossible to think that through the feeling I have of his lived experiences, an original knowledge of his experience could be accessible to me. Through this way of conceptualizing empathy, Stein distances herself from that vision that conceives of empathy as a full experience of the other's experience (1989, p. 13). According to Stein empathy is not "a feeling of oneness" (1989, p. 17), that is to say it fails to create a situation of ontological fusion, it does not make me feel at one with the other, but it does allow me to abide "by" the other (1917, p. 16). Lived experience and empathized experience remain two different experiences, in the sense that through the empathetic act I do not access the other's own lifeworld or lived experience but I can comprehend its tonality. If feeling the other's experience is essential to understanding the situation that the other is living, by accepting Stein's vision we must always consider the irreducible distance of the other person, the fact that it is only the other who has an originary experience of his/her past, while my bringing his/her past to the present is always non-originary, and inevitably filtered by the qualities and by the ways of my being present to the other.

Nonetheless, an indication of the distance within which the other dwells, together with the inevitable subjective filter that each one of us introduces into matters of relationship is not to be intended as a complete capitulation to distance. Whoever knows how-to-care-for goes towards the other while trying, as far as possible, to keep her/his own conceptual and affective filters permeable. This personal effort to reduce the assertive and self-referential way to be in a relationship with the other is a necessary condition to turn ourselves into an ethical tool, or in other words into a presence that gently makes itself felt by making room for the other, because if this were not to happen care would not be accomplished.

These clarifications, without wishing to detract anything from the cognitive and relational significance of empathy, are intended simply as a reminder of the need to critically monitor the way of being in a relationship with the other and the use that we make of empathetic intuitions.

Stein's theorization of empathy should also be read from another point of view: if in contrast with what is suggested by Edith Stein we were to interpret empathy as unipathy, assuming that is possible to experience in a complete and primordial way the other's lived experience, not only would we be have to admit the ontological disappearance of individual boundaries, but from the relational standpoint the risk of invasion from who-cares-for to the life space of the other would be a constant danger. The breakdown of individual boundaries, especially, but not exclusively, in the cases of health care operators who are often exposed to situations of pain and suffering would turn into an unbearable emotional burden, and this would induce the caregiver to silence any possible empathetic openness. Stein's vision, on the other hand, supports the theory that is not possible a complete coincidence with the lived experience of the other (Stein 1917, p. 13). If in one respect we are reminded that we shall never have complete knowledge of the other, by emphasizing ontological non-permeability and therefore the occurrence of reciprocal invasions of the subjects in the relationship, an emotionally sustainable vision of empathy is restored. Empathy conceived of as a feeling-with the other does not presume that the subject of the empathic action and the subject to whom it is addressed are related in such a way as to produce a blurred fusion, but generates a situation that we can define as intimately relational separateness.

The empathetic experience is not mere irrational sentimentalism, but a way of thinking with the heart (Stein 2002, II Vol, p. 437). Thinking with the heart means thinking that allows itself to be touched by the other's being, it is a turning towards the other that is realized in the form of an intensely receptive attention, an attention where even the smallest details of the external experience are meaningful. It is therefore a way of thinking that feels the other's feeling and this makes understanding possible. Its generative matrix can be identified in the mind's readiness to concentrate intensely on the other, to search for a comprehension that reaches the core of his lived experience. Thinking with the heart is a capability of whoever knows how to embrace thought in depth, since "[people] who live collectedly in the depth of their personalities are able to see even the little things" (Stein 2002, II Vol, p. 440). The "wisdom of the heart" (Psalm 90, 12) does not indicate a simple emotional tonality of the mind, but a way of thinking that is nurtured by a feeling founded on comprehension. Meditating on our own experience so as to understand its affective meaning is an essential condition, even if not sufficient, of understanding the other's lived experience. To concentrate ourselves within the depth of our feelings does not mean wallowing in narcissism, but practising the comprehension of experience beginning with a constant focusing on and listening to reality; this exercise is the roadmap to find other threads from which to weave existence, other paths on which to meet the other, to gain deep contact with reality.[5]

---

[5] Among the scholars who theorize the ethics of care, there are those who maintain that it is the valorization of feelings that characterizes this way of conceiving ethics (see in particular Noddings 1984 and Held 2006), and this valorization is expressed not only in the theoretical acknowledgement of the function played by those defined as moral feelings, but also in the invitation to cultivate them (Held 2006, p. 190). In order to avoid romantic distortion, during the construction of a theory of care, it may be useful from the point of view of philosophical matters, to regain the neo-stoic conception of emotions (Nussbaum 1986) and on the psychological side the cultural theory (Oatley 1992), that both agree in supporting the idea that we need to go beyond any dualism between reason and emotion, because every emotion includes

Feeling Compassion

We can empathize with the other's well-being, but also with her/his malaise, with her/his positive experiences like joy or negative ones like pain. Empathy can be defined as the ability of feeling the other's feelings and their differences and, if the empathy is particularly heightened, their shades of difference. Then there are situations where we not only feel the negative feelings of the other, her/his pain, but this feeling-together is accompanied by an assessment of what is happening; and when this estimate makes clear that the other's suffering is something that any sense of justice could not tolerate then the empathetic experience is defined as compassion. To be compassionate means to feel the other's pain and judge it to be something that cannot be accepted.

Compassion is feeling the injustice of the experience that is provoking pain to the other. Feeling something that is hurting. It is a characteristic of compassion to feel the other's condition as unjust and to take action to alleviate the other's pain (Carse 2006, p. 41); for this reason, compassion has strong ethical and political implications.

The ancient Greek term *eleos* [ἔλεος] is translated as compassion. Aristotle says that "eleos" indicates "A feeling of pain aroused in oneself when someone is perceived as meeting undeservedly with trouble of a life-threatening or pain kind, and which seems close at hand" (Aristotle, *Rhetoric*, II, 8, 1385b). Furthermore, compassion is generated when "some misfortune comes to pass from a quarter whence one might have reasonably expected something good" (*Rhetoric*, II, 8, 1386a). If we accept the Aristotelian thesis according to which we feel compassion only towards people not too close to us (*Rhetoric*, II, 8, 1386a), then professional relations of care are indeed relational situations where it is possible to experience compassion.

According to Aristotle, the ability to be delighted by someone else's joy and to suffer for someone else's pain are states of mind characteristic of an honest person, and he defines these moments as "just things" (*Rhetoric*, II, 8, 1386b). Therefore, if caring for involves the ability of empathy and compassion, and if this way of feeling is typical of the just person, then care is no different from justice, but has, in point of fact, an intimate relationship with this virtue and with the ethics that embraces it as its fundamental idea.

a cognitive nucleus, and it is the type of vision of things that are implied in these concepts that induces a certain way of feeling. Cultivating moral feelings is the same as cultivating a certain conceptual horizon on which depend the evaluations of situations of experience that generate moral feelings.

This is what is meant by "the realism of compassion" (Murdoch 1997, p. 354) because feeling the other's feelings helps us to grasp the quality of reality. Every human being knows from experience that compassion is at the root of acting in favor of someone else, of acting to help her/him and for her/his own good. In the gospels, every time that Jesus does a miracle to meet someone else's need, it is said that he is moved by compassion. When he did the miracle of the multiplication of the loaves and the fishes and the healing of the sick (Mt 14) it is written that when he saw how many people there were "he was moved by compassion" and he healed them all. In the parable of the Good Samaritan it is written that when the latter saw the other on the ground he felt compassion and for this reason he took care of him (Lk, 33).

At the root of the ability for compassion there is the readiness to be touched—not invaded but touched—by the other's suffering, and instead of avoiding the experience of the other's pain because it is too great, knowing how to transform this feeling into an urge to act with care. I do something for the other when I know how to feel her/his situation, when I don't just look at her/his face, but I feel the quality of his lived experience. I am capable of care when I hear the other's call to be cared for.

On the subject of the way of being-there of compassion, and by extension of empathy, there are now many points of view and one which is particularly debatable should be mentioned, the one defining empathy and compassion as putting ourselves in the other's place. If healthcare-workers were informed that the right way of acting is to feel all the other's pain in an original way, they would be overwhelmed by the burden of the lived experience that they would find themselves bearing and they would have no strength or energy left to spare. Feeling-with is not an immersion in the other's world, but both an emotional and a cognitive capacity to let the quality of the other's past echo in our minds.

Regarding compassion, Plutarch tells Paccius (the recipient of the text): that it is necessary to manage compassion in the right measure and that happens when we comprehend the lived experience of the other and give him help, but without her/his pain permeating our mind (Plutarch, *On the Fragility of Mind*, 468d). A good action of care needs a good state of mind and an educated mind is filled with "salutary thoughts" (470d). Feeling the other is all very well, but at the same time we should keep a form of distance, that is granted by reflexive thinking motivated by the intention of keeping things in proportion. The way of being that is necessary to a relationship of care is not a state of fusion with the other—the relationship would simply fail—but staying in touch with her/him. Being in touch with the other does not mean investing the other with our own way of thinking and feeling, nor trying to obliterate ourselves for the other. It means being present and making our presence felt, but both with respect for the other, or in other words without invading her/his living space, and also with respect for ourselves, or in other words without trying to smother our subjectivity, since in that way we would not help the other at all.

According to Aristotle, people who have suffered too much, and for this reason have a gloomy attitude towards life, are not capable of feeling compassion because too much suffering makes the soul incapable of feeling the other's pain. Arrogant people are also impervious to the pain of others (*Rhetoric*, II, 8, 1385b). It is interesting to notice that among those able to feel compassion Aristotle names "the educated persons, for they reckon rightly" (II, 8, 1385b); if we accept this thesis and we develop its implications, we can hypothesize that the ethical and political feeling of "pietas" is something that can be cultivated. And therefore, the cultivation of care should be the object of a politics interested in constructing a community of care.

Feeling-With in the Right Measure

The theoretical action of valuing empathy nevertheless requires an emphasis on the constant risk of drifting into excessive involvement while in a relationship of care. The good depends on the principle of proportion, whereas both shortcoming and excess are harmful. A lack in the capacity of feeling the other's feelings both obstructs the weaving of a relationship and hampers complete comprehension; on the other hand, investing too much might be transformed into an invasive presence that damages the action of care.

Joint emotional participation is also suspect because of the effects that it would have on who-cares-for, since it would jeopardize interior equilibrium. Nonetheless it should be pointed out that affective sustainability is not a problem because of the possible occurrence of empathetic experience, as it is of the repetition of those experiences of compassion that activate a strong ethical and political involvement. Joint empathetic participation alone does not endanger the person experiencing it, because the other's feeling is not lived in an originary way and however intense the affective involvement created is, the quality of the empathetic experience remains inferior compared to the fullness of vitality that characterized the other's experience. In this sense, empathy contributes to understanding without jeopardizing the subject who experiences it. On the contrary, when the feeling of the other's quality generates compassion, then the simple belief that her/his experience is not justifiable engages the life of the mind in an intense search for the conditions necessary to the relief of the other's pain. When the act of compassion is repeated often and with intensity, it causes an emotional exhaustion that could become unbearable.

For the very reason that there are risks connected to the situations of emotional involvement, many doubts are being voiced regarding a theory that emphasizes emotional closeness in care relationships and in many cases a non-affective education of the operators might seem to be best. This theoretical option is based on the hypothesis that in order to operate correctly it is probably better to suppress our feelings. Nevertheless, if we consider the affective life as a burden, inasmuch as it possesses the characteristics of an irrational phenomenon that interferes with the possibility of a presence that is rationally guided, it means that we become hostages of the modernist and positivistic myth of a mind that is purified from any feeling.

Acting in a way that is neutrally affective is not only impossible, but also impoverishes any relationship. It is not possible to deprive an act of any emotional resonance because being-there is always modulated by emotion and this is inevitably communicated to the other. The feeling that at all times accompanies being there is a phenomenon which is not without ontological significance, but it is a form of intelligence about the real because it reveals the quality of what is happening (Heidegger 1962, p. 172). It is through feeling that thoughts alert us to the quality of reality. In other words, emotional experience allows us to understand the qualities of the phenomena we live through.

If we accept the thesis that promulgates the cognitive value of emotions, then the right way to stay in a relationship of care presumes an affective competence that is not intended as the ability to suffocate every feeling in the encounter with the other, but actually to develop a reflexive competence necessary to understand our own affective functioning and, as much as possible, to keep it under the check of a constant critical analysis. The comprehension of what we feel is essential to exist as relational subjects utilizing to our best the resources of being. If the ordinary way of being in the world is the irreflexive one and if the lack of reflexivity makes us passively dependent on what happens, then the quality of being-there that must be gained is that of a posture that is reflexively present at the happening of things, either out in the world or inside us. It is not just a post-action reflection that is necessary, or in other words a way of thinking that focuses the attention on what has happened, but a reflexive thinking that happens as the action is taking place, because a reflection that is almost contemporary to experience is the only possibility for saving the relationship of care from the distortions that can occur.

Feeling with Attention

There is no encounter with the other unless it is emotionally modulated, because we are affective beings. If it is true that feeling "is that through which all things think" (Heraclitus, 14[A14], in Colli 1993, p. 31). The meaning of experience is always affectively defined. But the treatment of the topic of affectivity in a philosophy of care needs caution. It could be and actually is, all too easy to say that good care is what happens in a relationship nurtured by positive feelings. The danger is that of forcing the discussion towards "a must be" that does not work, besides that of sliding towards a deceptive vision of the life of the mind. However, simply because of the importance of feelings in experience, it is impossible to avoid making a brief mention of this topic.

It is evident from the moment we are born that the emotional quality of a relationship carries out an essential task. The first relationships that we experience are fundamental, in the sense that the intimate quality of our existential posture derives from them. When at the moment we come into the world we experience a positive welcoming of our own being-there, because the person who receives us makes us feel the joy of being in his/her arms and he/she knows how to give us a welcoming look that tells us that we are always in his/her mind and therefore in his/her heart, then we experience the pleasure of being-there. Feeling welcome calms the soul and when the soul is calm it relaxes and in doing so it finds its roots in the world.

When on the other hand we fail to experience this first acceptance, when the other expresses no pleasure in our presence, we suffer a sense of uncertainty that makes the soul fold in upon itself and in doing so it struggles to put down roots. The failure to put down roots leads to bewilderment and from this to anxiety and the fear of not being able to give a complete form to our own being-there. This fear makes people incapable of giving life to a truly generative movement of being. There is the possibility of moving about in the world, to form ties, whenever there is a safe internal space from which to set out and to which to return, or where simply to move around. But when there is no solid foundation that nurtures the soul with energy, action becomes extraordinarily difficult, especially when it is a matter of taking an initiative, because to begin something new, if it is admitted as a natural movement of the human being, since each of us is born to begin at our beginning (Arendt 1958, p. 9), evokes in the soul the first beginning, that of biological birth. It is easy to venture into inaugurating something good if at the beginning of our existence we experienced something good at our origin; on the other hand, it is difficult to face something that evokes a primordial anxiety because of which, if we fail to control it, we risk muddling around without accomplishing anything.

Winnicott supports the thesis of the importance of a good relation with the mother as a necessary condition for a healthy psychological development. Indeed he affirms that the primary relationship with a "devoted mother", that is a mother who "likes having a baby to look after" offers the prevention of mental disorder (1987, pp. 12-13); Indeed feeling our mother's pleasure to take care for us helps us to open up positively to life. Although wishing to avoid a deterministic vision which endorses the theory that the quality of existence depends solely on what happens during the first months of life, we cannot deny the importance of the role that primary experiences have. Biological birth is a primary experience, but not less important is our introduction to the external world when we start going to school. The affective position of the teacher who welcomes us outside our comfort zone stays in our heart when s/he is a positive figure. Indeed, when discussing the caring and non-caring experiences that shaped their lives, people often go back to the years of primary school to notice how important the teacher was and how influential her/his way of being-there. The figure of a competent teacher who knows how to harmonize with the other is constructive one. S/he knows how to help the students to find their own place in the world of knowledge by asking how to go beyond where they are, starting from the acceptance of their original shape of being-there. The skilled teacher knows how to find the right balance between adjusting to the immanent quality of being-there of the other and fostering a drive to transcend what is given in order to go further. Strictness and determination become ways of care when they are encouraged by gentleness and trust in the other.

Without trust we could not exist: it is trust that makes us open to the other and that, as adults, gives us the necessary energy to bind ourselves in an act of love. It is only by trusting in the possible that we can bring our being-there into the world. There may be disappointment or hopelessness, but the act of continuing to exist needs to trust in the possibility of giving form to being-there.

There is a close relationship between being trustworthy and knowing how to accept the other. Who-cares-for manages to communicate trust only if s/he knows how to accept the other within her/his own being-there. Knowing how to accept the other with her/his qualities restores her/his sense of worthiness of self and in its turn it promotes the capacity of self-acceptance. Knowing how to accept is a feeling for reality that puts us in touch with our existence. The call to transcendence, or in other words to go beyond what has been given to seek the best form possible for our existential experience, alerts being-there. In order to positively answer the call to becoming our potential being, the person needs to know how to keep alert for further possibilities. Staying alert in order to explore other ways of actualizing our own humanity is exhausting and requires energy; it can jeopardize the being-there of a person if s/he lacks a solid basis in the deepest part of her/himself, a foundation that is created by knowing how to accept her/himself. Only when we are able to accept ourselves for what we are, does it become possible to be guided in a positive way by the drive towards something further. When the reverse is the case, each psychopathological experience is indelibly marked by the loss of the ability to accept reality.

Self-acceptance conciliates one with life and helps the soul to find a sense of intimate relaxation that is a fundamental element of the ability to open up positively to the movement of being-there, which is constantly driven to go further. Feeling at peace with being-there makes us experience the particular form of ease that helps the soul to find the vital energy which is necessary to the movement of living.

Self-acceptance has nothing in common with resignation. To accept does not mean to renounce something, but realistically to understand that we must start from what we are. Knowing how to accept reality as it is, without relinquishing anything but simply to begin from oneself, is learned in the relationships of care: when a mother accepts her child as s/he is, when the teacher accepts the student for the qualities s/he effectively possesses and invents ways to facilitate learning starting from these qualities, when the physician accepts the patient's limitations and accompanies her/him with understanding throughout the therapeutic procedures. Accepting reality as it is in no way signifies rejecting the different, but discovering different threads with which to weave time starting from where being-there is. This is the unmistakable interaction between immanence and transcendence. The teacher who accepts the student according to the ways of her/his being-there is not going to refuse to look for teaching methods that can help her/him explore other ways to stay in the world among things, s/he will try to draw the map of what is possible from the exact point at which the student finds her/himself. The movement of becoming her/his own possible being is fostered by a balance between tension and relaxation, and therefore between the search for something else and the acceptance of reality.

Being-There with a Faraway Closeness

To take care means to answer positively to the other's needs, one of which is to be protected from potentially dangerous situations. The patient who is in a state of intense vulnerability needs to be protected from events that can worsen his condition even further or that cause useless pain: for this reason a health-care worker who is looking after a patient, also monitors the context to avoid mistakes in the administration of therapy or to prevent the patient from unnecessary intervention. There is also the damage that the person may inflict on her/himself, as in the case of a child who, if left alone, might fall into all sorts of danger.

According to Noddings (2002, p. 32) one of the essential qualities of a good practice of care is the commitment to prevent the other from harming her/himself; in this case we mean a type of care whose purpose is prevention. The position inspired by liberalism however, maintains that nobody has the right to interfere in the decisions that a person takes regarding her/himself, even when there is the risk of harm to her/his own person. Thus, the intention to protect the other could mask a paternalistic approach that interferes with the other's freedom. These two different positions confirm the existence of a problem that requires much more attention than it is usually given: it is a case of understanding in which situations and to what degree who-cares-for can and must intervene in decisions that the other generally makes for her/himself.

To do something to protect the other is not always easy, because some dangers are clearly visible, whereas others—like psychological violence for instance—are less noticeable, and because of this very intangibility, even when possible harm is perceived as it happens understanding how to intervene and protect the other can be extremely difficult. In some cases, it is a case of protecting the person who needs care from deprivation, for which the care-giver her/himself is responsible, for instance when s/he causes the other to be unable to express her/his own personality, her/his own essential qualities. Even this is a type of violence, although it is subtractive.

Some actions that are usually defined as caring actions can be dangerous; Noddings (2002, p. 39) talks about pathological forms of caring and when the damage is hidden beneath actions that are presented as legitimate it becomes difficult to find a way to protect the other, especially in the case of minors (the baby who is not able to express himself) or in serious difficulty (the patient in severe pain who is no longer rational).

In this case too, the problem is finding the right degree of being with and for the other, in other words finding the point of balance between actively present being and standing aside to make room for the other and for the integrity of her/his existential movement. Finding the way to stay in touch, to be ever-present, without invading the other's space, her/his territory, to demonstrate our being-there from the right degree of distance to do what is necessary to accompany the other in her/his becoming, while leaving her/him enough room for her/his personal project for being-there. Staying close to the other is feeling the duty not to leave, but simultaneously to remain on the frontier of her/his field of action with discretion. In short, to allow the other to feel cared for but to stay in her/his vicinity, within reach and ready to help.

Responsiveness should not be confused with replacing the responsibility the other has for her/himself, but should instead be understood as the readiness to implement the cognitive, emotional and practical tools that enable her/him to care for her/himself. Care calls for a discreet presence. In some cases, the other simply needs a silent presence, but one that communicates its availability to be-there and to be involved in the experiential space of the other when s/he feels the necessity. The teenager in difficulty who needs time to understand her/himself or the patient who looks at us in silence and seems to want to remain distant are not looking for isolation but rather an unexacting presence, one that even if it is wordless, communicates all the care of being-there at the opportune moment. Daniel Siegel

(1999, p. 94) talks about an emotional "alignment that permits a nonverbal form of communication to the patient".

The intense existential presence that is discreet at the same time is actualized in the knowledge of how to cultivate a relationship with the other that will preserve her/him in her/his transcendence, or in other words a relationship that finds its just proportion between showing closeness and keeping at a distance. Discreet vicinity is one that provides all possible support to the other without reducing the space of her/his free movement; it is a matter of knowing how to stand aside when the other shows the desire to loosen the bonds of the relationship but still to maintain contact, and to be able to return to a state of active presence should it be necessary. A good, and therefore just practice of care is one that defends the other's subjectivity and facilitates the establishment of conditions that allow the realization of her/his being-there in singularity.

There is a way of interpreting care that is activated as a kind of interference in the other's space, a replacement of that type of care-of-self that is idiosyncratically hers/his. Replacing the other and taking away the responsibility of her/his care work, could be interpreted as an expression of extreme dedication; in reality, the action of relieving the other from her/his responsibility for care actually creates an ontological expropriation. The effect of an expropriating action can range from the loss of the possibility to develop our own way of being to finding ourselves to be dependent and dominated.

Finding the right degree of care constitutes one of the difficulties of education. "Student-centered" theories tend to emphasize the importance of privileging the full development of the other without interfering in her/his vital space, in her/his feelings and in the creative spaces of her/his mental life. If the dangers inherent in the possible appropriation of the other should never be underestimated, monitoring the risk of impoverishment of the educational process because of an excessive reduction of adult presence is no less important. Today we are being challenged by the ever-increasing trend to reduce educational care—a care that finds its existential sense in taking the other's being to heart with all its potential—to the mere action of instructing; in this way, the educational process becomes reductive and could even diminish the other's possibilities. Beneath the useful layers of knowledge that fill the mind, the other's possibility of being finds no sustenance. The soul is in danger of remaining inactive. If we agree in identifying the soul as the living point that feels the aspiration towards transcendence and the impulse to search for meaningful horizons, then starting from this perspective, educative care must undertake to devote itself to offering experiences that stimulate being-there to recognize its real problems. Even with extreme discretion, in search of a non-intrusive way to maintain a relationship with the movement of the other's being, educative care cannot escape from the task of fostering the passion for what is beyond. Following this path means soliciting the noetic work of asking questions about being-there; about life that is happening and about life that could be. Asking questions activates the life of the soul. Here, though, is the true problem: to stimulate questioning without exaggerating and giving room to problematization that is too difficult or complicated for the other's soul to bear. To know how to stay in the area of development that is workable for the other without ceasing to open her/his mind to other regions of thought.

If in educational care the risk of ontological expropriation of the other is high, in the case of health care the doctor or the nurse are in the position of having to take the place of the other when s/he is not physically or psychologically able to take care of her/himself. However, even in cases of radical dependence of the patient upon whoever cares for her/him, the focus on the patient must always be kept at a high level in order to avoid any form of replacement by the medical staff when the moment comes that s/he seems able to assume the responsibility for her/himself. Those practices that in the sanitary field are defined "education of the patient" are finalized towards enabling the development of a command over the self in order to acquire the capacity to take care of one's own being. A useful interpretation of the practice of care is the one that "it helps the Other to become transparent to himself *in* his care and to become *free for* it" (Heidegger 1962, p. 159). Education towards self-care signifies that action for the other that is motivated by the desire to promote the passion to become one's own most possible being through the search for things that are of the greatest value for life.

Being Gentle but Firm

Since in the asymmetrical relation of care one always finds oneself dependent on the other, Eva Kittay (1999, p. 30) defines care-work as "dependency work" and "dependency workers" are those who assume the responsibility to carry out the work of care. Defining care-work as actions that deal with others, who are in situations of dependence gives us the chance to home in on the relational and ethical difficulties of care work. Consequently, on the one hand, who-receives-care sees her/his state of vulnerability accentuated because it takes on a relationship of dependency and on the other, who-cares-for becomes vulnerable because s/he is subjected to obligations imposed on her/him by the state of dependency of the other.

The vulnerability of who-requests-care means that dealing with her/him requires tact and sensitivity. Sensitivity in treating her/his body and sensitivity in getting in touch with his spiritual dimension. When touching the other her/his transcendence must be respected. This means that the other should be approached without dominating her/him. We should evidently share our own thoughts, our own vision of things but never impose our opinion as the truth. Acting according to the principle of sensitivity means taking time to find the right word, and when necessary keeping quiet, without silence being transformed into distance, but letting the other know that we are simply waiting to find the right moment for the right word, so that our dialogue may continue fruitfully and be of real help to the other. Whether with our words we are trying to obtain information, or we are fostering the possibility of the voicing of life experience, or attempting to soothe past hurts, we must always choose these words with care, because expert and sensitive use of the lexicon of care is quite another thing from simply parroting senseless commonplaces. Respect is measured in the search for a terminology that is true, not trite.

We are spiritual beings because we go in search of the sense of things and the words we are able to speak are the evidence of our human search since it is not only through actions but also through words that our spiritual substance takes shape. Caring for the other implies, therefore, Caring for the words we pronounce, because they can create breathing spaces in the relationship. Too many words overrun the space between me and you, and too few words prevent the relationship from taking shape. It is not just a matter of quantity, either, but also of quality: inexact words, that are carelessly chosen do nothing but make the space where we meet the other less transparent. If they are too sophisticated they can hinder the attempt at dialogue, if too emotional they can disorientate the other, and if they are too laconic they end up by merely creating distance. To transform words into an experience of care we need to allow our words to be guided essentially by the search for truth of experience.

Sensitivity is also a possible way of implementing an approach of the other with respect but also with distance; and indeed the kind of sensitivity that is an expression of tenderness is an actual source of care. Tenderness is manifested on the border between being and not being, a sweet warmth within which being radiates. The depth of the dimension of tenderness prevents it being confused with kindness, even if they both seem very similar. A soft heart knows how to make room for the other because it modifies itself and becomes something that welcomes the other's identity, whereas hardness of heart creates distance, diffidence, and negativity.

By the same token, vulnerability is also experienced by the care-worker. It is not only the prerogative of the person who occupies a dominant position in the relationship of care to be abusive and transform her/his power into violence towards the other, but who-receives-care can possess this dominance, too. Just because s/he is in a position of vulnerability, does not exclude the possibility of behaving in an abusive way towards the helpfulness of the caregiver. In some cases the erosion of the other's substance comes, on the contrary, from who-receives-care. The other we care for is not an angel, but a human being with all her/his weaknesses. The teenager who keeps on needing care, but at the same time tries to break free from the ties of dependence to find her/his proper path often reaches the point of putting the adults who are taking care of him in great difficulty. The child in custody who is feeling all the precariousness of her/his situation can endanger the stability of the family that welcomes her/him. The sick person can be tyrannical, can entertain unreasonable expectations, can behave aggressively, can fail to respond with courtesy and exhibit false necessities. In these cases, the person who detains the responsibility of care has the duty not only to be tender but also to be resolute, and in some cases should decide to redefine the action of care when it represents a useless waste of energy, and, without abandoning the other, try to identify different solutions of care.

In Diemut Bubeck's opinion the term care should only be employed when the other shows needs that s/he cannot deal with her/himself, otherwise what is requested is not care but service (1995, p. 129). Being subjected to too many demands from who-receives-care implies an erosion of energy not only useless but also dangerous, which should be prevented. Knowing how stand firm, starting from an analysis of the situation, requires care work that precludes feelings of guilt on our part and keeps the mind focused on the search for the right proportion in our acting with care.

Acting with firmness means to know how to say no to the other's demands whenever necessary. Even if the price of refusal is high, because it might set off a conflict or break a relationship, when our own decision is carried out in a "loving and reasonable way" (Noddings 2002, p. 42), the action of care achieves an important objective and is worth the effort.

There might be also long periods of time where who-receives-care rejects our determined way of being in the relationship; in these cases, who-cares-for needs training, besides the courage to make difficult decisions, and, naturally, the virtue of patience.

The danger of being dominated by who-receives-care is greater in cases where there is an affective relationship between the people. The relationship of care is always meaningful on an emotional level, and who-cares-for is required to manage the relationship with the other with balance, but the exercise of emotional command becomes more difficult when the action of care is long-term and the relational boundaries are eroded, thus creating a significant emotional tie (Kittay 1999, p. 36). In these cases, it is important that the person who cares for knows how to restrain her/himself so that the emotional investment does not affect the way in which he/she reacts to the behavior or to the requests of whoever-receives-care in

a negative manner. Virtues are ways of being that are implemented not only towards the others, but also towards ourselves, and who-cares-for is expected to cultivate the virtues towards himself in order to act well: and one of these, indeed, is
defined as "self-respect" (Kittay 1999, p. 37).

The Effort of Care

How Care May Be Difficult

Care work is tiring. It requires much cognitive, emotional and in some cases physical and organizational energy. This is because not only does it make us even more
vulnerable, but also requires us to operate in a context of great uncertainty.

There can be no care if there is no sensitivity towards the other's feelings; but
sensitivity also signifies exposure to the other and being exposed increases the level
of vulnerability that is typical in inter-dependent beings. Because being sensitive
exposes, and in doing so put us in danger, who-cares-for may often ask her/himself
whether it is worth the risk. However if care is to exist, this risk is inevitable. As life
entails the constant gamble of exceeding one's own limits, in the same way the
existential position of taking care entails the same thing.

Simply because we are relational beings and thus as we lack complete being, we
need the other, to be able to sustain the effort of care work we need a form of recognition for this. This occurs when the other shows us with words or gestures that
s/he accepts our actions in a positive manner.

Sometimes we actually receive acknowledgement. The adult in a condition of
awareness of the care s/he is experiencing can recognize this with a smile, a hand-
shake or words, but a newborn, too, is capable of recognition, when with her/his
gestures s/he shows pleasure in receiving care. The student has many different
ways of displaying appreciation for educational experiences that are organized in
order to facilitate the development of her/his specific potentialities, but also a person who is experiencing difficulty on the psychological level can manage to find
her/his way to express gratitude for the care actions received. In some elective situations, as in any relationship between friends, besides acknowledgement there is
reciprocity, or in other words who-cares-for becomes in turn the recipient of care
actions and vice-versa who-receives-care assumes the role of the caregiver. But
sometimes the acknowledgement comes later and sometimes the other even if s/he
may usually be able to reciprocate cannot manage to at that particular moment.
Perseverance in a care relation when acknowledgement is missing becomes difficult

and requires of who-cares-for a great deal of self-control to keep the necessary energy alive and active.

The phenomenological analysis of care practices makes evident their intrinsic difficulties. Care, just like any other practice, is a form of action which is also an example of the fact that it is not possible to develop full control of actions. When we create something material, it is usually possible to undo it and, in some circumstances, to start the work all over again. But it is not possible to control processes that are started by an action that takes place in a relationship, because the recipient of the action is another human being, who not only reacts to my actions with her/his own intentionality, but is located in a precise context where whoever practices the caring action is not able to control what is going on.

Since the effects of human actions, even if carried out with good intentions, are unpredictable and in many cases irreversible, the work of care needs our attention on what we do. We must be particularly alive to what happens to the other when our gestures and our words enter her/his life space. The difficult part of acting with responsibility is that vigilance should be constant, not only because there is no guarantee that the quality of the intention would guarantee the desired effect, but also because the gesture and the apparently most insignificant word can give rise to processes of some importance for the quality of the other's being-there and for the care relation as a whole. The responsibility of caring for is therefore an attitude that involves the cognitive and emotional life profoundly.

Just because of the unpredictable nature of actions, according to Hannah Arendt (1958, p. 175) it is important to understand, in case we fail to achieve the desired result, that we can be forgiven. Certainty of comprehension and forgiveness would be enough for us to find the strength to take action in the ocean of incertitude represented by the relationship with the other. Indeed, the power to forgive is essential for the actions that we share with others, either in private or in public, because feeling forgiven is the overriding condition for us to find the strength to resume action. But the drawback to Arendt's thought, as well as that of a great deal of political philosophy, is that it presupposes an autonomous subject as a reference, one that is fully aware and free to move around. Reality, however, doesn't correspond to this picture, relationships do not always occur among subjects that possess equal rights in negotiation; in the relationships of care, simply because they are asymmetrical, who-cares-for can find himself taking the responsibility for someone who is not autonomous and not able to actively participate in the procedures that makes the experience meaningful. Consequently who-cares-for has to take the whole responsibility for her/his actions and this overwhelming responsibility makes us feel that we face our decisions and their results alone. Responsibility for the other very first at all involves complete responsibility for our actions and therefore for the ability to bear the consequences of our actions by ourselves. In this sense, the decision concerning caring for another person is always hazardous.

Being in a hazardous position signifies the need for constant vigilance over our own way of handling our role in the care relationship. This should indeed take the form of a sort of critical self-analysis both of our thoughts and feelings and of our actions. Understanding the need for self-analysis and carrying it out should not be transformed into the misapprehension that vigilance is the same thing as full control over the development of the care action, because the specific quality of action is its unpredictability. It is the lack of power over action that really shows how who-cares-for must put up with her/his own fragility, because it is impossible for her/him to have full control of her/his own actions. The power of care is inseparable from a condition of increased vulnerability that is the consequence of the non-sovereignty that we must admit to regarding action.

It is difficult to decide on the appropriate degree of action not only because it is difficult to gain a clear idea of what is the right thing to do, but also because the result of an action does not depend solely on the subject who decides but also on contextual variables. Who-cares-for is always working in a condition of uncertainty, because the reaction to his action is not predictable, but in spite of this, s/he is always personally responsible for her/his own actions. The greater the condition of weakness and dependence of the other, the greater is the sense of responsibility that weighs her/him down.

The Necessary Reason of Care

Thus, maintaining one's responsibility for care is difficult: difficult because we are unable to control action, difficult because we cannot always be forgiven, difficult because we may have to go without recognition. Nonetheless reality only survives through acts of care.

The mere fact that acting with care entails such problems would be enough to make one decide not to take on this form of responsibility. However, it is a fact that many people dedicate their time to care actions, and in some cases they are ready to guarantee an availability requiring a considerable investment of energy, that almost constitutes an ontological and ethical danger. If we examine social reality, especially in little known places, far from the limelight, we may come across situations where someone takes the responsibility of care despite a high level of risk. I am thinking particularly of those families who open their homes to strangers and know how to welcome people going through hard times with complete and immediate hospitality.

If the concern of every human being should be that of trying to eliminate the factors that increase the level of vulnerability of life and if in care relationships this possibility not only disappears, but the vulnerability of who-cares-for becomes greater, then why venture into forms of responsibility that imply taking upon oneself dangerous situations? What causes people to abandon patterns of life that are adequate and secure to opt for a way of being-there entailing a huge investment of energy? It can only be the passion for the good. The passion to discover the good responds to the awareness that, if nobody lives as a unit but is always fostered by the other, the search for the valuable things in life that makes it worth living can only be that of a project that involves us in our intimate plurality.

Affirming the passion for the good as a value obliges us to refer to what Tzvetan Todorov (2010) defines the "temptation of the good", that corresponds to the certainty of possessing the concept of the good and to the belief of knowing how to actualize it; this has the consequence of wanting to impose it perforce on the other. The temptation of the good, meant as the presumption of doing something good by oneself, can cause great harm. The concept that lies behind the philosophy of care here sketched out is that care work is driven by the passion for the good, but also that we are fated not to have a sufficiently clear idea of the good to be able to establish it as a horizon for our actions. For this reason, the search for things that do good opens possibilities of action that are highly problematic.

Seeking for the good is often a gamble. But gambling is inevitable, because it is a part of being. It is a part of human existence to seek for the good and avoid the evil, to search for what brings us joy and helps avoid pain. We must be on the side of the search for the good. It is the quality of the human condition and the inner impulse that moves it that evinces that the search for the good should not frighten us but rather excite us. A meaningful search is the one that is understood by those who, day after day, constantly dare to deal with the difficult job of care, or in other words pay attention to the desire of the good that the other feels, and certainly not as ethics and politics nailed to the will of goodness. This search is not about constructing theories of good action, that in truth become dangerous impositions upon reality, but it concerns reinforcing and protecting the disposition to do what helps our life to find its best form.

Given the difficulty of envisioning the good, the problem is not so much one of avoiding the challenge of this idea, but in point of fact it has more to do with keeping alive an awareness of the fragility of human reason, which prevents a full grasp of the essence of ideas that are so important for the quality of life such as the idea of the good. To be in search of the good does not mean assuming a deliberately saccharine attitude and avoiding dealing with the negative; in actual fact, we are on the side of the good if we really try to focus on the difficulties it brings. There can be no problem in admitting that some sorts of presumptuous voluntary work give a distorted idea of goodness but this is not a sufficient reason for what I call the passion for the good to be considered with diffidence. Because it is the desire for the good that keeps us in the world.

Diffidence towards the search for the good can reach the point of sanctioning a defeatist way of being, that distances itself from reality and wherever it perceives evil being-there, it steps aside because, according to this school of thought, the only sensible way to react is passivity. I consider this a terribly dangerous political option. Whenever evil strikes we need to "roll up our sleeves", even knowing that we might make mistakes. It is reality itself that, if we listen to it, asks us to have the courage to get our hands dirty and deal with difficulties while thinking of the good.

From the theoretical point of view, to keep close to reality means that we must begin bearing in mind less sophisticated ways of thinking, but that it is these that really do the work of existing. From the phenomenological analysis of good practices of care, it ensues that who-cares-for, while trying to do what is good for the other, does not have any general theory to promote, nor does s/he have any universal vision of the good. S/he is not concerned with holding discussions that produce theories that are formally defined by ethics. What counts is listening to the other and to ourselves trying to find in that specific situation to do the best that possibility and the limits of reality allow. There are no rules to apply, no categorical imperatives to guide reasoning; the only thing that helps me is the quality of the experiential situation of the other, the ontological necessity of good that I can see in her/his eyes.

Interpreting the practice of care in a situational perspective can be labeled as relativism or situationism, but this conceptualization is incorrect. Keeping one's eyes on the other, on her/his individual need and on her/his own desire, does not imply failing to reason on a general level. To focus on detail does not mean to forget to wonder: "What is good?", "How must I do what is just?". The difference between systematic thinking which builds up theoretical scenarios and the practice of care is in the thoughts that accompany the care work, the confrontation with general questions is never aimed at creating theories; what matters is the way of reflection that permits the drawing of horizons that help us to stay in reality.

In care, it is the attention for the other and the obedience to necessity everyone feels to be-there-with others in the world that guides it. We can say that the daily ethics of care is realized by efforts of a patient attention directed upon the other; an attention without fantasies and capable of obedience to reality (Murdoch 1997, p. 332). This attention for the other and her/his singularity together with making decisions according to a situational logic is not lack of a wider horizon (the general principles of Enlightenment ethics) nor of a fragmented situationality, because behind attention for the person and his singularity and the avoidance of the mechanisms of pre-judging there is a constant working of the mind to find a good and just degree of action. A type of thinking that is neither systematic nor occasional can be defined as realistic and empirical, to indicate its quality of attention to reality. And reality is made up of unique and single encounters:

> I was teaching the first year of primary school. As I did every morning, I arrived early at school so that the children getting there by the school bus could find me already in the classroom. While I was waiting there was always something to do. That morning I was busy writing a report. The pupils arrived and greeted me happily. Alessandro, the youngest of the group, came to me and said: "Hello teacher. I have an important thing to tell you". "Fine, tell me. I am listening to you." Alessandro started to tell me his story, while I kept on writing the report. "Listen to me, teacher!" "Yes, it's alright I am listening to you, go ahead." And as I said these words, I kept on writing my report. Alessandro started again, but then he stopped; I could feel his little hands on my face, he turned it towards him and says: "If you don't look at me, it means that you are not really listening. But the things I have to tell you are important". He was right. "Sure, I am listening." I put the pen on the table and I closed my notebook. Alessandro started to tell me his story again and I was listening with the attention he deserved.

Care is care for another specific person. The good is what the other needs to feel good at that specific moment. Life is not a system, it doesn't need general complicated knowledge. It needs attention and dedication at that specific moment for that specific person. We live in time and our soul sustains itself with concrete and singular moments of goodness.

Bibliography

Arendt, H. (1958). *The Human Condition*. Chicago (Ill.). The University of Chicago.
Aristotle in 23 Volumes, Vol. 22, translated by J. H. Freese. Aristotle. Cambridge and London. Harvard University Press; William Heinemann Ltd. 1926.
Baier, A. (1985). *Postures of the mind. Essays on Mind and Morals*. London, UK: Methuen.
Bubeck, D. (1995). *Care, gender, and justice*. Oxford: Oxford University Press.
Carse, A.L. (2006), "Vulnerability, agency, and human flourishing". In Taylor, C., Dell'oro, R. (a cura di), *Health and Human Flourishing*. Georgetown University Press, Washington DC, pp. 33-52.
Colli, G (1993). *La sapienza greca*. III Eraclito. Milano: Adelphi.
Heidegger, Martin (1949). "Hölderlin and the Essence of Poetry" and "Remembrance of the Poet". In *Existence and Being*. Trans. Douglas Scott. Ed. Werner Brock. Chicago: H. Regnery, 270-91 and 233-69.
Heidegger M., (1949). *Hölderin and the Essence of Poetry in Existence and Being, with and introduction by Werner Brock Dr Phil*, London: Vision Press Ltd.

Heidegger, M. (1962). *Being and Time*. Translated by J. Macquarrie and Edward Robinson. New York, NY: Harper Collins Publishers.

Heidegger, M. (1988). *The basic problems of Phenomenology*. Translation, Introduction, and Lexicon by Albert Hofstadter. Bloomington & Indianapolis: Indiana University Press.

Heidegger, M. (1992). *History of the Concept of Time: Prolegomena*. Stati Uniti: Indiana University Press.

Held, V. (2006). *The ethics of care*, Oxford: Oxford University Press.

Kittay, Eva (1999). *Love's labor. Essays on Women, Equality, and Dependency*. New York and London: Routledge.

Lévinas, E., (1969). *Totality and infinity*. Translated by Alphonso Lingis, Pittsburgh, Pa: Duquesne University Press.

Lévinas, E. (1996). *Martin Heidegger and Ontology*. Diacritics, Springs, 1996, Vol. 26, No. 1 (Spring 1996), pp. 11-32, Baltimora, MD: The John Hopkins University Press.

Lévinas, E., (1998). *Otherwise than being., or, Beyond essence*. Pittsburgh, Pa: Duquesne University Press. Originally published as Autrement qu' être. Dordrecht, Netherlands: Martinus Nijhoff, 1974.

Lévinas, E. (2006). *Humanism of the Other*, translated from theFrenc by N. Poller, Urbana and Chicago, IL: University of Illinois Press.

Murdoch, Iris (1997). *Existentialists and Mystics*. London: Chatto & Windus.

Nancy, J-L. (2004). *All'ascolto*. Tr. It Torino: Einaudi.

Noddings, Nel (1984). *Caring. A Feminine Approach to Ethics and Moral Education*. Berkeley: University of California Press.

Noddings, N. (1992). *The challenge to care in school: An alternative approach to education*. New York: Teachers College Press, Columbia University.

Noddings, Nel (2002), *Starting at Home*. Los Angeles: University of California Press.

Nussbaum, M. (1986). *The Fragility of Goodness. Luck and Ethics in Greek Tragedy and Philosophy*. Cambridge: Cambridge University Press.

Nussbaum, M. (1996). *The Therapy of Desire*, Princeton: Princeton University Press.

Oatley, K. (1992). *Best Laid Schemes. The Psychology of Emotions*. Cambridge: Cambridge University Press.

Siegel, D. (1999). *The developing mind*. New York: Guilford Press.

Slote, Michael (2007). *The ethics of care and empathy*. London and New York: Routledge.

Stein, E. (1989). *On the Problem of Empathy*. In *The collected works of Edith Stein, Sister Teresa Benedicta of the Cross. Discalced Carmelite, Volume Three*. Translated by W. Stein. Washington, D.C.: ICS Publications.

Stein, E. (2002). *Finite and Eternal Being: An Attempt at an Ascent to the Meaning of Being*, translated by (Vol. I). Washington: Ics Publications.

Stein, E. (2002). *Finite and Eternal Being: An Attempt at an Ascent to the Meaning of Being* (Vol. II). Washington: Ics Publications.

Todorov, T. (2010). *Memory as a Remedy for Evil*. Translated by Gila Walker, London: Seagull Books.

Winnicott, Donald W. (1987). *Babies and Their mothers*, The Winnicott Trust.

Zambrano, M. (2008). *Per l'amore e per la libertà*, Genova-Milano: Marietti, 2008.

Made in the USA
Las Vegas, NV
01 December 2023

81953519R00105